Financial Management for Episcopal Parishes

Financial Management for Episcopal Parishes

James B. Jordan

Morehouse Publishing
NEW YORK · HARRISBURG · DENVER

Unless otherwise noted, the Scripture quotations contained herein are from the New Revised Standard Version Bible, copyright © 1989 by the Division of Christian Education of the National Council of Churches of Christ in the U.S.A. Used by permission. All rights reserved.

Material quoted on pages 157–161 copyright © the Association of Certified Fraud Examiners, *Report to the Nations on Occupational Fraud and Abuse 2012*. Used by permission.

Morehouse Publishing, 4775 Linglestown Road, Harrisburg, PA 17112

Morehouse Publishing, 445 Fifth Avenue, New York, NY 10016

Morehouse Publishing is an imprint of Church Publishing Incorporated.
www.churchpublishing.org

Cover design by Laurie Klein Westhafer

Library of Congress Cataloging-in-Publication Data

Jordan, James B.
    Financial management for Episcopal parishes / James B. Jordan.
        p.   cm.
    Includes bibliographical references.
    ISBN 978-0-8192-2825-3 (pbk.) — ISBN 978-0-8192-2826-0 (ebook)
1. Church finance.   2. Episcopal Church—Finance.   I. Title.
BV770.J67   2012
254'.808828373—dc23

2012034604

Printed in the United States of America

Disclaimer

No part of this book should be relied upon as legal or tax advice. Laws change frequently at the national, state, and local level, and widely differ. As a result, the reader should not rely on the information in this book as it relates to his or her particular situation. The reader must consult competent legal counsel and/or a Certified Public Accountant in his or her locale. In considering searching for advisors, obtain at least two opinions, ask only those specializing in the area of concern, and document the advice received. Information in this book is general in nature and not intended to address the intricacies of a particular situation, regardless of how similar it may appear.

Notice Pursuant to Treasury Circular 230 Regarding Use of Written Tax Advice: Please note that no tax advice is intended or given to the reader in this book. This book cannot be used to avoid penalties that the Internal Revenue Service might impose, as it does not include all of the information required by Circular 230, nor does it offer services that rise to this level of assurance.

Contents

Introduction

This book is intended to be read by clergy—bishops, priests, deacons; by staff—canons to the ordinary, diocesan finance committee members, parish administrators, senior wardens, parish finance directors or finance committee members, other diocesan and parish staff members; by laypeople—vestry members, ushers, bookkeepers, secretaries, committee chairs, volunteers, and parishioners.

This resource is as much about leadership and roles as it is about internal control and processes. Without the desire at the top to implement good internal controls, the rest of the organization will not easily follow through. This requires real leadership. The clergy must take the initiative to insist that the assets of the church are properly accounted for, properly identified, and properly maintained and protected. It is the leadership of the clergy that can set the tone of the parish—including the financial tone.

Most clergy enter the presbyterate from walks of life that do not prepare them for the financial and procedural tasks required to safeguard the assets of the church. Most do not have accounting or business degrees. If they do, they are ahead of the game. However, the not-for-profit organization has major differences in its management and accounting practices from other organizations, much the same as there are major differences among retail, manufacturing, and construction companies. So, too, is the not-for-profit different from all other businesses (yes, the church is a business). The church is a not-for-profit organization (usually a corporation), and has its own lexicon, mission, customer set, management objectives, accounting methods, and definitions of success—large and small.

Further, religious not-for-profit organizations are different from other not-for-profit organizations such as the Red Cross or United Way. And each denomination is different; each diocese is different; each parish is different. Herein lies the rub.

While there are many texts, treatises, canons, church publications, and personal opinions regarding *what* to do to protect the church's assets, there are none that deal with *how* to design and implement the processes and procedures, accountability, checks and balances, and oversight to actually accomplish protecting the assets. This is a *how* to book.

Even if all those in the church at all levels could agree on exactly *what* to do, the implementation of the *how* is left to those in each organization at each level of the church. This means that the interpretation of *what*, and the translation into *how*, are left to those in charge of the implementation—the local staff or volunteers. The plot thickens.

Consider now that each of these staff or volunteers all have varying backgrounds. Most are not trained in accounting procedures or safeguarding assets, and are left to make it up as they go along. Have you heard that before? Additionally, every time new members are elected to the vestry, one-third of the memory of the *what* and/or *how* is lost. In three years, the slate is clean and we start afresh recreating varying aberrations of a process to accomplish the same protection that may have been created and implemented better four years ago, but of which no one is aware. Or worse, maybe the *what* and *how* are simply no longer addressed.

Hence, the need for this book as a blueprint that any church organization can use to design processes and procedures that are lasting, documentable, hold people accountable, provide for the separation of duties, record and protect the assets, and provide oversight on a regular basis. This book addresses many things that must be clear in your mind before you can begin designing and implementing your own processes. You do not need a business or accounting background to use this book in your church organization. You do need common sense because much of this *is* common sense mixed with observations of churches from my CPA auditing practice, combined with sound tried-and-true methods from businesses and theories from academia.

The chapters in this book build upon each other, sometimes are parallel to each other, then come together at the end to provide an understanding of the elements necessary (and how to implement them) to build your own processes that work for *your* church organization. It is important to remember that the principles in this book work for organizations as small as three people and for ones that are as large as thousands. The difference is scale of effort. The scope of effort—the *what* and the *how*—does not change.

The principles in this book apply to a church of any denomination and faith. However, the references to canon and church publications are specific to the Episcopal Church.

We must first establish the authority on which the contents of this book are based, both in religious terms and in earthly terms. Chapter 1 deals with the religious authority. Being Christians, we give the most credence to the words and actions of our Lord Jesus Christ. The Bible is loaded with references to money, but in this book we focus on the gospels as the source of authority for the attention to and about money in the church.

Chapter 2 moves from the religious to the earthly authority. In the Episcopal Church, those are the canons. We examine the canons closely to understand *what* the church has already charged us to do—but, by design, without telling us *how* to do it. As we will see, the national canon is explicit, but the interpretations by dioceses range from strict to loose.

In chapter 3 we discuss roles within the church organization and the related associated leadership necessary. Comparisons are made with other businesses to assist in comparing the church organizational structure with those with which you are probably more familiar. And, we examine the relationships among the roles, their accountability, and their oversight responsibilities.

Chapter 4 examines what money belongs to the church and categorizes donations of all kinds. It is important to understand the different characteristics of unrestricted, temporarily restricted, and permanently restricted funds before proceeding with subsequent chapters.

Chapter 5 establishes the accounting lexicon of a church and how to read a church financial statement. Financial statements are the records of all the transactions of the church—including donations, expenditures, assets, and liabilities. There are those who will want to skip this chapter, understandably, but there are some concepts that must be comprehended in order to understand future chapters. I encourage you to muddle through this as I try to put it into plain English as much as possible.

Chapter 6 examines the canonical requirement for annual audits and the resulting audit reports. It also highlights the need to report to the Bishop the results of each audit and the vestry's responses to the auditor's comments.

Chapter 7 looks at conditions for fraud in the church and the characteristics of those who perpetrate fraud. This chapter explains why you should read the rest of the book to safeguard the church's assets. The Association of Certified Fraud Examiners consistently finds one in six not-for-profit organizations have fraud perpetrated on them. My demonstrated audit experience is that one in three churches experience fraud. In the words of a canon to the ordinary, "This is a disaster of preponderous proportions."

Chapter 8 introduces The Three-Legged Stool™ of internal control. This is the model we will use to properly design processes to safeguard the church's assets in later chapters. Understanding the concepts provides the basis for understanding of the elements of internal control.

In chapter 9 we start with donations and other revenue of the church. I advise how to design a set of internal controls to ensure that money given is money received. Roles, responsibilities, accountability, and oversight are recalled from chapter 3 and applied in the specific areas of the processes, along with the concepts from chapter 8.

We focus in chapter 10 on expenditures and the processes necessary to ensure that funds are being expended as intended and approved. Again, we rely on roles, responsibilities, accountability, and oversight from chapter 3 and the concepts in chapter 8.

The remaining chapters address other specific issues, including taxation in chapter 11 and budgets in chapter 12, while chapter 13 discusses fixed assets, insurance, endowments, bank accounts, payroll, and change management.

I invite you to obtain the companion workbooks and other materials (www.financialmanagement4churches.com) that contain more detailed examples and templates to use in implementing your own church's processes and procedures.

CHAPTER
1
The Gospels and Money

Jesus did not despise money, nor did he love money. Jesus had no problem with money. His interest in money was how we, you and I, regard money. Do we love money as the Israelites loved and worshipped the golden calf? Has money taken a place in our hearts as well as our heads? Is money a tool or an instrument by which we accomplish good, or is it a means to an end for power, purchased obedience, and admiration? Are our decisions in life based on money or matters of the heart?

Money has been much maligned by the church. But money is not bad in itself. Jesus had no more problems with money than he had with sandals. To illustrate, we should examine what the gospels and New Testament have to say regarding money. It is vital to have an understanding and agreement of the legitimacy of money in the life of the church. We look to Jesus himself concerning how money should be regarded in our lives—spiritually and secularly.

When I teach courses on parish finances, we begin with the gospel witness. One cleric in the course could not remember having preached a sermon about money based on the appointed lectionary readings. That may be a choice, but the lectionary does contain many opportunities to preach about money.

While there are exceptions with individual parishes, by and large Episcopalians avoid discussing money. Some people think it is a private matter—between them and God. Some people are embarrassed for others to know their involvement in the church financially. Some wear their gifts on their sleeve like a badge of honor. Others regard it as a matter of the heart, like the widow in the parable of the widow's mites in Luke 21:1–4.

Most people have heard that "money is the root of all evil" and claim it comes from the Bible. The correct quotation is, "For the *love* of money is a root of all kinds of evil, and in their eagerness to be rich some have wandered away from the faith and pierced themselves with many pains" (1 Tim. 6:10).

With the proper inclusion of "the *love* of money," the passage takes on a different meaning. The entire subject of the sentence changes from money to the *love* of money.

Money has been maligned, but should no longer be considered a scapegoat. It is our human emotion and intent that are judged on the last day, not the amount we gave. We are the culprits, not the dollars themselves, with whom the Bible takes issue when schooling us about money. The thirty pieces of silver that Judas got for betraying Jesus is not as important as the intent of his heart and the actions he took to gain reward.

When Jesus launched into his tirade at the temple, it was not about the money itself.

> In the temple he found people selling cattle, sheep, and doves, and the money changers seated at their tables. Making a whip of cords, he drove all of them out of the temple, both the sheep and the cattle. He also poured out the coins of the money changers and overturned their tables. He told those who were selling the doves, "Take these things out of here! Stop making my Father's house a marketplace! (John 2:14–16)

While I do not blame him for wanting livestock and birds out of the temple, it sounds like Jesus was angry with the people and their *love* of money, not the money itself.

Another observation is the use of *them*, which is more clearly defined by the use of the word *both*. Jesus drove out both the cattle and the sheep. It does not say he drove out the people selling the cattle and the sheep. He told the sellers of the doves to take them out of his Father's house. He did not drive out the sellers. Is it because Jesus perceived the *love* of money in their hearts, but loved them as he loves all of us, each with our individual sins?

The Jewish temple required taxes and offerings be given in Hebrew shekels, but Roman money—denarii—was the currency of conducting business transactions outside of the synagogue and Jewish community. This is much like the difference between the U.S. dollar, an internationally recognized currency used and accepted in international business transactions, and the *baht* of Thailand, used only in that country. The money changers extracted a plentiful fee for their services from those paying taxes to the temple and from the temple priests who then had shekels from the taxes and needed Roman money for other transactions. This policy of "get you going and coming" made the money changers rich while preventing a sizable amount of money from reaching the priests for use in the synagogue.

I believe it was this *love* of money in the hearts of the money changers that drove Jesus to react the way he did, not the fact that money was present in the temple. Had there been no money changers, the money would still be present on the Temple Mount to pay the temple its taxes and offerings. By overturning the tables of the money changers, Jesus ruined the possibility of an exchange rate. With the money strewn about, the money changers would not know how much was their initial investment and how much was their profit, as they kept those in stacks on the tables. Interestingly, the English word *bank* comes from the Greek word used in the Scripture *trapeza* (*Τράπεζα*) that today is still used interchangeably in modern Greek to mean both table and bank.

Money was a large part of daily life during the life of Christ. It was, and is, how we humans exchange things in an orderly fashion. Taxes were necessary and rendering unto Caesar what was Caesar's was as desirable as rendering unto God that which is God's.

As we read in Matthew's gospel:

> When they reached Capernaum, the collectors of the temple tax came to Peter and said, "Does your teacher not pay the temple tax?" He said, "Yes, he does." And when he came home, Jesus spoke of it first, asking, "What do you think, Simon? From whom do kings of the earth take toll or tribute? From their children or from others?" When Peter said, "From others," Jesus said to him, "Then the children are free. However, so that we do not give offense to them, go to the sea and cast a hook; take the first fish that comes up; and when you open its mouth, you will find a coin; take that and give it to them for you and me." (Matt. 17:24–27)

Jesus made sure he paid his taxes to the temple. There was no fanfare about it. It was a matter-of-fact reference that paying temple taxes was what Jews did. Interestingly, Jesus was exact in his choice of words. The Greek word used for the coin that was in the fish's mouth is *stater* (*στατήρα*), which means two didrachma, or the exact amount of tax for two people at the time—Peter and Jesus.

Is this beginning to sound like how we deal with money today in our secular lives, too? We earn it, save it wisely, invest it, take to heart how we spend it, and pay taxes. So did the Jews at the time of Christ. Then why be surprised that the gospels deal with these events involving money in our lives?

We have created an entire vocabulary in the church that allows us as clergy, vestry, volunteers, and parishioners to avoid acknowledging that money is what enables the church's activities. It is both necessary and desirable, not for our personal gain but as a tool for compassion and good. We have created a vocabulary unique to the church that is used in sermons, vestry meetings, and coffee gatherings to avoid having to say the word *money*.

Needs of the parish, parish life, and *outreach* are examples of terms we all know involve money. We employ them to imply the need for, and the use of, money without having to discuss the topic of money or use the word itself. We speak of budgets as if they are something for which we have no personal concern or knowledge.

Money is the tool used by the church to pay the utility bill, buy flowers, repair the building, or put gas in the church bus. Money is used to pay the priest, reimburse parishioners for Wednesday night supper purchases, or buy formation supplies. It is money that is used to outfit the church with pews, an altar, prayer books, and hymnals. And it is money that buys the music and robes for the choir, candles for service, and the envelopes for tithing.

Think about your parish. From the moment you step onto the church grounds, everything you see has been purchased with money at some point. True, some of the items were donated, but someone purchased them originally. When articles made by hand, such as kneelers at the altar or baptismal font, are donated to the church, we record the donation and include the value of the raw materials that were purchased. If the person were in the business of making fonts, kneelers, whatever was donated, we probably include the value of their time as well.

The Bible is full of hundreds, even thousands, of references to money. Jesus spoke a lot about money: gold, silver, mites, drachmas, shekels, treasure, taxes, and the like. He recognized that money was necessary for life in the world, but not of value in heaven. He alluded to the difference between treasures stored in the bank versus the treasure in the heart that is stored in heaven. Matthew 19:21, Mark 10:21, and Luke 12:33 all refer to "treasure in heaven," while Matthew 25:27 and Luke 19:23 refer to the investing of money in a bank. Jesus wanted us to understand that it is what we do with our money, how we treat each other concerning the use of money, and the intentions of the heart regarding money that determine whether we are acceptable in the sight of God.

Jesus wants us to use wisely the money we have. In the parable of the talents (Matt. 25:14–30), we are given instructions regarding how to deal with the secular side of money. Investing what is entrusted, even if only earning interest in a bank, is the right thing to do. While the servant with the one talent did protect it, he did not provide for its oversight for which he was held accountable. Oversight and accountability are concepts we will examine a number of times in later chapters.

The point is that talk of money should not be ignored in the church. Money is not the "thing that shall not be named." However, there is one verse of

Scripture that I have never heard discussed openly in the church. In John 12, there is the confrontation by Judas about the cost of the nard that Mary Magdalene used to anoint Jesus and provide fragrance to Jesus' feet.

Nard is made from the root of a plant found in India. Because of its enormous value, it was transported by camel in caravan for protection. The route was a long one because the camels had to get to Jerusalem and Galilee by going the long way around the mountain trails of Lebanon, making it about an eight months' journey. Once a sealed jar of nard was opened, it lost its fragrance and usefulness quickly. The entire contents of the jar had to be used or the remaining amount would quickly be of no value.

"But Judas Iscariot, one of his disciples (the one who was about to betray him), said, 'Why was this perfume not sold for three hundred denarii and the money given to the poor?'" (John 12:4–5). Mary used about a pint of nard to anoint Jesus. The value is about $35,000 in today's currency. "(He said this not because he cared about the poor, but because he was a thief; he kept the common purse and used to steal what was put into it.)" (John 12:6).

Wow. Not only did Judas betray Jesus to the Romans for money, he *loved* money itself. Judas committed fraud. He helped himself to the funds of Jesus and the disciples for his own use. Was Judas concerned about selling the nard to get the cash to put in the money bag just so he could help himself to some of that $35,000, too?

Judas was one of the twelve called by Jesus. He was their accountant, in a similar position of access to the funds as a parish bookkeeper today. Yet, he took money from the band of disciples much as those who steal money from the church do today—through willfulness and deceit. If Judas stole from the inner circle—in the vicinity and presence of Christ—then why are we surprised when we discover fraud in our own parishes? Returning to the parable about taking care of the money by investing, depositing, and spending wisely, we see that neither Judas nor we are excused for mismanagement, lack of accountability, and lack of oversight.

There is another Scripture reference regarding Judas and the money: "Some thought that, because Judas had the common purse, Jesus was telling him, 'Buy what we need for the festival'; or, that he should give something to the poor" (John 13:29). This further confirms that Judas was the keeper of the money and bookkeeper for the twelve and Jesus.

The Old and New Testaments contain many more references to money. What we have in the gospels is the clear indication that money is a part of life. We are responsible for tending to the church's needs for money to operate just as each of us needs money to operate our own households.

Jesus did not condemn money. He did identify that matters of the heart and matters of the wallet intersect, and there will be treasure in heaven created, or not, based on our heart's approach to and use of money. In Matthew 19:24, Jesus said that it was easier for a camel to pass through the eye of a needle than for a rich man to enter the kingdom of heaven. This is not meant literally, but rather for understanding that it is hard for a person who treats money as an idol for their affection to see the real value of God.

CHAPTER

2

Church Canons and Financial Matters

We have seen in the last chapter that money is biblically established as a component of our lives with which we must deal like any other. Jesus legitimized money in the church and our lives through his examples and teaching. We now turn our attention to the church and the legitimate authority and responsibilities given to us by the church itself in the handling of money in our parishes.

The Episcopal Church (TEC) is a member of the Anglican Communion. This Anglican Communion has no oversight or great influence in the workings of TEC. Until the Revolutionary War, the colonies' churches were a part of the Church of England. After the Revolutionary War, the churches were autonomous and formed their own organizational structure. Drawing upon their roots, they formed their own rules and regulations known as canons. Canons, or canonical laws, are what guide the operations of the church in most instances.

There is one canon in particular—Title I, Canon 7—that must be carefully examined if we are to understand the financial requirements of dioceses and parishes. We will also look at other canons, but this is the primary one. To help us in our discussion, I have reproduced Title I, Canon 7 as of the 76th Convention (2009) below.

Title I, Canon 7:
Of Business Methods in Church Affairs

Sec. 1. In every Province, Diocese, Parish, Mission and Institution connected with this Church, the following standard business methods shall be observed:

(a) All accounts of Provinces shall be audited annually by an independent certified public accountant, or independent licensed accountant or such audit committee as shall be authorized by the Provincial Council. The Audit Report shall be filed with the Provincial Council not later than September 1 of each year, covering the preceding calendar year.

(b) Funds held in trust, endowment and other permanent funds, and securities represented by physical evidence of ownership or indebtedness, shall be deposited with a National or State Bank, or a Diocesan Corporation, or with some other agency approved in writing by the Finance Committee or the Department of Finance of the Diocese, under a deed of trust, agency or other depository agreement providing for at least two signatures on any order of withdrawal of such funds or securities. But this paragraph shall not apply to funds and securities refused by the depositories named as being too small for acceptance. Such small funds and securities shall be under the care of the persons or corporations properly responsible for them. This paragraph shall not be deemed to prohibit investments in securities issued in book entry form or other manner that dispenses with the delivery of a certificate evidencing the ownership of the securities or the indebtedness of the issuer.

(c) Records shall be made and kept of all trust and permanent funds showing at least the following:

(1) Source and date.

(2) Terms governing the use of principal and income.

(3) To whom and how often reports of condition are to be made.

(4) How the funds are invested.

(d) Treasurers and custodians, other than banking institutions, shall be adequately bonded; except treasurers of funds that do not exceed five hundred dollars at any one time during the fiscal year.

(e) Books of account shall be so kept as to provide the basis for satisfactory accounting.

(f) All accounts of the Diocese shall be audited annually by an independent Certified Public Accountant. All accounts of Parishes, Missions or other institutions shall be audited annually by an independent Certified Public Accountant, or independent Licensed Public Accountant, or such audit committee as shall be authorized by the Finance Committee, Department of Finance, or other appropriate diocesan authority.

(g) All reports of such audits, including any memorandum issued by the auditors or audit committee regarding internal controls or other accounting matters, together with a summary of action taken or proposed to be taken to correct deficiencies or implement recommendations contained in any such memorandum, shall be filed with the Bishop or Ecclesiastical Authority not later than 30 days following the date of such report, and in no event, not later than September 1 of each year, covering the financial reports of the previous calendar year.

(h) All buildings and their contents shall be kept adequately insured.

(i) The Finance Committee or Department of Finance of the Diocese may require copies of any or all accounts described in this Section to be filed with it and shall report annually to the Convention of the Diocese upon its administration of this Canon.

(j) The fiscal year shall begin January 1.

Sec. 2. The several Dioceses shall give effect to the foregoing standard business methods by the enactment of Canons appropriate thereto, which Canons shall invariably provide for a Finance Committee, a Department of Finance of the Diocese, or other appropriate diocesan body with such authority.

Sec. 3. No Vestry, Trustee, or other Body, authorized by Civil or Canon law to hold, manage, or administer real property for any Parish, Mission, Congregation, or Institution, shall encumber or alienate the same or any part thereof without the written consent of the Bishop and Standing Committee of the Diocese of which the Parish, Mission, Congregation, or Institution is a part, except under such regulations as may be prescribed by Canon of the Diocese.

Sec. 4. All real and personal property held by or for the benefit of any Parish, Mission or Congregation is held in trust for this Church and the Diocese thereof in which such Parish, Mission or Congregation is located. The existence of this trust, however, shall in no way limit the power and authority of the Parish, Mission or Congregation otherwise existing over such property so long as the particular Parish, Mission or Congregation remains a part of, and subject to, this Church and its Constitution and Canons.

Sec. 5. The several Dioceses may, at their election, further confirm the trust declared under the foregoing Section 4 by appropriate action, but no such action shall be necessary for the existence and validity of the trust.[1]

Now comes the fun for some of you and the drudgery for others. We need to carefully examine each section of this most important canon as it relates to financial matters in the church. This is the principal canon that gives authority to the dioceses for financial matters. The dioceses write their own canons

1. *Constitution and Canons: Together with the Rules of Order: For the Government of the Protestant Episcopal Church in the United States of America, Otherwise Known as The Episcopal Church,* adopted and rev. 2009 (New York: Church Publishing, Inc., 2009), pp. 39–41.

that most of the time are not a direct quotation of ECUSA canons, but address many of the same issues. Many diocesan canons incorporate parts of the canon verbatim. Others try to interpret the canon. However, there are clearly some parts of the canon that are not left to the dioceses to interpret and some that are. Then again, there are some dioceses that choose to ignore the imperatively obvious and risk things on their own, either deliberately or well intentioned, but with potentially unintended consequences.

Explanation of Title I, Canon 7: Of Business Methods in Church Affairs

"Title I, Canon 7"

The canons of the church are aggregated into titles that group similar topics. A canon is actually a subgroup of the title. Canons are then broken into sections with further subdivisions. You might have heard the terms *canon law* or *canonical law*. The structure of the canons is similar to that of U.S. or state laws—titles, sections, and sections with further subdivisions. This particular Canon 7 is contained in Title I, Organization and Administration.

"Of Business Methods"

What does this mean? In the language of business, it means processes and procedures that are implemented based on strategic or policy statements. The U.S. Patent Office will actually patent a business method.

"In Church Affairs"

The ECUSA 76th Convention has prescribed policy statements and some directives of procedures and processes by which it expects the church to conform. These are not just good business methods, but ones that all the dioceses of this legal entity called The Episcopal Church in the United States of America have agreed to be governed by in conformity. As we shall see, we have already entered into the realm of a sticky wicket.

> "Sec. 1. In every Province, Diocese, Parish, Mission and Institution connected with this Church, the following standard business methods shall be observed . . ."

This part is explicit—"every Province, Diocese, Parish, Mission and Institution" leaves no room for interpretation. If there is an organization of any kind—province, diocese, church, mission, thrift house, school, preschool, bazaar, Sunday school class, church camp, or any organization—that is "connected with this Church," then everything that follows "shall be observed": Yet, there is a lack of conformity in the church that is sometimes unintentional and sometimes outright defiant.

> "(a) All accounts of Provinces shall be audited annually by an independent certified public accountant, or independent licensed accountant or such audit committee as shall be authorized by the Provincial Council. The Audit Report shall be filed with the Provincial Council not later than September 1 of each year, covering the preceding calendar year."

This language is repeated again with respect to the rest of the church—dioceses, parishes, missions, and institutions connected with this church.

> "(f) All accounts of the Diocese shall be audited annually by an independent Certified Public Accountant. All accounts of Parishes, Missions or other institutions shall be audited annually by an independent Certified Public Accountant, or independent Licensed Public Accountant, or such audit committee as shall be authorized by the Finance Committee, Department of Finance, or other appropriate diocesan authority."

I will address the preceding paragraphs together, albeit out of the sequence of the canon. *All accounts* is problematic. Some would interpret that to mean all bank accounts or all financial institution accounts. From an accounting and auditor's perspective, it is much broader than that. *All accounts* is meant to include all accounts in the chart of accounts in the bookkeeping records of the Church. Auditing solely the bank accounts is not permissible by any stretch of imagination per any form of auditing standards, and particularly not those of the Financial Accounting Standards Board (FASB) or the American Institute of Certified Public Accountants. The way the canon is written indicates that everything be audited.

In addition, the canon means for each organizational part of the church to be subject to audit annually. The intent is clearly that the performance of the audit be done by those in the order presented, that being first and foremost by a Certified Public Accountant.

The Licensed Public Accountant (LPA) is no longer in use by most states. It was a holdover designation from those people who began practicing accounting before there was a uniform CPA exam, a grandfathered approach. They have not met the requirements to be a CPA and are not legally permitted to sign audit opinion letters. The only person who can express an opinion on financial statements and sign an opinion letter is the CPA. LPAs do not have a competency exam they must complete and are not bound by the professional ethics or methods of practice by the American Institute of Certified Public Accountants. That is not meant to imply they are not competent or ethical. It does mean they legally cannot sign audit opinion letters. In the past, most LPAs performed bookkeeping services or tax services and did not perform audits.

Finally, we arrive at the last and least preferred method of examining the record keeping. We should pay attention to some key words, *Diocesan authority*. This specifically states that the diocese is directly involved and charged with the oversight of the examination of the books if that examination is not performed by a CPA. We will discuss audits in depth in chapter 6, but let me conclude here with this: There is no audit unless it is performed according to the Statements on Auditing Standards and other bodies of professional work and practice of the American Institute of Certified Public Accountants. There is no shortcut to an audit and no substitute for an audit.

> **(b)** Funds held in trust, endowment and other permanent funds, and securities represented by physical evidence of ownership or indebtedness, shall be deposited with a National or State Bank, or a Diocesan Corporation, or with some other agency approved in writing by the Finance Committee or the Department of Finance of the Diocese, under a deed of trust, agency or other depository agreement providing for at least two signatures on any order of withdrawal of such funds or securities. But this paragraph shall not apply to funds and securities refused by the depositories named as being too small for acceptance. Such small funds and securities shall be under the care of the persons or corporations properly responsible for them. This paragraph shall not be deemed to prohibit investments in securities issued in book entry form or other manner that dispenses with the delivery of a certificate evidencing the ownership of the securities or the indebtedness of the issuer.

For the rest of this chapter, I will use "Church organization" to represent "Province, Diocese, Parish, Mission or Institution connected with the Church."

"Funds held in trust"

All monies and other assets received by the church are held in trust. Donors entrust the church to use the funds for the purposes for which the money is given, even if it is broadly implied as "go do God's work." In addition, the implication in the word *trust* is that there is a fiduciary responsibility on the part of those who have any form of governance or control over the funds. This fiduciary responsibility is one that has legal implications. When we get into the roles of those in the church, we will discuss this in more detail.

"Endowment and other permanent funds"

This refers to a specific class of assets held by the church organization. *Funds* usually means money in the vernacular and does here, too. *Held in* . . . *endowment* means that the funds are held by the church organization, usually for some purpose designated by the donor. *And other permanent funds* gets into a use of words with a specific meaning from an accounting perspective. In the vernacular, the term "endowment funds" is used loosely, and often incorrectly, to mean a large sum of money set aside for some purpose. However, the proper use of the word "endowment" is defined as money or other financial assets given via either bequest, extreme generosity of an individual or family, or possibly a group of donations aggregated for a specific purpose— most likely permanently or for a long period time, if not in perpetuity.

We have a modifier, *and other permanent funds,* that now puts these endowment funds into a specific category from a legal and accounting perspective. Permanent funds are those that usually have a corpus—an initial amount of the donation that the donor specifies must be invested and can never be spent. Only the income derived from the investment of the corpus can be spent for the designated purpose for which the money was given in the first place. Most often, there are monies left in a will by someone who intends for there to be a permanent amount of money in perpetuity that when invested will generate income to the church organization for the purpose for which the donor has specified. The canon has set these permanent funds into a special category different from checking or savings accounts. The implication of an even higher fiduciary obligation to oversee and account for these funds is clearly implicated by nature of the definition of permanent funds.

And securities represented by physical evidence of ownership or indebtedness refers to stocks and bonds, such as IBM stock and U.S. Treasury, municipal, or corporate bonds.

"Shall be deposited with a National or State Bank, or a Diocesan Corporation, or with some other agency approved in writing by the Finance Committee or the Department of Finance of the Diocese"

Why would the canon require trust, endowment, other permanent funds, stocks, and bonds be deposited in a national or state bank? For oversight and accountability. The banks are highly regulated and inspected by states and the Federal Reserve. The probability of their safekeeping and accurate recordkeeping in a bank is substantially higher than other methods, such as prospective oil drilling, swamp land, the Brooklyn Bridge, or a jar in the sacristy. Implied, the canon introduces the requirement for oversight and accountability; first, with the audit of the church organization's records and, second, with deposit in a financial institution. However, *or a Diocesan Corporation, or with some other agency approved in writing by the Finance Committee or the Department of Finance of the Diocese* indicates that a financial institution is not an absolute requirement.

In the absence of depositing the assets in a financial institution, they can be deposited with the diocese. However, the diocese is now also as fiduciarily liable as the vestry who received the donation. Hence, many dioceses have provided for a diocesan foundation or some other entity or vehicle in which to pool the assets for investment. Most likely, these accounts are invested with a financial institution in the aggregate. Notice that this still provides for oversight and accountability because all aspects of the diocese are to be audited annually. Finally, the diocese has the authority to provide written approval for depositing the assets in some place other than a bank or a diocesan corporation.

Notice that a stock brokerage house is not approved automatically by the canon. I am not sure why in today's environment with the heightened regulation and oversight by the Securities and Exchange Commission (SEC), the canon does not also authorize the depositing of funds with a financial institution such as an investment brokerage. It could be that the canon has not kept up with the times. Or, it could be deliberate. Stock brokerages allow for much more risky investment vehicles such as mortgage backed securities, derivatives, and stock options. They also allow for margin accounts from which to borrow funds from the brokerage company while using the assets deposited with it for collateral. In addition, they are not bound by the wishes of the bequest. In other words, the fiduciary responsibility to the donor's estate or the church does not extend to the brokerage company. Regardless, the canon says the church organization must get diocesan finance approval before using any financial institution other than a national or state (chartered) bank or a diocesan corporation.

"Under a deed of trust, agency or other depository agreement"

This requires there be formal agreement establishing the fiduciary responsibility, and, hence, fiduciary liability on the part of the institution holding the funds and the person or persons who are the legally constituted authorized person or persons on the accounts. Bank signature cards for a checking account establish a fiduciary liability on the part of the person or persons named on the card, and also that of the bank. When we get to roles, I will identify those who are fiduciarily liable for these funds in the church.

"Providing for at least two signatures on any order of withdrawal of such funds or securities."

On the surface, this is straightforward. If the church has a deposit somewhere of any kind of funds, then there must be two authorized signatures to withdraw the funds. However, financial institutions have changed. Most banks no longer will honor the request by a church for two signatures, and will allow the withdrawal of funds with only one signature. Therefore, the likelihood of this portion of the canon being practiced in the church is one of diligence on the church's part, not the bank's. The church bears the sole responsibility for having two authorized signatures for withdrawal. This part of the canon is not only a control point for the protection of funds, but also a point of oversight for the purpose of the withdrawal in the first place. There is much more to come in later chapters on oversight and control.

"But this paragraph shall not apply to funds and securities refused by the depositories named as being too small for acceptance. Such small funds and securities shall be under the care of the persons or corporations properly responsible for them."

What sort of funds could this be? Some churches will have a Sunday school account. Some will have a coffee money jar. Some will have no brokerage account because donations of stock certificates have never been made before—until someone gives a share of stock. More likely, banks are doing away with free checking except for larger accounts. This makes it imprudent to put a small amount of money in a bank account, for example a Rector's discretionary account, just to have it dwindle due to bank fees. Nonetheless, the canon does allow for that.

"This paragraph shall not be deemed to prohibit investments in securities issued in book entry form or other manner that dispenses with the delivery of a certificate evidencing the ownership of the securities or the indebtedness of the issuer."

This last portion of the paragraph is disjointed from the rest. It uses language that has not been used before, and implies the existence of types of accounts that have not been previously authorized. The term "book entry form" comes from the securities industry—stocks and bonds. It refers to the lack of presence of a physical stock certificate or a physical bond. It means that the shares or bonds are recorded electronically at the brokerage company, and the church does not have physical possession of them. If you personally own stocks for investments, in your 401(k) or your IRA, you most likely own them in book form. You get a statement every month showing the shares you own, but you do not physically have those shares. Neither does your broker. They probably do not physically exist anywhere, but are in the data processing systems of the brokerage house and the stock registrar or bond issuer. Any further explanation is beyond the scope of this book. Previously, I posited that the canon probably meant it was okay to deposit money, stocks, and bonds in a brokerage house and not a bank, but the canon did not specifically allow it. These last sentences of this paragraph basically authorize it, albeit in the negative by providing that such deposits are not prevented.

> "**(c)** Records shall be made and kept of all trust and permanent funds showing at least the following:
> (1) Source and date.
> (2) Terms governing the use of principal and income.
> (3) To whom and how often reports of condition are to be made.
> (4) How the funds are invested."

Because endowment or other permanent funds are often received from the estate of a deceased person, a foundation, a trust, or other legal entity, it is important to keep a permanent record of the information specified. Without this information, vestries can lose sight of the purpose for the gift and its specific investments and expenditures required. If the wishes of the bequest are not kept, the estate of the deceased can petition the court to retrieve the money from the church, for example. It is wise counsel to always keep a copy of the actual bequeathing or gifting documents handy and review them annually with the new vestry to ensure the vestry is adhering to the terms and conditions of the gift. We will spend more time discussing restrictions on gifts in another chapter.

> "**(d)** Treasurers and custodians, other than banking institutions, shall be adequately bonded; except treasurers of funds that do not exceed five hundred dollars at any one time during the fiscal year."

The treasurer is easily identifiable, but who are *custodians*? Anyone who has control over the money, including parish administrators, bookkeepers, and those who are authorized signers of financial institution accounts.

Adequately bonded is subjective. How much bonding is adequate? Twenty-five percent of annual revenue is a good start. Bonding is done by insurance companies and basically comes in two flavors—fidelity bond or surety bond. A fidelity bond will likely involve taking the fingerprints on those to be covered along with a background check performed by the insurance company. This is the type of bond that is fiduciarily prudent as it is designed to protect the church from dishonest employees. Interestingly, in Australia the fidelity bond is more accurately called the "employee dishonesty insurance coverage."

Most churches think that liability insurance provides bonding. It does not. A specific insurance policy, or a specific insurance rider on a more pervasive insurance policy is required.

Except, that is, for treasurers of funds that do not exceed five hundred dollars at any one time during the fiscal year. I know of no mission so small that it has less than five hundred dollars at one time. Basically, this paragraph requires fidelity bonding of all the church organizations.

> "**(e)** Books of account shall be so kept as to provide the basis for satisfactory accounting."

Books of account mean the bookkeeping of the church. *Satisfactory accounting* may seem to provide a great deal of leeway to the church organization regarding how they accomplish the bookkeeping. It does not. Because the church is a not-for-profit organization, the proscribed method according to Generally Accepted Accounting Principles (GAAP) is the use of the fund accounting method. This method provides that donations given for a specific purpose are segregated in the accounting records. There are FASB, AICPA, auditing, reporting, and other accounting rules that are to be followed. Failure to do so does not provide for *satisfactory accounting*. There are those who disagree with this view, but my usual answer is, "Tell it to the judge presiding over the donor's lawsuit against the church." When the accounting industry provides standards of practice and prudence, it would be imprudent, or unsatisfactory, to do otherwise. There is much more in this book regarding GAAP, fund accounting, and how to read financial statements prepared in that manner.

> "**(g)** All reports of such audits, including any memorandum issued by the auditors or audit committee regarding internal controls or other accounting matters, together with a summary of action taken or proposed to be taken to correct deficiencies or implement recommendations contained in any such memorandum, shall be filed with the Bishop or Ecclesiastical Authority not later than 30 days following the date of such report, and in no event, not later than September 1 of each year, covering the financial reports of the previous calendar year."

All reports of such audits refers to the auditor's prepared financial report. This includes the signed auditor's opinion letter, required (by GAAP) financial statements, and the required Statements on Auditing Standards (SAS) Notes to the Financial Statements.

Including any memorandum issued by the auditors or audit committee regarding internal controls or other accounting matters. A CPA is required to issue findings from the audit regarding the internal controls of the church organization. Additionally, the CPA is required to determine if the accounting transactions are recorded according to GAAP, and if not, to report their findings either way.

Together with a summary of action taken or proposed to be taken to correct deficiencies or implement recommendations contained in any such memorandum. This is most often referred to as the letter to management. A CPA will make recommendations regarding how to correct the internal control deficiencies found and any inappropriate accounting practices that would cause the financial statements to be misleading.

Shall be filed with the Bishop or Ecclesiastical Authority not later than 30 days following the date of such report means that the CPAs prepared audit report—opinion letter, financial statements, and Notes to the Financial Statements—and the accompanying letters regarding internal control, accounting practices, and recommendations are all to be sent to the bishop within thirty days of the delivery of the audit to the vestry or other governing board.

Together with a summary of action taken or proposed to be taken to correct deficiencies or implement recommendations contained in any such memorandum. I deliberately addressed this portion of the paragraph out of sequence to make a point. It is not only everything the auditor gives the church in the form of reports, findings, or recommendations, but also what the church organization's governing body is going to do about correcting the deficiencies and addressing the recommendations. When we get to roles and responsibilities we will see how this impacts the fiduciary responsibilities of the parties.

And in no event, not later than September 1 of each year, covering the financial reports of the previous calendar year is self-explanatory.

"**(h)** All buildings and their contents shall be kept adequately insured."

The operative word *adequately* adds emphasis to this requirement. It also implies that accurate records be kept about the fixed assets of the church organization. When we discuss insurance, I will give some terrifying but real examples of the impact of not maintaining accurate fixed asset records.

"**(i)** The Finance Committee or Department of Finance of the Diocese may require copies of any or all accounts described in this Section to be filed with it and shall report annually to the Convention of the Diocese upon its administration of this Canon."

The Finance Committee or Department of Finance of the Diocese may require copies of any or all accounts described in this Section to be filed with it means all of the accounting records, insurance and bond policies, fixed assets accounting, all audit documents, and all the underlying supporting documentation such as invoices, payroll records, bank statements, cancelled checks, and donor records. These are the records of the church and the diocese is entitled to all of them when they request them. There is no limitation on the age of the documents and no limitation on the documents themselves.

And shall report annually to the Convention of the Diocese upon its Administration of this Canon puts the onus on the diocese to report to the Annual Convention whether it has adequately overseen the implementation and adherence to this canon, not only by the diocese, but also by every church organization within it. This is quite a burden. However, the rest of the canon in this Section 1, if adhered to by the church organizations within the diocese, lessens the reporting of abnormalities to a great degree. In my opinion, most diocesan Finance Departments do not report to the Annual Convention in enough detail to satisfy this canon.

"(j) The fiscal year shall begin January 1."

The last paragraph in Section 1 sets the financial accounting year for all church organizations as the calendar year ending December 31. There are some church schools that would argue their operating year is July 1 to June 30. That may be true, but the canon requires the financial records and subsequent reporting and audit be done on a calendar year basis. There is no room for misinterpretation of this paragraph.

"Sec. 2. The several Dioceses shall give effect to the foregoing standard business methods by the enactment of Canons appropriate thereto, which Canons shall invariably provide for a Finance Committee, a Department of Finance of the Diocese, or other appropriate diocesan body with such authority."

Each diocese is required to provide the person or office, from which the church organizations get the various approvals mentioned in Section 1, options for deposits of permanent funds, filing of audit reports and findings, and other financial matters. Section 2 requires that each diocese enact its own canons to further implement Canon 7. It is baffling to me that dioceses think this means it is acceptable to remove parts of Canon 7 requirements through their own canons. Section 2 is explicit: *Dioceses shall give effect to the foregoing standard business methods by the enactment of Canons appropriate thereto* does not say "if the diocese so chooses" or "is not inconvenienced by." For example: diocesan canons that modify the requirement for an annual audit every year by every church organization into something less than that are in direct violation of Canon 7, Section 2 and Section 1. When we discuss fraud and audits, we will see the dire consequences of not providing for the full implementation of Canon 7.

> **"Sec. 3**. No Vestry, Trustee, or other Body, authorized by Civil or Canon law to hold, manage, or administer real property for any Parish, Mission, Congregation, or Institution, shall encumber or alienate the same or any part thereof without the written consent of the Bishop and Standing Committee of the Diocese of which the Parish, Mission, Congregation, or Institution is a part, except under such regulations as may be prescribed by Canon of the Diocese."

Without joining the debate over church property, Section 3 is clear about how real property is to be treated. It specifically says that a church organization cannot get a loan of any kind against the real estate of the church organization without both the bishop and the Standing Committee's written approval. Since church real property is held in trust for the diocese (see Section 4 below), this makes sense in that the diocese has the authority over the pledging of the real property as collateral, securing of loans against real property, or otherwise causing title to the real property to be encumbered in any way. This includes donated real property as well as purchased real property.

> **"Sec. 4**. All real and personal property held by or for the benefit of any Parish, Mission or Congregation is held in trust for this Church and the Diocese thereof in which such Parish, Mission or Congregation is located. The existence of this trust, however, shall in no way limit the power and authority of the Parish, Mission or Congregation otherwise existing over such property so long as the particular Parish, Mission or Congregation remains a part of, and subject to, this Church and its Constitution and Canons."

*All real and personal property held by or for the benefit of any
Parish, Mission or Congregation is held in trust for this Church
and the Diocese thereof . . .*

Most people think it is only the real property that is held in trust for the
diocese. It is also the personal property. That pretty much makes everything
the property of the diocese. Real property is the real estate—including land,
buildings, and parking lots. Personal property is everything else. Some examples of personal property are: furniture, computers, copiers, refrigerator,
playground equipment, musical equipment, books, bank accounts, cash,
and other donated funds or items. Every asset of the church is held in trust
for the diocese. Based on this section of Canon 7, we begin to see the importance of the paragraphs in Section 1 that require proper accounting methods and audits.

*The existence of this trust, however, shall in no way limit the power
and authority of the Parish, Mission or Congregation otherwise
existing over such property so long as the particular Parish, Mission
or Congregation remains a part of, and subject to, this Church and
its Constitution and Canons.*

This section gives the use of these assets to the respective church organizations, but does not give title or ownership to them. What the church organization should understand by now is that the fiduciary responsibility on the
part of the governing board to church members, donors, and the diocese
cannot be ignored.

> "**Sec. 5**. The several Dioceses may, at their election, further confirm the
> trust declared under the foregoing Section 4 by appropriate action, but no
> such action shall be necessary for the existence and validity of the trust."

The final section of Canon 7 further illuminates that the diocese owns the
assets whether or not the diocese's name is on the deed or the bank account.
In absence of any document explicitly acknowledging the diocesan ownership of the assets, rest assured the diocese owns it anyway. This brings us to
the end of Title 1, Canon 7.

Title III (Ministry) Canon 9.5.b.6: Alms and Offerings

> The Alms and Contributions, not otherwise specifically designated, at the Administration of the Holy Communion on one Sunday in each calendar month, and other offerings for the poor, shall be deposited with the Rector or Priest-in-Charge or with such Church officer as the Rector or Priest-in-Charge shall appoint to be applied to such pious and charitable uses as the Rector or Priest-in-Charge shall determine. When a Parish is without a Rector or Priest-in-Charge, the Vestry shall designate a member of the Parish to fulfill this function.[2]

Title III, Canon 9, Section 5, Paragraph b, item 6 deals with money, but is found in the ministry title of the canons. Basically, this is a canonically required allocation of the undesignated offering—cash and checks—on a monthly basis to what is commonly called the rector's discretionary fund. In fact, the entry in the index of the canons for discretionary funds refers specifically and only to this part of the canons.

Right about now, many of the clergy who are reading this book are experiencing a return on investment in purchasing it. Note that, unlike Title I, Canon 7, there are no caveats or possibilities for deviation from this canon. While additional sources of funds for the discretionary fund may be used, this one is not to be deleted or altered. There will be a further discussion regarding the discretionary funds, and the proper and improper use of them in later chapters.

By now, you probably have taken exception to one or more of my comments in this chapter. I have confidence in that because often church organizations are lax in adhering to each tenet of the canon, particularly as it relates to money. That approach works until you have to explain it to the bishop or the judge. The canons are there for a reason, and I hope you see the necessity for conforming to them. If not, the ensuing chapters will have you revisit the validity of those disagreements by further explaining the implications and perils in failing to obey the canons with respect to money and personal liability. This will be true for laity as much, or more so, than for the clergy.

---

2. *Constitution and Canons for the Government of the Episcopal Church* (New York: Church Publishing Inc., 2009), p. 88.

CHAPTER

3

Roles and Responsibilities

Church Organization

This chapter discusses roles and responsibilities within the church at the diocesan and local church organization levels, paying particular attention to canonical requirements. These are observations of typical trends, but in no way intended to cast any one diocesan or church organizational standard as the only way. Because this is a generic aggregation of observations, this description probably will not look exactly like your organization. However, what I describe in this chapter will ensure the proper tone and execution of oversight, accountability, and fiduciary prudence and obligation. If this chapter differs greatly—not just in named role, but in functions being performed at all—from yours, then I submit there is a heightened need for immediate examination of those roles, tone, and functions to ensure oversight, accountability, and fiduciary responsibility.

The Episcopal Church is organized similarly to, but not entirely like, the mother Church in England. In the United States (and the 15 other countries where TEC is found), the church is divided into provinces that are subsequently divided into dioceses with bishops at the head of the dioceses.

Canons

Title IV: Ecclesiastical Discipline
Canon 1: Of Accountability and Ecclesiastical Discipline.

By virtue of Baptism, all members of the Church are called to holiness of life and accountability to one another. The Church and each Diocese shall support their members in their life in Christ and seek to resolve conflicts by promoting healing, repentance, forgiveness, restitution, justice, amendment of life and reconciliation among all involved or affected. This Title applies to Members of the Clergy, who have by their vows at ordination accepted additional responsibilities and accountabilities for doctrine, discipline, worship and obedience.[3]

Notice the word *restitution* in this canon. Restitution is often a financial and legal community word for "pay back the loss of money." Further, this canon includes "vows at ordination . . . accountabilities . . . and obedience."

Title IV, Canon 3: Of Accountability

Sec. 1. A Member of the Clergy shall be subject to proceedings under this Title for:

(a) knowingly violating or attempting to violate, directly or through the acts of another person, the Constitution or Canons of the Church or of any Diocese;[4]

It is the canonical requirement that any ordained person (Canon 1) follow the canons, and that includes Canon 7, which requires audits each year and requires accountability and oversight of the assets of the church.

Title IV, Canon 4: Of Standards of Conduct

Sec. 1. In exercising his or her ministry, a Member of the Clergy shall:

. . .

(e) safeguard the property and funds of the Church and Community;[5]

It is a direct violation of the standards of conduct for those ordained to fail to:

---

3. *Constitution and Canons for the Government of the Episcopal Church* (New York: Church Publishing Inc., 2009), p. 123.

4. *Constitution and Canons for the Government of the Episcopal Church* (New York: Church Publishing Inc., 2009), p. 126.

5. *Constitution and Canons for the Government of the Episcopal Church* (New York: Church Publishing Inc., 2009), p. 127.

- provide the proper tone at the top for fiscal fidelity and prudence
- provide for and enact oversight of the funds and assets
- establish standards of performance and require accountability of their staff, employees, and volunteers
- design and set in place the internal controls (safeguards)
- establish the expected levels of performance
- inspect those persons and processes for adherence to standards as designed and implemented

Title IV, Canon 17: Of Proceedings for Bishops

Sec. 1. Except as otherwise provided in this Canon, the provisions of this Title shall apply to all matters in which a Member of the Clergy who is subject to proceedings is a Bishop.[6]

Bishops are just as subject to the above canons as any other ordained person in the church.

Constitution
Article IV

In every Diocese a Standing Committee shall be elected by the Convention thereof, except that provision for filling vacancies between meetings of the Convention may be prescribed by the Canons of the respective Dioceses. When there is a Bishop in charge of the Diocese, the Standing Committee shall be the Bishop's Council of Advice.[7]

The bishops are charged by the constitution of TEC as the authoritative head of the diocese. Neither standing committees or councils of advice are specifically identified in the constitution and canons of TEC as having the fiduciary responsibility over the safeguarding of the assets of the church, as are the bishops and other clergy.

The canons do provide for dioceses to expand upon the above as long as it is not contradictory, and many have. You will need to consult your own diocesan canons for any further definition and requirements. Using the above, I will compare the roles and responsibilities within the church to their corporate counterparts.

---

6. *Constitution and Canons for the Government of the Episcopal Church* (New York: Church Publishing Inc., 2009), p. 150.

7. *Constitution and Canons for the Government of the Episcopal Church* (New York: Church Publishing Inc., 2009), p. 5.

Diocesan Roles

Bishop

Diocesan bishops are elected by the diocesan clergy and laity whenever a position comes open in a diocese. Diocesan bishops have much more control over the daily workings of the diocese than does the national church or Presiding Bishop. The real tone in a diocese lies with the bishop (hence the meaning of the word *Episcopal*) who determines all sorts of policy for the workings of the diocese. While it may not be a formal authority, when it comes to a decision of what to do in a situation, the question often asked is what does the bishop think?

Clergy serve within a diocese at the pleasure of the bishop. While a church or organization may pay the salary of the rector, vicar, and priest-in-charge, the cleric reports to the bishop for direction.

Just like the CEO of a commercial company, the clergy of a parish help to shape the vision and mission of that parish. Clergy also help set the tone organizationally—in developing the structures, measurement criteria, and policies that guide the parish and in continuing to actively support the implementation of those structures, criteria, and policies. They work with the vestry to define the strategy, develop an organization to execute the strategy, establish ways of measuring the performance of the church, monitor the performance, and set policy.

A bishop, along with the standing committee and other groups and individuals, sets the tone for the diocese. The bishop, in consultation, determines the structure of the diocesan staff, hires the individuals to fill those positions, sets goals, objectives, and priorities, and will monitor the success or lack thereof in meeting those. There will be reporting requirements of one kind or another that indicate to the bishop the health of the diocese in terms of those priorities. Over time, a bishop and diocese will draw priests who share those priorities and discourage those who do not. That shaping occurs either consciously or subconsciously.

If the bishop sets the tone, then a bishop who cares more about the fiscal health of the church in his or her diocese will let that be known. If the tone from the diocese is focused on diocesan commitment or pledge, then that will be the focus in the parishes and other church organizations.

How does the bishop cause a heightened sense of fiscal responsibility in the rest of the church organization? It is through the observation of his or her behavior and conversations, and through the diocesan staff. Who at the diocese receives the letters of recommendation and indications of internal control issues resulting from the annual audits in the parishes and other church organizations in the diocese as required annually in Canon 7? Who demands the audits be done in the parishes and monitors their completion as required in Canon 7? Who sets the tone that September 1 is the real deadline for having them completed and turned in to the diocese as required in Canon 7? And who reminds the churches in advance of the deadline and after the deadline? If the answer is no one, then likely there is a general lack of tone for fiscal responsibility in the parishes.

Few will take it on themselves to create effort or expense for an audit when the higher-ups do not care. That is human nature. In my classes, priests and others who have been in the church all their lives tell me that no one in the diocesan office cares about the audit reports or internal control letters. Some have even told me the last time they looked at Canon 7 was in seminary—or even that they have never studied the canon. No one has told me that they had ever examined Canon 7 as closely as we did in the last chapter. Who is responsible for that behavior? The bishop sets the tone for the rest of the diocese. If the bishop is fully knowledgeable about the canon and causes his or her staff to be fully knowledgeable, if the bishop puts in place the monitoring and reporting procedures for compliance, then the majority of the parishes will follow suit. Again, why should the bishop do this? Reread chapter 1 of this book if there is any doubt. Money was not in the background but in the forefront of Jesus' life and teachings. If Jesus cared, then we should also. And so should the bishop and everyone in the church.

So the bishop sets the tone for compliance with Canon 7. What might the actions be that set the tone for the approach to money on the part of the diocesan staff? We will look at a number of examples in the church at the diocesan level starting with the staff.

Canon to the Ordinary

One of the most obvious staff members impacting the tone of the diocese regarding money is the canon to the ordinary. The canon to the ordinary is the advocate at the diocesan level for the parishes and other church organizations within the diocese. The roles of canons to the ordinary are broadly defined from diocese to diocese. If the canon to the ordinary is knowledgeable about financial matters and helpful in that regard when someone calls from a parish, then word will get around that the canon has expertise and interest in financial matters. The canon to the ordinary is akin to the turnaround expert or consultant in the business world. He or she is often a "been there, done that, nothing surprises me" kind of individual.

Often, it is the canon to the ordinary who gets called when there are concerns of fraud in the parish. The canon to the ordinary interacts with the parishes more on operational daily matters and has more opportunity to advise the parish regarding operational matters than the bishop. The tone set by the canon to the ordinary in conversations and other communications with the parish is critical. If the canon to the ordinary is interested, concerned, can quote Canon 7 and diocesan canons, expects full accountability and reconciliation (monetary), and provides counsel regarding oversight and the expectation thereof, the parish gets the message that the diocese has expectations of fiscal and fiduciary compliance.

Canon or Director of Finance—Diocese

Another office in the diocese with parochial interaction regarding financial matters is the diocesan director (or canon) of finance. Audit reports and audit letters received by the bishop often are forwarded to this office. Sometimes, the bishop or diocesan canons will specify the reports be sent to this office. This person carries the banner of accountability, oversight, and fiduciary responsibility before the parishes, missions, and other entities of the diocese. This office is usually where the approval, or at least a recommendation to the bishop, originates.

First, if there is to be an audit in the church organizations by any group other than a CPA, the director of finance is usually the "Ecclesiastical authority" referred to in Canon 7 who recommends or approves such committee of auditors. That authority may have been delegated fully by the bishop, in which case the director of finance must be a CPA, for reasons I will explain in chapter 6. Or, the director may simply recommend actions to the finance committee and/or the bishop.

Second, the office of the director of finance often aggregates investments for the church organizations into a pooling of funds for management by professional money management companies, often the large brokerage houses. Third, this office is often where the diocesan pledge, or diocesan commitment, is made to the diocese by the church organizations. This office uses those pledges in the budgeting process for the diocese and tracks the payments by the church organizations throughout the year. Fourth, this office is often where diocesan loans are originated and subsequent accounting is done.

Hopefully, this office is not merely ceremonial, but actually is staffed with CPAs, experienced bankers, or financial managers. This office requires skills and experience that cannot be gained by on-the-job training. The tone for this office is also set by the amount and quality of expertise it brings to its interactions with the rest of the diocese. Once again, the bishop is ultimately responsible for the tone and performance of this office. The bishop chooses the staff, directs the staff, holds the staff accountable, and is ultimately responsible for the staff's performance. So, we come full circle to the importance of the tone as set by this office.

Finance Committee—Diocese

Sometimes the functions of the director of finance are blurred with those of the finance committee, if the diocese has one. Usually, the finance committee is a diocesan-only internal organization that has little interaction with the parishes and other church organizations. The diocesan treasurer is often a member of, if not the head of, the diocesan finance committee. This organization usually oversees the audit of the diocesan financial records by choosing and hiring an independent CPA firm for the diocesan audit. Many times this committee prepares and/or approves the diocesan budget, loans, investment firms, and other more long-term financial matters in contrast, but in support of, the director or canon of finance.

While not usually having a direct interaction with the parishes, this committee often oversees the operations of the diocesan finance office. If no one is overseeing the diocesan finance office, then who is setting the tone of the office that does interact with the parishes? Sometimes the bishop will delegate this oversight of the finance office to the finance committee. If so, as the senior member of the diocesan organization, according to Title IV, Canon 4, Section 1(e), it is still the bishop's obligation to periodically inspect the operations of both the finance office and finance committee for compliance, and for proper tone. Clergy at any level cannot abdicate this responsibility by delegating its oversight to someone else, and they are not relieved of their obligation. It is clear—"In exercising his or her ministry, a Member of the Clergy shall: . . . **(e)** safeguard the property and funds of the Church and Community . . ."[8]

There are other opportunities in the diocese for the tone for oversight, accountability, and financial responsibility to be reinforced. Examples include: at clergy conferences; at Fresh Start initiatives; upon the turnover of rectors, priests-in-charge, camp directors, and the like; at the diocesan convention; at ministry fairs; and other times when there is a gathering of the faithful.

---

8. *Constitution and Canons for the Government of the Episcopal Church* (New York: Church Publishing Inc., 2009), p. 127.

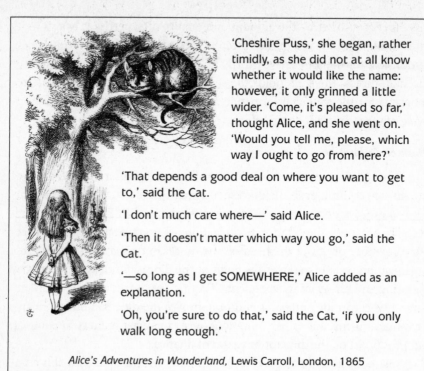

'Cheshire Puss,' she began, rather timidly, as she did not at all know whether it would like the name: however, it only grinned a little wider. 'Come, it's pleased so far,' thought Alice, and she went on. 'Would you tell me, please, which way I ought to go from here?'

'That depends a good deal on where you want to get to,' said the Cat.

'I don't much care where—' said Alice.

'Then it doesn't matter which way you go,' said the Cat.

'—so long as I get SOMEWHERE,' Alice added as an explanation.

'Oh, you're sure to do that,' said the Cat, 'if you only walk long enough.'

Alice's Adventures in Wonderland, Lewis Carroll, London, 1865

Local Church Organization—Parish, Mission, Camp and Conference Center, Soup Kitchen, Preschool, Thrift Shop

The strategy of an organization starts with a vision statement, followed by a mission statement, from which goals are derived that, when accomplished, will mean a successful accomplishment of the mission.

You say your church organization does not have a set of statements for vision, mission, and goals? I am reminded of Alice and the Cheshire cat.[9]

Without a vision statement, mission statements have no principles by which to be guided. Without mission statements, goals are aimless, literally. As the Cheshire cat said, ". . . Depends a good deal on where you want to get to." With no targets to hit, how do you know when you have achieved success and should set new targets? If, in the vision/mission/goals there are guiding principles and objectives set with measurable targets that pertain to how money is viewed, protected, and overseen by the vestry and parish, then money will come out of the shadows and into the light as a part of the church.

---

9. Lewis Carroll, *Alice's Adventures in Wonderland* (London: n.p., 1865).

Priests and Other Clergy in Church Organizations

Priests hire a staff and gather consultants who assist in implementing the parish strategy. A priest (I use the term generically for clergy-in-charge), along with the vestry, sets the tone for the church, the tone of worship, the tone of inclusiveness, the tone of conversations, and the tone of financial oversight and adherence to internal control processes. Leaders lead by example in all respects, not just in the areas they choose to lead.

If the priest does not follow internal control procedures, abide by the processes, and respect the roles of others in the process, then the staff and volunteers will not consider them important and will not abide by them either. For example, if the priest does not think the discretionary checking account is subject to the audit, but everything else is, then not only is the priest wrong canonically ("all money" means all money shall be subject to the annual audit), but also exhibits the wrong behavior to be emulated by the rest of the parish.

The priest generally manages paid and volunteer staff. This management includes giving proper direction, instruction, and inspection that financial processes and procedures are performed as designed and correctly. What is often not done where financial procedures are concerned is the inspection. Without inspection, those who might be inclined to commit fraud get a sense that no one is watching; no one is going to ask; there is no accountability, so why not "borrow" the money "just this once." Because there is no inspection, the thief thinks, *I will pay it back before anyone notices.* Rarely is this the case. Once a theft occurs, the tendency is for the perpetrator to continue to steal and not pay it back. We will discuss fraud in more detail in chapter 7.

Just as the priest sets the overall tone of the parish, so, too, does the priest set the tone for the implementation of internal control, oversight, accountability, and fiduciary responsibility. Because the priest directs the activities of staff and volunteers, the priest is responsible for the *implementation*, not the design of, internal control procedures. The priest needs to know what is the expected process and performance so he or she can direct, instruct, and inspect the staff and volunteers. This does not mean examining everything every day or every person's minute task performance, but it does mean management by walking around: being aware of what processes are supposed to be in place, where the checks and balances are, and every once in a while stopping by to "see how it's going" and showing interest in the current activity of staff and volunteers. Yes, even showing interest in the counting and bookkeeping. This is a subtle way to inspect without micromanaging.

By nature of being clergy, the priest exerts influence over the congregation and volunteers as well. It is a violation of internal control for someone who exerts so much influence pastorally to also influence the handling of or accounting for money. This may sound contradictory to the last points made, but there is a subtle difference. The priest should inspect the workings of the checks and balances, but not actually perform any of the functions. While the priest should inspect the internal controls, the priest should not have access to the accounting system or be in the position of having his or her name on an account at a financial institution. Definitely, he or she should not be a check signer. When we get to processes, I will detail a way that even discretionary funds are dispersed without the priest having a signature in the mix. A properly designed internal control system will have the necessary elements to allow the financial functioning of the church to occur without "hands on the money" by the priest.

Vestry

When vestry members hear that their own personal finances are at risk simply by virtue of being on the vestry, their responses range from confirmation of what is already known to sheer horror. Each vestry person, singularly and as a whole vestry, is fiduciarily liable for the finances of the congregation. Allow me to say that again. If you are on the vestry, you are personally liable for the finances of the parish, in addition to being personally responsible. That means that if there is a shortfall for any reason—theft or mismanagement—and the funds cannot be replaced from any other source, each and every vestry member is liable to the church for the full amount of the loss, personally and/or collectively. For vestries that have never heard this before, there are usually three possible reactions: "I knew that from other boards to which I have belonged"; "Really? Oh, my . . . "; or "How do I resign?"

> **Title I, Canon 14: Of Parish Vestries**
>
> **Sec. 1**. In every Parish of this Church the number, mode of selection, and term of office of Wardens and Members of the Vestry, with the qualifications of voters, shall be such as the State or Diocesan law may permit or require, and the Wardens and Members of the Vestry selected under such law shall hold office until their successors are selected and have qualified.
>
> **Sec. 2**. Except as provided by the law of the State or of the Diocese, the Vestry shall be agents and legal representatives of the Parish in all matters concerning its corporate property and the relations of the Parish to its Clergy.

Sec. 3. Unless it conflicts with the law as aforesaid, the Rector, or such other member of the Vestry designated by the Rector, shall preside in all the meetings of the Vestry.[10]

With this new knowledge, suddenly each vestry member has an invigorated interest in the proper management of the church's finances—the internal control, the processes and procedures, oversight, accountability, and fiduciary responsibility. If you are on the vestry, probably by now I have your attention.

The vestry must hold accountable everyone who has contact with the finances of the church. They set the tone for the transparency of the church's finances through their openness and communication with the rest of the congregation. This may be done, for example, by directing the posting of the financials on the bulletin board in a conspicuous place, in the newsletter, or on the website. They also set the tone by *establishing* the internal control process, accounting practices, and financial policies of the church.

Remember, the priest, via the staff and volunteers, *implements* what the vestry has *established* as internal control. The priest, staff, and volunteers are not the ones fiduciarily liable and should not have the latitude to deviate from what the vestry determines as the internal control procedures. For example: If proper receipts and authorizations are required to be turned in before a check is cut for payment or reimbursement (something the church absolutely should do), then vestry members should see that this documentation is properly attached to the check before the check is signed.

Most of the time, vestry members sign checks for a congregation. According to canon 7, two signatures are required. As we discussed earlier, banks do not require two signatures, only one. However, before signing the checks, each signer (presumed to be vestry members) should ensure the proper documentation and authorizations are present, and if not, *don't sign the check*. It is for internal control purposes, specifically inspection, that each signer examines all the documentation for completeness and reasonableness. The vestry has put in place this policy of two signatures for inspection because Canon 7 requires it. They have the responsibility for execution, because they are now a part of the process (signing checks).

See the difference between policy and process? The policy is that there will be two signers. The process is the attaching of documentation to the

---

10. *Constitution and Canons for the Government of the Episcopal Church* (New York: Church Publishing Inc., 2009), p. 52.

check, the inspection of the package, and only signing the check if everything required is present and reasonable. You probably do this at your home or business; the church is no different from the amount of scrutiny you give your own money.

The vestry is responsible for budgeting, hiring, and causing to occur and receiving the annual audit from an independent CPA auditor. The vestry should have the auditor present his or her findings and recommendations to the full vestry—not just the finance committee, treasurer, or any other subset. The vestry is fiduciarily liable. The treasurer, the finance committee, and the priest are not. The vestry must take its role seriously for the protection of donors, employees, volunteers, and themselves.

The vestry is ultimately, if not directly, responsible for approving all expenditures of the church. In some large churches, vestry commission chairs delegate invoice approval to committee chairs or individuals. For example, the music minister may be delegated authority to approve invoices for music as this person would know best if the invoice is valid. Or, the parish life commission chair may delegate approval authority to the formation committee chair for invoices for classroom materials. In either case, the vestry commission chair is responsible for the transactions, should review the transactions, and question any that are not reasonable. In most churches, the commission chair's review of the month's transactions does not take much time and can be sent out in advance of the vestry meeting. In small congregations, the responsibility is not lessened because of its size and the approval/reviews should take even less time. Complacency is the enemy of internal control, and the friend of a perpetrator.

The vestry must maintain diligence in its inspection and accountability. Previously, we said that the priest does not devise the internal control policies, but rather implements them. The vestry is responsible for establishing the internal control policies.

Because the vestry does handle the money, they are a part of internal control. There will be more about that later in chapters 8 through 10. No congregation is too small to protect the assets of the church. As we will see in the internal control materials later in the book, the number of people required to properly implement internal control is small, but they should be properly trained and given properly documented policies and procedures to perform their task.

A final note, the vestry is also charged with preparing the Parochial Report and making an annual report to the parish and the diocese.

**Title I, Canon 6: Of the Mode of Securing an
Accurate View of the State of This Church**

Sec. 1. A report of every Parish and other Congregation of this Church
shall be prepared annually for the year ending December 31 preceding, in
the form authorized by the Executive Council and approved by the Committee on the State of the Church, and shall be filed not later than March
1 with the Bishop of the Diocese, or, where there is no Bishop, with the
ecclesiastical authority of the Diocese. The Bishop or the ecclesiastical
authority, as the case may be, shall keep a copy and submit the report
to the Executive Council not later than May 1. In every Parish and other
Congregation the preparation and filing of this report shall be the joint
duty of the Rector or Member of the Clergy in charge thereof and the
lay leadership; and before the filing thereof the report shall be approved
by the Vestry or bishop's committee or mission council. This report shall
include the following information:

(1) the number of baptisms, confirmations, marriages, and burials during the year; the total number of baptized members, the total number of
communicants in good standing, and the total number of communicants
in good standing under 16 years of age.

(2) a summary of all the receipts and expenditures, from whatever
source derived and for whatever purpose used.

(3) such other relevant information as is needed to secure an accurate
view of the state of this Church, as required by the approved form.[11]

Note that Canon 6, Section 1(2) requires the "summary of all the receipts
and expenditures, from whatever source derived and for whatever purpose
used" be reported. Basically, the vestry is certifying all financial matters are
properly and prudently entered into the financial records of the church. Why
would a vestry not want an independent CPA audit annually? To not do so
is a huge risk.

Treasurer—Parish or Other Church Organization

The treasurer position is found in commercial business as well. Sometimes
the Chief Financial Officer (CFO) is also the treasurer. The distinction between the two, when the two positions exist, is minor, and we will not delve
into them here.

The treasurer should not be a member of the vestry. Neither should the
treasurer in a congregation or other entity be in a position of control over the
expenditures or in a position of influence. The treasurer is then free to report

to the priest and the vestry as an independent resource. The treasurer should not be related to anyone who is in a position of influence—any member of the clergy or any member of the vestry.

Many times, the treasurer will attend meetings of the finance committee, vestry, stewardship committee, planned giving committee, or audit committee, but does not vote or influence the committee. The treasurer's primary function is to reconcile all financial statements monthly and provide oversight of the church's finances from an independent perspective.

All communication from any financial institution should be opened only by the treasurer. The treasurer should also examine the general ledger transactions monthly to ensure proper recording of transactions. For example, one church recorded all payments made on a loan to expenses. This caused net income to be drastically understated and the loan to never decrease in balance outstanding. In addition, interest expense was never recorded. The proper transaction is to reduce the loan by the principal amount and increase interest expense by the proper amount. Over a year's time, improper recording of the loan payment as an expense can materially distort the income statement and the balance sheet of an organization.

There are times when a journal entry is necessary to correct an item or to record new items. Under no circumstances should the bookkeeper record any journal entries that are not approved by the vestry, and the treasurer should be the one to bring them before the vestry for approval. Each of these processes will be discussed in detail in chapter 5.

Bookkeeper

The bookkeeper never handles money. If he or she does, you have a highly likely opportunity for missing funds. The bookkeeper never counts money, never deposits money, and never receives the signed checks back from the vestry. A signed check is negotiable and is money.

The bookkeeper posts the transactions of the church and writes the checks for the entity—*only* after proper written approval from the person who provides oversight of that part of the budget (usually a vestry member) and documentation are received. The bookkeeper should never be allowed to write checks not previously authorized and properly documented. We will address proper approval and documentation later in chapter 10.

The bookkeeper posts transactions to the books and causes some non-cash transactions to be recorded, such as depreciation or the addition of fixed assets and loans. The bookkeeper should have mastery of the software and knowledge of generally accepted accounting principles and fund accounting to provide accurate and useful financial statements and reports, not only for vestry meetings, but also in advance of vestry meetings for commission chairs, the finance committee, the treasurer, and clergy. In many cases, the bookkeeper is a part-time salaried position or a volunteer position. That does not relieve him or her from the preceding comments.

Parish Administrator

What happens if the bookkeeper is also the parish administrator who also makes the deposits and reconciles the bank statements? First, there is no internal control. Second, should money become missing, the first place to look is the person previously described with the big target on his or her back. And who is responsible for this situation? It is the vestry's responsibility to properly design the system of internal control to prevent such a potentially disastrous situation. It is the priest, generally, who sees that the vestry designed system of internal control is implemented by staff and volunteers.

One task the parish administrator can take on regarding church finances is posting the pledges and the contributions into the donor records. Notice I did not say counting the money, making the bank deposit, carrying the deposit to the bank, or reconciling the bank statement. However, as we will see in the processes that are described later in chapter 9, the parish administrator can play a significant role in keeping donations of cash and non-cash items properly recorded.

Volunteers

Volunteers are everywhere. They are not paid, and are obedient to directions only to the extent they choose to follow them. Because they may not understand the rationale for processes, be careful when using volunteers to perform financial functions.

Title I, Canon 17:
Of Regulations Respecting the Laity
  Sec. 8. Any person accepting any office in this Church shall well and faithfully perform the duties of that office in accordance with the Constitution and Canons of this Church and of the Diocese in which the office is being exercised.[12]

Although the canon calls on laypersons to "well and faithfully perform," only the vestry is fiduciarily liable. Volunteers have *no* fiduciary liability to

---

12. *Constitution and Canons for the Government of the Episcopal Church* (New York: Church Publishing Inc., 2009), p. 58.

the church. Abdication of vestry duties to a volunteer, no matter how well known, how well-liked, or how trusted is done so at the exposure of liability for each vestry member and the vestry as a whole. <u>Volunteers are never used to count money unless at least one vestry member is present at all times with the money</u>—from the altar to the bank.

So, how do we use volunteers around money? There are certainly times when it is more convenient for volunteers to handle money, such as Wednesday night suppers, fund-raising events, taking tuition in the church school, handling the till at the thrift shop, and receiving donations for a memorial or dues for the Scouts. Also, volunteers could be in a position of approving expenditures from a budget that has been delegated by the vestry chair. The way we can use volunteers around incidental money is with proper internal control procedures, oversight, and accountability. To do otherwise is not prudent and creates a potential liability for the vestry.

In summary, the tone for financial prudence and responsible fiscal management starts at the top. Hopefully, the bishop sets the tone for the clergy in the diocese and for the staff at the diocesan offices. Even if that is not the case, the priest or person in charge is responsible for setting the tone of fiscal and fiduciary prudence at the local church organization level—parish, mission, or other church organization.

Positions of authority within the church have definite roles in financial management for the church. There is not much overlap in the roles. If performed as described, then the environment is established by which internal control, accountability, and oversight can be accomplished more readily.

4

Parish Monies

One confusion for most parishes and vestries is what money really belongs to the church. There also is a lack of understanding of the proper categorizations for the money and the accurate terms with which to discuss it. For example, the word *fund* has one meaning in the vernacular, a different meaning when speaking in accounting terms, and still another meaning when used by the vendor of the accounting software used by the church.

Even different software vendors use the word *fund* differently. No wonder we cannot seem to get on the same page of the conversation. If there are three people in the room with different backgrounds, there will most likely be a misunderstanding regarding the use of the word *fund*. A banker and an accountant will use the word differently in the same context. Besides *fund*, there are many other words that carry the risk of misunderstanding: *designated, endowment, permanent, temporary, restricted, cash, account, reserve, discretionary*, among others.

So with all these opportunities for misunderstanding, how do we have a conversation about money in the church? The answer is that we all use the same lexicon and work from the same operating definitions when speaking of financial matters in the church setting.

But, even before we can develop a common lexicon, a more basic question must be answered. What money really belongs to the church? Not in generic terms, but specifically. As an accountant, I tend to look at things from the accounting definition, which is usually more exacting than the vernacular. Also, it is the accounting definition that the legal community often draws upon when looking for an exact definition of terms.

Before we can discuss the lexicon of money, we must discuss the lexicon of accounting. This is partly because this is a book about financial management, which generally uses accounting definitions, and partly because a wealth of other material from the accounting community is available using that vocabulary.

In the accounting profession there will often be a reference to Generally Accepted Accounting Principles (GAAP). GAAP is a combination of the codification of accounting standards promulgated by the Financial Accounting Standards Board (FASB), and the de facto practice of accounting methods as conducted by the particular industry, in this case not-for-profit churches. The codification of this knowledge is found by researching the Financial Accounting Standards Board (FASB) pronouncements and American Institute of Certified Public Accountants (AICPA) published literature, as one would research court cases for precedence in the legal profession or professional studies and journals in the medical profession.

In addition, these principles (GAAP) reflect widespread practice throughout the industry, consistent with FASB. It does not mean that because everybody else is doing something, they are correct. For example, failing to record fixed assets in the books of the church is not correct according to GAAP (or to canon) even though most churches do not record fixed assets. Or, having a discretionary account that no one but the rector reconciles is not right, although many clergy feel that the account is so private that only they can see the bank book or bank statements.

Donations of Money

Probably the most misunderstood part of church finances is donations. How could that be? Everybody knows the term *donation*. If it were only that simple. You already know that a donation is an object or noun that refers to the actual thing or an amount of money given. For the purposes of this chapter, we are going to address the noun only, not the act of giving. However, there are different kinds of donations. This is where we begin to get more precise with the lexicon.

Pledges

Pledges are promises to give. Legally, pledges can be enforced as a contract between the donor and the church. Although I know of no one who took someone to court to enforce a pledge to a church, it has been done.

Pledges fall into two categories—undesignated and designated. Undesignated pledges are what we normally refer to as a general pledge that is made without any specific purpose being identified. Sometimes this type of pledge is referred to as a "tithe." This is where the church gets the majority of its revenue for operating expenses, for example, electricity, salaries, and office supplies. When the pledge is undesignated, the vestry has the full use of the money as it sees fit—within the bounds of their fiduciary responsibility. Although *undesignated* is the commonly used term, the correct accounting term is *unrestricted*. We will see this in chapter 5 when we discuss reading financial statements.

Designated

Designated is a term appropriate to both pledged income and ad hoc donations. Designated pledges are those that are made for a specific purpose. For example, pledges that are made to the building fund, organ fund, or memorial garden are designated pledges and donations. These must be accounted for separately in the church accounting records and on the donors' statements.

In general, it is a breach of fiduciary responsibility to spend money donated for designated purposes for anything other than that purpose. In other words, if someone gives money specifically for the building fund or memorial garden and it is spent on electricity or salaries, that is a breach of fiduciary responsibility. Also, failure to provide for the proper accounting to segregate the money for its purposes is irresponsible if not also a breach of fiduciary responsibility. And who is liable for that breach? The vestry is, both individually and collectively. *Designated* is the commonly used term. The correct accounting term for our consistent lexicon is *temporarily restricted*.

Many of the audits I have performed were for churches that either had not had an audit in recent memory or had never had one. In the course of the audit, I take the opportunity to teach the vestry about proper financial management. As an added bonus, I reconcile designated and undesignated funds (temporarily restricted and unrestricted). About half the time, the vestry had already spent all of the unrestricted funds to keep the doors open and the lights on, and were dipping into and spending temporarily restricted funds for operating expenses.

According to canon law, if that occurs, it is up to the vestry to come up with the additional money to put back into the church coffers so the designated funds are made whole and there are operating funds to pay the church's bills. I know of no church that has done this, but the fiduciary liability is there. There are some diocesan canons that require this to be done before the close of business on December 31 each year.

Scenario: The Youth Building   The youth of the church do not have a place to call their own. The youth minister feels that the youth need a wing off the parish hall designated as their space. There have been suggestions for decorating the Senior High Sunday school room, even suggestions that the youth be allowed to paint the room (much to the dismay of the junior warden). There have also been concerns raised about the teenagers holding EYC meetings in the same room where they attend Sunday school—at least those that come to Sunday school.

After all, Sunday nights or other times, a larger room would be nice for four square, foosball, guitar corner, lock-ins, sitting in a circle that is not knees-to-elbows, and other activities. With an older-youth-only facility, maybe Boy Scout and Girl Scout troops could be started, bringing in other families in the community.

Apparently a number of people in the parish have agreed. Seven families have donated $10,000 each for the beginning of the capital campaign for the youth building. Finally, the youth minister will have an office and some storage space.

While the vestry has been on board with this, and the finance committee has been helpful, a curveball was thrown at last night's vestry meeting. Now the formation commission chair wants to use the building, before the plans are even drawn, as an expansion of Sunday school rooms. There could be a new nursery with a playground, and the Stephen Ministry could have a room. The ideas kept pouring out. The parish outreach commission chair agreed. Even AA could have a place to meet away from the parish hall itself. Unfortunately, the junior warden went along in support. The next thing you know, there was general support, a motion, a vote, and approval to convert the proposed youth building into an expanded formation building. How did that happen so fast?

After the dust settled, the youth minister asked, "What about the seven donations of $10,000 each? There are going to be some upset people who gave that money for a youth building, not a Sunday school expansion building." The formation commission chair retorted that once the money is given, it is in the purview of the vestry to use capital campaign funds for buildings as they see fit.

Analysis Bad move. There are seven upset people. The vestry cannot take that money and redirect the purpose of the building, altering the physical plans and converting it into a Sunday school expansion. What if the money had been given for a gymnasium? Could the vestry redirect the building to be built as Sunday school classrooms or a preschool? Absolutely not, if they ever expect those seven people to donate anything else ever again.

The seven people need to be contacted and given an opportunity to either receive their donation back in full or specifically alter (in writing) their designation for the use of the funds for a Sunday school building. The prudent thing to do is to get permission from the seven *before* the vote. The obvious part is that this scenario provides for seven easily identified donors. What if the following were the case?

Scenario: Christmas Poinsettias   The flower guild has decided that the church should be decorated for Christmas with as many poinsettias as possible and has ordered two hundred plants, costing $1,000. The hope is that each family will donate specifically designated money for the Christmas poinsettia fund at $5 each to cover the cost of the plants. The donations flowed in with an extra $500 donated over the actual cost of the flowers and three hundred donors participating. Assume that each donor gave exactly the same $5 amount for one plant. With three hundred donors, the amount received was $1,500, or $500 more than was needed to pay for the poinsettias. What does the vestry do with the extra $500?

Analysis   Does the flower guild try to contact the three hundred donors to ask if any would like their money back? If so, which are the first one hundred contacted to the exclusion of the rest? In this case, it is not realistic to try to take that approach. There are several options. The first is to keep the money in the flower guild fund for Christmas flowers for next year. Since this is the end of the year and all designated funds are rolled over as starting balances into next year, the second option is to keep the money in the flower guild fund for flowers to decorate the church throughout next year. If the flower guild feels they do not need the money for next year, the vestry may take the money out of the flower guild fund and use it for some other purpose (not recommended). However, it would be prudent to make that well known before actually taking the money out of the flower guild fund.

For example, publish in the service bulletin for four Sundays, in the monthly newsletter, on the website for a month, announce from the ambo for four weeks (and any other regular means of communication), that there was an excess and anyone not wanting their funds used for other purposes could either get their money back or designate it for another purpose. In reality, you will most likely hear from no one.

However, think about the message this sends to the congregation about tone and transparency. The message that comes across is: "We care about your donation and the purpose for which you gave it. We want to give you the opportunity to see that your money is used as you intend. Please let us know if you have a preference. Thank you and bless you for your donation." If the vestry takes the money without any communications and spends it on polishing the floors, what kind of message does that send?

And do not think that this transferring of designated funds to operating funds is only known to the vestry. There are no secrets in the church. What may seem like an innocuous use of money to some then becomes a big flap. Personally, when I give money for flowers in thanksgiving for, or in memory of, a loved one, I expect that to be spent on flowers and not on polishing the floors.

Other Designated Donations

Basically, any donation, whether pledged or not, that is made for a specific purpose is a designated (temporarily restricted) donation. All of the preceding comments regarding designated pledges also apply to the unpledged gift of a designated donation. A one-time gift for flowers is still a designated donation and is recorded as such in the accounting records of the church as well as the donor records indicating that the money has been donor-restricted for a particular purpose.

Plate

Plate donations are often referred to as loose change or cash in the offering plate. But plate donations also include any checks not designated for a specific purpose. If there is nothing written on the face of the check that identifies the purpose of the check donation, then it is considered plate income. It is not correct to assume that Susie meant for the check to go toward her pledge. Because of your fiduciary liability, do not try to second-guess donor intentions; instead, follow what is written, or not, on the face of the check. The person posting the contributions could also call or email Susie and ask her intentions. I recommend documenting Susie's response in some way, such as keeping a copy of the email or a phone log. This is one of the banes of existence for anyone who posts contributions into the church records. It is also a bane for the finance committee and the vestry who try to keep the accounting straight. Why is this important?

Title III (Ministry) Canon 9.5.b.6:
Alms and Offerings

The Alms and Contributions, not otherwise specifically designated, at the Administration of the Holy Communion on one Sunday in each calendar month, and other offerings for the poor, shall be deposited with the Rector or Priest-in-Charge or with such Church officer as the Rector or Priest-in-Charge shall appoint to be applied to such pious and charitable uses as the Rector or Priest-in-Charge shall determine. When a Parish is without a Rector or Priest-in-Charge, the Vestry shall designate a member of the Parish to fulfill this function.[13]

First, there is a canonical reason for plate donations to be identified correctly. Specifically, *The Alms and Contributions, not otherwise specifically designated* is clear: if there is nothing specifically designating the funds for pledges or other purposes, the check is considered a plate offering, just like loose cash.

Second, some dioceses require in their canons that the alms and contributions not otherwise specifically donated go to the bishop's discretionary fund on the day of the bishop's visit. The bishop is going to expect that the checks that are not otherwise designated for pledges or for other designations, along with the cash, be sent to the bishop.

Third, the parochial report filed annually with the diocese separates pledge and plate income. Canon 7 requires the accurate accounting of all funds, and that includes properly identifying and recording plate income.

Endowments

Another term misused in the church is *endowments*. Properly used, an endowment represents a sum of money that has been given in perpetuity, usually for a specific purpose. The most common misuse of the term *endowment* is when a collection of money, usually large, is held for a specific purpose, usually a building campaign. Properly, that would be a designated account and a temporarily restricted fund. The misconception is that whenever there is a large amount of money set aside for a specific purpose, it is an endowment. That is incorrect. Part of what you must do in the church, particularly at the local level, is to correctly use terms that have exacting meanings financially. Otherwise you cannot accurately communicate among the vestry, congregation, and diocese your intentions or those of the donors.

So what is an endowment? An endowment can be recognized by how it is created, the terms and conditions of its creation, how the money is to be used, and the perpetuity of the donation. Notice that I did not mention anything about the dollar amount of the endowment.

An endowment is most frequently created from a last will and testament as a bequest to the church. It does not always have to be created that way, but that is most common. An endowment could also be created by a donor or a

---

13. *Constitution and Canons for the Government of the Episcopal Church* (New York: Church Publishing Inc., 2009), p. 88.

group of donors, but it has to have some of the following elements to be an endowment rather than a designated donation.

An endowment usually has an initial amount of money that is given to the church in perpetuity. In other words, that initial amount can never be spent by the church, but rather must be fiduciarily invested with the proceeds from the investment being spent for the purpose for which the initial donation was made. That initial donation also has a financially exacting name—the *corpus*. This name becomes important later when we get to the financial statements because the corpus, if from an endowment in perpetuity, has specific accounting rules. Separately, the earnings from the corpus also have their own accounting rules.

What follows is an example of the Church of the Holy Smoke's™ scholarship endowment from Ma Barker's last will and testament.

> The Rev. Faith H. Charity
> Church of the Holy Smoke
> 123 Elm Street
> Paxtown, Agape 12345
>
> Dear Faith:
> Please find enclosed a check made payable to the Church of the Holy Smoke in the amount of $150,000. This represents a disbursement under the Estate of Mrs. Ma Barker. Mrs. Barker, under item Twelve of her will, left the rest, residue, and remainder of her estate to the Church of the Holy Smoke for the following purposes, and I quote: "All of the rest, residue, and remainder of my estate, I give, bequeath and devise to the Church of the Holy Smoke, Paxtown, Agape, for the purpose of creating and maintaining a scholarship fund to be known as the 'Ma Barker Scholarship Fund.'"
> "It is my desire that an education committee be composed from the members of Holy Smoke to govern said scholarship fund and that the income of such scholarship fund is to be used to establish as many annual scholarships as will be permitted by the available funds."
> If you have any questions, please do not hesitate to contact me.
>
> Sincerely yours,
> I. M. Willum
> Willum, Shakum, and Down P.C.
> Attorneys at Law

Notice that the establishment of the fund states ". . . the *income* of such scholarship fund is to be used to establish as many annual scholarships . . .". It does not state that the $150,000 corpus may be used to pay out scholarships. It implies that only the income earned on the corpus can be paid out. This is an endowment, permanently established from a bequest, with a corpus in perpetuity, the purpose of which is specifically scholarships. When we get to financial statements, you will see that the corpus is permanently restricted while its earnings are temporarily restricted.

Endowments do not have to come from bequests. Someone living could donate money and put a permanent restriction on the corpus. Each gift of an endowment-like nature needs to be examined individually to determine if there are terms and conditions that make it an endowment. This is not meant to imply that a corpus in perpetuity must exist for there to be an endowment. There are some endowments in which the corpus is capable of being spent, but usually over a long period of time. There is usually some expectation that the funds will be invested to yield some return, the benefit of which will be used for some purpose. If in doubt, consult a local CPA for proper classification—endowment or designated donation.

Donations Other Than Money

Property Donations

Donations can also be in a form other than cash or checks. Some donations are in the form of publicly traded securities—stocks and bonds. Other donations are in the form of personal property—a refrigerator, baptismal font, or hymnal—or, real property—land for a church or parking lot, rectory, or cemetery plots. Further, there are differences in the amount recorded as a donation based on whether the item is real or personal property, new or used. How does the church determine the value at which to record the donation and the fixed asset? This is trickier and involves an inexact science. (Technically, accounting is considered an art, not a science.) Since the donor is most likely interested in the value for tax deductions, and the church needs to comply with tax law when issuing donor statements, we need to look to the Internal Revenue Service Code for guidance.

IRS Publication 561—Determining the Value of Donated Property

This publication is designed to help donors and appraisers determine the value of property (other than cash) that is given to qualified (not-for-profit) organizations. It also explains what kind of information you must have to support the charitable contribution deduction you claim on your return.[14]

---

14. *IRS Publication 561: Determining the Value of Donated Property* (Washington, D.C.: Internal Revenue Service, 2012), p. 1.

IRS Publication 561 categorizes property donations into the following:

- household goods
- used clothing
- jewelry and gems
- paintings, antiques, and other objects of art
- collections
- cars, boats, and aircraft
- inventory
- patents
- stocks and bonds
- real estate
- interest in a business
- annuities, interests in life of terms of years, remainders, and reversions
- certain life insurance and annuity contracts, and partial interest in property not in trust

In addition, there are rules regarding appraisals, and special documentation requirements when the donated value exceeds $5,000 and when it exceeds $500,000. Leave it to the IRS to take something that appears innocuously simple and convert it into something extremely complicated. If the donation transaction is not done according to the tax law, it puts the donor and the recipient at odds with the IRS.

For those who are so inclined to self-persecution, the following is the U.S. Code citation from which Publication 561 is derived: *Title 26, Subtitle A, Chapter 1, Subchapter B, Part VI, Section 170, Charitable Contributions.* I recommend saving the reading of it for a time when penitence is required. However, it is the law from which most interpretations about charitable contribution transactions for tax purposes will be derived. IRS Publication 561 puts into more readable English the intentions of the U.S. Congress and §170.

Fair Market Value

When goods are donated rather than cash, both the church and the donor need to determine the fair market value (FMV) of the donation. In some cases the FMV may be different for the donor and the church. To determine the value at which to record the donation of property in the fixed assets of the church and into the donor records, the church must first establish the FMV on the date of donation. For some assets, such as publicly traded securities like stocks and bonds, this is easier than, say, a used Ping-Pong table. While the IRS has a great deal of detail for each category of asset mentioned above, I will address only the most popular ones where there seems to be confusion and leave the rest for you to research on your own now that you have the publication reference and U.S. Code.

From IRS Publication 561, "Fair market value (FMV) is the price that property would sell for on the open market. It is the price that would be agreed on between a willing buyer and a willing seller, with neither being required to act, and both having reasonable knowledge of the relevant facts. If you put a restriction on the use of property you donate, the FMV must reflect that restriction."[15] The last part is one that sometimes causes donations of land to be valued incorrectly, particularly by the donor.

Scenario: Parking Lot   Church of the Holy Smoke™ needs a parking lot for its growing membership. However, the church is landlocked in an increasingly urban area. Land is at a premium. Finally, the small frame house and lot across the street became available for sale, and an individual bought the parcel and donated it to the church. The donor paid dearly—a price that reflected a fully constructed and usable residence in an area that was surrounded by commercial property. However, it was known at the time of purchase and donation that the house would be razed and the land used for a parking lot. The donor restricted the donation to the use of a parking lot.

Analysis   From the perspective of the IRS, the fair market value of the donation is the lower value of an empty lot, not the higher value paid for a residence and lot surrounded by commercial property. However, had the donation been for the purpose of a rectory, then the price paid for the lot and house would likely be FMV. In absence of a qualified appraisal to the contrary, the IRS rules give clear indication of FMV. The scenario also assumes that the purchase and subsequent donation occur within a short period of time, such as a month or two. It should be a short enough period of time that another parcel of property of similar value is not sold that would call the value of the donated property into question, or a market condition that would also call the value into question.

If the property is donated from a bequest, or other than within a short period from purchase, then the prudent thing to do is have the property appraised by a certified real estate appraiser who will provide the necessary documentation to defend the appraisal should the donor need to appear

---

15. *IRS Publication 561: Determining the Value of Donated Property* (Washington, D.C.: Internal Revenue Service, 2012), p. 2.

before the IRS to substantiate the deduction. Failure to do that gives the IRS the right to make the determination of the FMV on its own.

While the burden of the valuation rests with the donor, the church should be a good citizen and accept the donation only after proper determination of FMV and record in its books that determination. The church should require the donation occur reasonably close to the purchase of the property or require that the FMV be established by certified appraisal or other means that are acceptable to the IRS. If the church really wanted to be a good citizen, they would offer to pay for the appraisal, considering the large value of the donation. Consult a CPA, particularly one who specializes in not-for-profit donations.

The above are not all the pitfalls of donating real property. IRS Publication 526 identifies several more that I will not address here. I highly recommend the donor and the church get a set of professionals involved—real estate appraiser, real estate attorney, CPA, a contractor if the property needs modification, and others that may have a bearing on the FMV determination—before the donation is made.

Stocks, Bonds, and Other Publicly Traded Securities

Determination of FMV for stocks, bonds, and other publicly traded securities is usually straightforward. If the security donated is anything other than a stock that is traded principally on the New York Stock Exchange (NYSE), a CPA should be consulted, preferably before the donation is made or immediately thereafter. However, if the donation is ten shares of IBM stock, then the FMV is relatively easily determined—but not by the value of the stock at the close of the trading day.

The FMV is correctly recorded this way: On the date of donation, the highest price and the lowest price traded on the NYSE are averaged to determine the FMV of the ten shares. Since it is assumed the church sells the shares at a later date, then the date of donation is used for the FMV determination by the donor. What usually happens is the church sells the stock within three days and records the donation at the value the stock brought from the sale: ten shares IBM sold at 190.25 less $45 sales commission = $1,857.50 received in a check from the brokerage house. The donation usually recorded by the church is $1,857.50, and in this case is different from what the donor would report as a contribution on his or her tax return per the previous calculation of averaging the values on date of donation.

In practical terms, the church should not be involved in the FMV determination for the donor. The church will probably record the donation at $1,857.50 and issue a donor statement accordingly. There are a number of other considerations regarding FMV and securities, and if your situation is not very similar to the above, do your own research and seek professional advice from a CPA.

Other Personal Property

Personal property donations are a great way to receive assets for the church and are often donated for a specific purpose. Many examples come to mind. If the church needs to refurbish or establish a kitchen, donations of a refrigerator, stove, dishwasher, and microwave can all be made by separate individuals to lessen the cost overall to the donor while allowing precious capital funds to be spent instead with the contractor on the renovation.

Establishing a band for contemporary worship services involves obtaining microphones, amplifiers, and other audio equipment, all of which are likely donated in pieces of the whole setup. Of course, sometimes money is given to buy those things, and that is clearly donor designated (temporarily restricted) funds for the purchase of the items for which the money is specifically given. But how does the church properly deal with physical goods that are donated, like the refrigerator, from a financial perspective?

The problem for the church is multi-faceted. Using the refrigerator as an example, if the donation is the physical refrigerator and not cash, the church uses FMV of the refrigerator as the amount to record. But, how do we know what FMV is? Is it at replacement cost? Is it the purchase price paid by the donor? The correct answer usually starts with determining whether the goods are new or used.

If new, then the amount to record for the donation in the books is easily determined. Have the donor bring in the receipt for the item and post the amount the donor paid for the item, including any sales tax, shipping, and installation fees in the contribution records of the donor. *Also*, record the item in the fixed asset records.

For example, I bought a new refrigerator and microwave for our youth room. I took the receipt to our parish administrator, who recorded it as a non-cash contribution of personal property. Included on the receipt were the purchase date, manufacturer's model and serial number, delivery fee, sales tax, and the price paid less a discount applied. The church has all the information needed to properly identify the asset in the fixed asset records (refrigerator with ice maker and water lines, date acquired, new, net price paid including sales tax and delivery/installation fees, estimated useful life). The total price is also recorded in my donor records as a non-cash contribution, the description, and the amount.

When I get my annual Statement of Donations, there is the value on the statement, which when totaled with my cash contributions, correctly reflects my giving to the church for the year. When the church's books are audited, the refrigerator shows in the fixed assets section, and the depreciation is calculated showing the net book value of the refrigerator as of the time of the financial statements. Some of these other points of fixed assets and depreciation are covered in chapters 5 and 13.

If the refrigerator had been used rather than new, then the determination of FMV becomes more difficult. The complications associated with the determination are several. Age and condition of the refrigerator are important in determining its FMV. Age has to do with determining its remaining estimated useful life. Condition has to do with determining its marketable value if the church were simply to turn around and sell it.

Determining its FMV is an inexact art, but there are some guidelines. If there is a used appliance dealer within the area, a quick call might determine its FMV. The Internet is an imperfect indicator, but may be your only option. Goodwill or the Salvation Army may be able to offer an idea of the FMV through one of their thrift stores. Regardless, there is one amount that is not FMV—replacement cost. It is never appropriate to determine what a new refrigerator would cost and record that as the FMV of a used one.

Some donations of personal property are larger than a Ping-Pong table and a lot more costly, such as a car. In short, if the car is donated and sold virtually immediately, then the value of the donation is what the car brought at sale. If any other conditions in your situation exist, get advice from a tax professional in your locale before accepting the car. Make sure the donor fully understands the valuation of the vehicle for tax purposes because there are special laws for vehicles.

For any donated vehicle with an estimated value greater than $500, the IRS has provided publications for both the donor and the organization receiving the donation: *IRS Publication 4302, A Charity's Guide to Vehicle Donations* and *IRS Publication 4303, A Donor's Guide to Vehicle Donations*. The IRS has gone on a witch hunt with vehicle donations. The church should seek local tax advice prior to accepting and valuing the donation.

I am not attempting to dodge the issues of FMV, but the donated item itself, whether new or used, how and when acquired, condition, age, and a myriad of other factors for each donation type cannot be fully covered within the scope of this book. Hopefully, you have begun to appreciate that this is an area that requires careful attention to properly record donations.

Required Donation Documentation
from the Church to the Donor

The donor needs written confirmation that properly values the donation. Another publication with which the church should become familiar is *IRS Publication 1828: Tax Guide for Churches and Religious Organizations*. The guide describes the substantiation requirements for the donor and the church as follows:

A donor cannot claim a tax deduction for any contribution of cash, a check or other monetary gift made on or after January 1, 2007 unless the donor maintains a record of the contribution in the form of either a bank record (such as a cancelled check) or a written communication from the charity (such as a receipt or a letter) showing the name of the charity, the date of the contribution, and the amount of the contribution.

A donor cannot claim a tax deduction for any single contribution of $250 or more unless *the donor obtains a contemporaneous, written acknowledgment of the contribution from the recipient church or religious organization* [emphasis added]. A church or religious organization that does not acknowledge a contribution incurs no penalty. However, the IRS regulations state that the charitable organization (the church in this case) must provide written acknowledgment for any single donation of $250. Without a written acknowledgment, the donor cannot claim a tax deduction. The church is allowed to provide this written acknowledgement via an annual statement of donations instead of each and every donation, so the burden on the church is not as large as it may originally appear. Although it is a donor's responsibility to obtain a written acknowledgment, a church or religious organization can assist the donor by providing a timely, written statement containing the following information:

- name of the church or religious organization,
- date of the contribution,
- amount of any cash contribution, and
- description (but not the value) of non-cash contributions. It is the donor's obligation to determine and defend the FMV of the donation.

In addition, the timely, written statement must contain one of the following:

- statement that no goods or services were provided by the church or religious organization in return for the contribution,
- statement that goods or services that a church or religious organization provided in return for the contribution consisted entirely of intangible religious benefits, or

- description and good faith estimate of the value of goods or services other than intangible religious benefits that the church or religious organization provided in return for the contribution.

The church or religious organization may either provide separate acknowledgments for each single contribution of $250 or more or one acknowledgment to substantiate several single contributions of $250 or more. Separate contributions are not aggregated for purposes of measuring the $250 threshold.[16]

For more substantiation requirements, the IRS has also provided another publication: *IRS Publication 1771: Charitable Contributions Substantiation and Disclosure Requirements*. For example, when there is value received that is purchased and a donation included at the same time:

. . . a charitable organization [the church] is required to provide a *written disclosure* [emphasis added] to a donor who receives goods or services in exchange for a single payment in excess of $75.[17]

Example

An example will help us understand this requirement. Church of the Holy Smoke™ has a St. Valentine's Day dinner and dance. The menu is lavish and includes lobster tail and filet mignon for a price of $100 per couple. The church's cost for the meal is $60, which approximates the cost at the local steakhouse. However, this is also a fund-raising activity for the youth who cook and serve the meal. The remaining $40 is a charitable contribution for the youth program at the church. The church is required by the IRS to reveal to the ticket purchaser that the FMV of the meal is $60 and that the amount of donation to the church is $40. This could be done on the donor statement or on the face of the ticket itself, or both.

Every church organization should become familiar with the IRS regulations for charitable donations—both from the perspective of the church for proper recording and reporting, and of the donor to understand the donor's intentions and potential tax benefit. The church doesn't provide tax advice, but if there is clearly a misunderstanding of the tax benefit on the part of the donor, the church might point the donor to a CPA for advice prior to accept-

---

16. *IRS Publication 1828: Tax Guide for Churches and Religious Organizations* (Washington, D.C.: Internal Revenue Service, 2012), p. 24.

17. *IRS Publication 1771: Charitable Contributions Substantiation and Disclosure Requirements* (Washington, D.C.: Internal Revenue Service, 2012), p. 1.

ing the donation. In addition, there are specific requirements for recordkeeping and reporting on the part of the church in some cases. It is also in the best interest of the church to become familiar with the donor's perspective of tax deductions and assist the donor by providing substantiated statements accurately and timely.

Another reason to become familiar with the viewpoint of the IRS is to provide a guideline to determine the appropriate FMV that the church should be recording for assets on its books. In addition, Generally Accepted Accounting Principles (GAAP) has specific rules regarding the recording of donations and the recording of fixed assets. It is important that the church follow those rules for each transaction. Otherwise, the auditor will have to make the determination, and the cost of the audit will go up, sometimes significantly. The purpose of financial statements is not to provide a guess at the value of the church and its possessions, but, according to Canon 7, to use GAAP in determining and making the proper entries into the books to fairly represent the value of the church and its assets, liabilities, revenue, expenses, and net assets.

When is a donation not a donation? When the donation has strings attached to the donor.

Scenario: The Vestryperson's Donation　Recently, I was called to a special meeting of the vestry at Church of the Holy Smoke™. The purpose of the meeting was to settle a dispute regarding the donation of $100,000 by a family, and the subsequent use of money by the church. It seems that one of the vestry member's mother had passed, leaving him with a large insurance payout. He wanted to share some of that with the church. The church was in a growth area of town and had leased several trailers for use as classrooms in lieu of building. The $100,000 was given for the purpose of constructing that building.

Simple so far? The trailer leases were about to expire, and a condition of the expiration of the lease was the return of the trailers by the church to the lessor at the church's expense ($5,000). There was also a lease expiration balloon payment that was $15,000. In other words, the church faced $20,000 in expenses related to the trailers before construction could begin and continue over the summer. The vestry wanted to use $20,000 of the $100,000 to pay the leasing company at the lease termination. The donor vestry member vigorously objected and threatened to withdraw the donation.

Analysis　It is the donor's prerogative to withdraw the donation if he wishes, since none of the money had been spent and the church had made no additional commitments in reliance on the donation. Unfortunately, the vestry had not planned well from a cash flow perspective, and $20,000 was not available from any other source. The lease was going to expire regardless, so the $20,000 had to come from somewhere. The donor had given the money in 2010, and had taken the charitable deduction on his 2010 tax return.

Here is the sticky wicket. The IRS rule states that if the donor still exerts influence over the money, there is no tax deduction allowed for the donation. I had to help the donor understand that if he withdrew the donation, he would have to file an amended tax return for 2010, removing the charitable donation from the itemized deductions of his tax return, and pay any taxes due thereon with interest. I further had to help him understand that if he exerted enough influence over the vestry or the church to cause the vestry to vote other than they would have without his influence, then the IRS construes he has not made a donation at all, thereby disallowing all of the $100,000 deduction outright. He would have to file an amended tax return for 2010, removing the donation from the return even though he did give the money, and pay any tax and interest due.

The rule is simple: Once something is given to the church, the church owns it free and clear of any influence by the donor, actual or perceived, but with the fiduciary duty to use the money as designated. The donor cannot retain any rights to the donation—including any form of influence over its use—without risking the contribution being disallowed as tax deductible by the IRS. In the end, the vestry "borrowed" the funds from the donation and paid it back when contributions were at higher levels in the fall. What seems like a simple rule was anything but in this case.

Clergy Discretionary Fund Bank Account

The church owns the discretionary fund, not the rector, vicar, or priest-in-charge. This is not the clergy's slush fund.

Title III Canon 9.5(b)(6) Alms and Offerings.
. . . to be applied to such pious and charitable uses as the Rector or Priest-in-Charge shall determine.[18]

The most common interpretation of the above is that the funds are for pastoral aid purposes. This is the fund to help the less fortunate in a crisis.

---

18. *Constitution and Canons for the Government of the Episcopal Church* (New York: Church Publishing Inc., 2009), p. 88.

However, some clergy think it is their money to spend on anything as they see fit. Clearly, according to the canon, it is not.

When I conduct audits, I look for several things in the discretionary fund. First, I make sure there are no condos in Florida being purchased by the clergy with discretionary funds. Second, I see if the funds are being expended for any purpose other than for pastoral (pious) aid reasons. What is my authority to audit the discretionary fund? Canon 7 states that "all monies" are subject to the annual independent audit. I do not know the name of the individual assisted; I simply am interested in the intent and purpose of the disbursement. Much as a cleric who is "under the stole" at confession and does not remember the transgression after confession, I could not tell you one single detail of any of the discretionary accounts I ever audited, except for what is in my auditor's work papers regarding the amounts and intent, not the individuals assisted.

Here are some of the things that create problems with discretionary accounts in an audit:

- Checks written payable to "cash." Unless there is detailed documentation—meaning all receipts are present—for which the cash was spent, then there is nothing to indicate that the money was not pocketed. Even the appearance of wrongdoing must be avoided. Significant documentation means a complete accounting of all the money cashed with receipts and purpose.
- Meals for meetings. While it is nice to have a business luncheon or coffee and doughnuts, fruit, and yogurt for a meeting, those are not pastoral aid (pious) uses of the funds. If that is considered by the vestry to be a legitimate use of church funds, then it must be paid from the operating funds, not the discretionary fund. Even if the vestry says it is okay to use discretionary funds in a manner other than for pastoral aid purposes, it is not okay according to canon. Vestries cannot trump the canons in these cases.
- Music or other non-budgeted operating items. There is nothing in the furthest stretch of the imagination that permits the use of discretionary (pious) funds for relieving the vestry of its obligation to properly fund the operations of the church. Something like the below scenario may have occurred in your parish.

Scenario: Music for Christmas The music minister at the Church of the Holy Smoke™ ordered the music for the Advent and Christmas services at the end of October. When the music arrived along with the invoices, after having gotten them properly authorized, she sent the invoices to the book-keeper for payment. When the bookkeeper began to prepare the checks, she discovered that the music budget would be exceeded by $800 for the year. The vestry did not allow invoices to be paid in excess of budget without prior approval from the vestry. When the bookkeeper advised the rector of the problem, the rector replied, "I will pay for it out of my discretionary fund."

Analysis That constitutes the use of discretionary funds for non-pious purposes and is a violation of Canon 9.5(b)(6). If there is no available money anywhere else, then the rector should write a check out of the discretionary fund back to the church operating account for $800 unconditionally.

This may appear to some that this is just a shell game maneuver to satisfy a canon. While that may be true to some extent, it has a more practical purpose. By writing the check back to the operating account for $800 and subsequently paying for the music invoice in its entirety from the operating account, it gives the vestry a clear view of what it costs to run the church. When the budgeting process begins for the following year, then the additionally needed $800 is visible to the vestry in the expense category of "music" in the financial statements and current year budget. If the music was paid for directly by the rector from the discretionary account, then the music expense would not be properly recorded in the operating expenses of the church, and there would be no view of the real cost of music needed to run the church. Most likely, this will become an annual problem until the real cost is recognized and a proper budget is provided.

Compound this one instance by several or habitually frequent instances of using the discretionary fund for operating purposes throughout the year, and the vestry's view of the cost to operate the church becomes clouded and inaccurate. Subsequently, stewardship campaigns will set targets below what is needed because of the lack of total cost being recorded. As costs rise each year, the problem compounds itself. Besides, if the operating budget properly included all costs to operate the church such that there is no shortfall, then the discretionary fund is left whole, and all money is available for the good pastoral aid (pious) purposes.

Club Dues or Memberships

While there is an argument to be made that being visible in the community is worthwhile, there is no argument that can be made that membership in a country club, Rotary, Kiwanis, or other civic organization is for pastoral aid purposes. Those are operating expenses (some may call it advertising expense). They should never be paid from the discretionary fund.

Checks Made Payable to an Individual

You would think this is common sense, however it happens. You should never write a check from the discretionary fund to an individual. If the purpose of writing the check to the individual is to reimburse them for church expenses, we have already discussed that it is inappropriate to reimburse someone for an operating expense from the discretionary fund. But what if it is for a pious purpose? If the person needs an electricity or gas bill paid, write the check to the gas company for account #1234567, for example. If it is for apartment rent, write the check to the landlord. If the need is for food or gasoline, gift cards that are not cashable are an alternative. Mark them as coming from the church "for the purchase of goods only" so the cashiers will not likely simply cash them. Have those on hand and provide an accounting of them to the finance committee monthly; the auditor will certainly ask for an accounting.

Discretionary Checking Account Titled Incorrectly at Bank

The money in the discretionary account belongs to the church, not the clergy. The checking account should be titled something like this: "Church of the Holy Smoke™ Rector's Discretionary Fund." Under no circumstances should it be titled in the name of the rector. Under no circumstances should the rector open the account or be the only signatory on the account. There must be someone else, usually the treasurer, who has access to the account for oversight purposes and reconciles the monthly statements. Then, it only takes a change on a signature card and not the closing of the account or extra expense of printing checks when a rector leaves and a new one comes.

Employee Loans

This one has the potential for unintended consequences of a tax nightmare. Under *no circumstances* should the discretionary fund be used for loans or bonuses to employees, be they full-time or part-time. Loans need to be made as an arm's-length transaction between the employee and the church. This means that the vestry will need to approve a loan, record the loan in the minutes, and obtain a loan agreement with repayment schedule from the employee. There are all kinds of problems a prudent person can envision in the absence of such an arm's-length transaction. If the loan turns into a gift, regardless of reason, then it becomes income to the employee from which taxes must be withheld, FICA taxes paid by the church and the employee, unemployment taxes, and others based on locale, unions, and so forth. The problem is that an employee is the recipient of the loan. Loan forgiveness has to be included in the W-2 and taxes have to be paid.

Employee Gifts and Bonuses

This one is definitely a tax nightmare. Again, the problem is that this is an employee. Many gifts of goods are taxable. Obviously, cash given to the employee is taxable, regardless of the intent of the gift or bonus. Gift cards are also taxable as are vouchers for merchandise. Anything that falls into the category of cash or cash equivalent is taxable. However, to write the check from the discretionary fund circumvents the payroll process and avoids paying the tax. That is tax evasion. I highly recommend the clergy and the church not be involved in tax evasion, no matter how well intentioned.

Paying Credit Card Bills

If done, the credit card bills and the underlying receipts need to be reconciled monthly by the treasurer and are going to be audited. In addition, most likely the credit card is used for the purchase of operating items. A word of advice: do not pay credit cards bills from the discretionary account unless you keep meticulous records. It is best not to do it at all. The temptation is too great, and the opportunity for error is compounded significantly.

Credit Cards

Credit cards in the name of the church are a potential for disaster. Aside from the lost or stolen credit card, they are tempting to be misused. I will cover credit card fraud in chapter 10. However, if your church does have credit cards, they must be treated similarly to a bank account—inspected and independently reconciled. Receipts—not credit card statements—must be turned in for every charge.

At the risk of being redundant, a credit card bill is not a receipt, and all line items on the credit card bill must have an original receipt turned in promptly. This needs to be a no-exceptions policy that is strictly enforced. The temptation is too great for an occasional misuse, which, if left undetected tends to grow larger.

For that reason, the receipts and the bill should be stapled together and turned in for payment as any other invoice for the church. There should be checks and balances in place where the approver of payment is not the person who holds the credit card and does not work for the person who holds the credit card. This means that the senior warden must approve the rector's credit card. The rector approves the parish administrator's card, for example. Experience tells me that <u>when a credit card is in the name of the church and the person using the card is not personally liable for the charges, obtaining receipts becomes a problem</u>.

The preferred method is to <u>require the employee to obtain a credit card in his or her own name, not the church's name, and to submit for reimbursement the expenses incurred on behalf of the church</u>. When that happens, it is amazing how much better the person is able to remember to turn in the receipt, and promptly.

Again, the credit card bill is not an acceptable receipt. <u>The original cash register receipt or online receipt is required</u>. Why the original? Because if the original is not turned in, then the person could return the goods to the store, getting a partial or complete refund, yet the church would have reimbursed the individual. A scenario illustrating why a credit card bill is not sufficient as a receipt may be helpful.

Scenario: Innocent Intentions? The Church of the Holy Smoke™ had a petty cash fund. It started as a small change jar in the parish administrator's desk drawer. It was used to pay for mail returned for postage, occasional cream or sugar for coffee, and other items. Over time, it grew to a small separate checking account with a nominal balance of $150. All the proper controls were in place with monthly accounting, and all receipts present at the time of month-end reconciliation.

When I conducted an audit the next year, I was surprised to learn the monthly balance maintained was $1,500. That is no longer a petty cash fund. The explanation was that in January, it was thought to be easier if the parish secretary, who had a personal Sam's Club membership, purchased the plates, cups, and napkins for the month's Wednesday night suppers. Buying in bulk is less expensive and keeps the number of receipts and checks down for reimbursement.

Interestingly, although this was a checking account, the parish administrator decided to use her personal American Express card to make the purchase so she could get the points. In reviewing January's submission for reimbursement during the audit, the original Sam's Club cash register receipt was there along with all the other original receipts for other purchases using the petty cash fund throughout the month. This was a large church, and the amount of paper products for the month's suppers was $250. However, for months February through December, the Sam's Club cash register receipt was not included with all the others. She "could not remember to bring that one in." All other cash register receipts were present as they should have been, but the

Sam's Club receipt was missing. Since she could never seem to remember to bring it in or find it, in its place the parish administrator included a copy of her American Express credit card bill with the amount for Sam's Club circled.

Analysis   What happens to attendance in the summer months, particularly at Wednesday night suppers? It declines. However, the summer months' paper products for the Wednesday night suppers were over $450. In fact, the amount had grown since January and seemed to level off at $450 for the rest of the year. Without the cash register receipt there was no way to know what was purchased. Were personal items purchased and that is why the receipt is missing for the next eleven months? Or, what does the cashier at Sam's Club ask when taking a credit card for payment: "Would you like cash back today?" Without the original cash register receipt, there is a potential for fraud.

Once you understand the precautions that have to be taken with credit cards, I hope you see that they are a lot of trouble. While they are a potential disaster if they are in the name of the church, due diligence requires a receipt *every time* no matter whose name is on the card. A better solution is to have employees use their own personal credit cards and submit promptly the proper original receipts, then reimburse the employee promptly. There should almost never be a problem with credit cards with that approach. That is the process that the church's volunteers use to buy products for the church and get reimbursed for them. Keep it safe and simple, and have only one process for reimbursement for volunteers and employees, including not having credit cards that belong to the church.

Other Organizations within and Affiliated with the Church

All organizations affiliated with the church that have bank accounts are the fiduciary responsibility of the vestry. Church camps, preschools and schools, thrift stores, outreach centers—all are entities that are subject to the fiduciary oversight and accountability of the vestry. Regardless of how an organization is related to the church, if the organization uses the church's Federal Employer Identification Number (FEIN) to open a bank account, it is the church's money, and the vestry is liable for it. There are as many different types of organizations as there are those who create them. Some examples include bank accounts held by:

- Sunday school classes
- Boy/Girl Scouts, if sponsored by the church

- Petty cash
- Discretionary
- Altar Guild
- Flower Guild
- Episcopal Church Women (ECW)
- Circles
- Social clubs
- Fund-raising projects
- Church Bazaar
- Youth

Why have separate bank accounts? I have heard all kinds of reasons, all of which are emotional, but none have convinced me any of the accounts in the above list are necessary. In chapter 9, I will get into the proper internal control and processes for handling church funds, but let me say here that there are no separate processes for any of them. They all have to follow the same reconciliation, signature, accountability, oversight, and inclusion in the financial statements monthly as much as the operating checking account does. Failure by the vestry to require independent reconciliation and oversee them and to see their inclusion in the mainstream of the financial matters of the church is a failure of fiduciary duty. It is much simpler to have a single process all must follow. However, it is simpler still if there is only one checking account for everything. The above list should be designated accounts in the general ledger chart of accounts, and not physically separate bank accounts. In chapter 10, we will get into the mechanics of how to make that work.

In this chapter we have discussed money in its many forms—cash, checks, stocks and bonds, and credit cards. A consistent thread throughout the chapter is that it needs to be accounted for correctly and safeguarded through oversight and independent inspection.

There were references to potential tax problems with how some money is handled. I have offered several solutions, such as a single bank account and not having credit cards in the name of the church. In the following chapters, these and other issues with money will be explored further.

Using the previous discussions of pledge and plate, unrestricted, designated, temporarily restricted, corpus, and permanently restricted, we have enough information to look at the financial statements.

5

How to Read Church Financial Statements

Why do we need to know how to read financial statements? They contain the only common language of the financial transactions of the church. Financial statements provide a detailed record of the history of the church from a financial perspective. And, they give us a record of how the church deals with donors and money.

The first known clay tablet with structured writing came from Mesopotamia five thousand years ago, even before the Mesopotamians created cuneiform. On this tablet was a record of crops grown and traded, and taxes paid thereon. One of the first written records of humankind was inspired by the need to keep track of commercial transactions and taxation. So it appears that accountants and tax collectors are among the oldest of professions.

Regardless of time, language, or product, financial records speak universally to all people everywhere. While mysteries still abound about the cultural life of the Mesopotamians and others in ages gone by, the financial records are less ambiguous. In demystifying the Mayan language, numbers were the first of the characters to be understood. As humans, we count things, keep track of things, and know our net worth financially.

Double-entry accounting, the use of debits and credits, was invented by an Italian monk in the twelfth century. I will not go into debits and credits, as it is not necessary for the understanding of the financial statements. But, should you be bitten by the accounting bug, there are numerous introductory accounting books available.

Reading church financial statements is not difficult. However, like the Mesopotamian records, it does require the use of exacting terminology, a lexicon of accounting, along with some understanding of accounting principles. This chapter is not intended to teach accounting, but my hope is that anyone who is familiar with commercial accounting or who can only balance a checkbook will understand the elements of church financial statements in the end.

As I have noted, this book is not intended to be an accounting text or to give accounting advice in the preparation of financial statements. Consultation with a CPA who is knowledgeable and specializes in not-for-profit organizations, and if possible, specifically churches, is always the best approach should you have questions about your own financial accounting situation.

Basis of Accounting

There are two fundamental bases of accounting—those that are in conformity with GAAP, known as the accrual basis, and others not in conformity with GAAP, known by names such as cash basis or modified cash basis.

Accrual Basis

Accrual basis accounting calls for recording receivables and payables. Several examples will help in understanding this better. In accrual accounting, when someone formally makes a pledge to give to the church, usually evidenced by a pledge card, the pledge is recorded as a receivable in the donor contributions subsidiary ledger and summarized in the general ledger. If an invoice comes into the church and will be paid in a few days in the future, it is recorded as a payable. Loans that have future payment obligations are recorded.

All of these transactions have a common element. They all have some *written* evidence that there is an expectation on the part of the church to take some financial action; that there is some future transaction that will occur to satisfy the expectation of the receivable or the payable. There is a high degree of certainty surrounding the transactions.

By contrast, if a person mentions to the rector on the way out of church one Sunday that she was so moved by the sermon she is going to pledge $2,000 to the church, that is not recorded in the books. How likely is that pledge to be fulfilled? However, if the individual fills out a pledge card, then it is recorded.

If a parishioner comes into the office and says he needs reimbursement for expenditures on behalf of the church, nothing gets recorded and no action is taken. However, if he brings in valid original receipts, fills out a re-imbursement form, gets approval from the Commission chair who oversees the budget from which the money will be taken, it becomes a payable and is recorded.

Notice that the money has not been collected nor paid yet in these examples. That is accrual. We accrue our likely future obligations (payables) and likely future collections (receivables). When we actually receive the money or pay the invoices, then the receivable or payable is eliminated off the books, and concurrently, the revenue or expense is recorded.

OCBOA and Cash Basis

OCBOA is an acronym for Other Cash Basis of Accounting. If accrual basis accounting is not followed, then by definition, it must be some other basis. OCBOA calls for recording transactions when they really occur. Some examples may help. Unlike accrual accounting, in OCBOA nothing gets recorded in the general ledger when the pledge card is turned in. (A record is kept of the intended contribution, but it is not a part of financial accounting.) Expectations are not recorded in the general ledger in OCBOA. There is no receivable recorded.

Only when the money is actually received is anything recorded in the general ledger—in the form of a deposit and as revenue. The receivable (the pledge) never gets recorded. Unlike accrual accounting, when an invoice comes into the church to be paid, in OCBOA nothing gets recorded. When a check is actually cut to pay an invoice, OCBOA records an expense. There is no payable recorded—ever. This is known as cash-basis accounting. Cash in and cash out—those are the only transactions recorded, exactly like your own personal checkbook.

OCBOA and Modified Cash Basis

If the church uses a combination of cash for some classes of transactions and accrual for others, then the two accounting bases are blended. This is called the modified cash basis and is also an OCBOA basis of accounting. A vast majority of churches and related religious organizations use this method. Even if the only accrual recorded as a liability is the mortgage and all other transactions are on the cash basis, this becomes a modified cash basis of accounting.

Canon 7 says that organizations below the diocesan level can use OCBOA. Some larger churches will use the accrual basis, but for smaller churches the accrual basis makes for a lot of needless work. Canon 7 also says that dioceses and provinces must use the accrual basis.

Not-for-Profit

The church is a not-for-profit (NFP) organization. It is automatically declared a non-profit entity by IRS Code 501(c)(3). Some people think that NFP means the organization must spend all that it takes in. That is not the meaning of NFP. In your own life, do you think it is a good idea to spend everything you take in? I hope not. Then why would it be a good idea for the church to spend everything it takes in?

NFP is not a management philosophy; it is merely a determination made by the IRS that taxes will not be paid on any profit generated. If there were no taxes, the NFP designation would have no meaning, as it is only a tax designation. Other organizations seeking to be NFP must make application to the IRS, who alone determines whether they are allowed to be NFP for tax purposes.

An organization other than a church cannot claim it is NFP simply because they want to be and not pay taxes. The approval process takes months and involves one of the longest IRS forms in use, spanning thirty pages. Thankfully, churches have an automatic designation as NFP. In the last several years, the IRS has required NFP organizations other than churches to file tax returns, regardless of whether there is taxable income or not. If you are an already designated NFP, why do you need to file a tax return? If you represent an organization that has had to file an IRS Form 1023 to gain NFP status, you are now required to file an IRS Form 990 in one of its aberrations annually. Failure to do so will cause you to lose your NFP status and have to pay tax on your income.

The Accounting Equation

There is an axiomatic truth in accounting that everything must balance. What does it mean to be in balance? There is a simple equation in accounting that explains this:

$$\text{Assets} = \text{Liabilities} + \text{Net Assets}$$

That is about as hard as it gets in accounting. Think about it this way. In your own checkbook you have cash, which is an asset. You have bills that need to be paid, which are liabilities. If that is all you have in your life and someone asks you your net worth, you take your bank balance (cash) and subtract the bills you owe (liabilities) and that leaves you with how much you have left after you have paid all your bills (net assets). Another way of expressing the same thing is:

$$\text{Assets} - \text{Liabilities} = \text{Net Assets}$$

The accounting equation is manifested on the face of the financial statements as we will see.

Financial Statements

There are three statements that comprise the financial statements of any organization whether commercial or NFP. Their NFP names are Statement of Financial Position (known commercially as Balance Sheet), Statement of Activities (Income Statement), and Statement of Cash Flows (Statement of Cash Flows).[19]

As you might imagine, since there are two different bases of accounting—accrual and OCBOA, the resulting financial statements will contain different information. The accounting profession requires that in order to eliminate confusion to the reader regarding which basis of accounting is used, the statements will be named differently. There is a prescribed name for the statements when representing the accrual basis, and the prescribed names are prohibited from being used in the absence of properly prepared accrual based statements. Virtually anything but those names are used for OCBOA statements. Remember, only the accrual basis is in conformity with GAAP.

Accrual Basis Financial Statements

Financial statements that conform to GAAP allow the reader to compare financial statements from one entity to another in the same industry, knowing that similar transactions within the two organizations are usually recorded consistently. This consistency within the company and similarity from one company to the next in the same industry is one of the underlying accounting principles that make financial statements in conformity with GAAP. *Within the same industry* is important because the accounting methods in retail companies are different from construction companies, which are different from banking companies, for example. The industry in our case is not-for-profit churches and church-related organizations.

It is not possible in this book to present a financial statement that contains everything your organization may have in its financial statements. If

---

19. A fourth statement is required of commercial stock companies (that is, corporations that issue ownership shares of the company in the form of stock): Statement of Changes in Stockholders' Equity. Since NFP organizations do not have stock, this fourth financial statement, by definition, is not valid for NFPs.

you really want to understand your organization's financial statements, I invite you to get a copy of your organization's audited financial statements and follow along. (However, if your financial statements are not prepared on the accrual basis of accounting, but on OCBOA, following along here will be confusing. Another section of the chapter reviews OCBOA statements.) There will be some accounts that look similar; there will be others that are not found in yours that are found in the example I have presented for the Church of the Holy Smoke™ and vice versa.

For accounts not found in the example, you may want to have a conversation with your bookkeeper to better understand those particular accounts. While there, it is also a good idea to ask about the accounts that are in order to fully understand the underlying composition of the items on the financial statements. Most likely, the items on your financial statements are the summarization of several general ledger accounts into a single item, such as cash and cash equivalents. You should understand what these are. Then proceed to the next item on the financial statements, and so forth, until you understand what general ledger accounts go into comprising which item in the financial statements. I will go through each of the items for the Church of the Holy Smoke™ as you follow along with your statements.

Statement of Financial Position

Refer to Exhibit 5-1 Statement of Financial Position at the end of this chapter.

Accrual Basis: Statement of Financial Position

The Statement of Financial Position is a snapshot as of a moment in time. If the vestry receives a Statement of Financial Position monthly (and they should), then the date of the statement will be the date on which the snapshot is taken, usually the last day of the preceding month. It is always dated with one particular date. Annual statements are dated at the last day of the financial fiscal year, "December 31, 20XX." A church's annual statement will always be dated December 31, 20XX. Why? Canon 7 says that the fiscal year of all entities of the Church starts on January 1, thus ending on December 31 of the same year. Annual Statements of Financial Position always end on December 31, 20XX. From a diocesan, provincial, and denominational perspective, if all statements end on the same day, and all are according to GAAP, then the comparison of one church to another with respect to financial statements is reasonable and reliable.

Looking at the sample Statement of Financial Position referenced above, notice the three components—Assets, Liabilities, and Net Assets. The Total Assets are equal to the Liabilities plus Net Assets. To put the numbers back into the equation:

$$\$3,276,188 = \$561,413 + \$2,714,775$$
Assets = Liabilities + Net Assets

or

$$\$3,276,188 - \$561,413 = \$2,714,775$$
Assets – Liabilities = Net Assets

Heading

One of the first things you should notice about the Statement of Financial Position is its name. If *Statement of Financial Position* is used, it implies that the financial statements are prepared in conformity with GAAP. If any other title is used, then the implication is that the statement is *not* prepared in conformity with GAAP, for example, *Statement of Assets, Liabilities, and Fund Balance—Modified Cash Basis*. The proper name for the commercial company equivalent is *Balance Sheet*.

Assets

An asset is anything of value that the church owns. The building, checking account, church van, pews, vestments, organ, endowment brokerage account—all that has value. Notice most of these are tangible assets. You can reach out and touch them. Some are financial institution accounts but could be converted into cash. Assets are things of value. I will explain each asset in the sample Statement of Financial Position as of the close of church business for the year on December 31.

Cash and cash equivalents   The designation of "cash and cash equivalents" is the sum of money in the jar in the parish secretary's office, all the checking and savings accounts, certificates of deposit, U.S. savings bonds, UTO boxes on hand, checks not yet deposited, for example. From the accounting perspective, cash and cash equivalents are defined as cash or something that can easily and quickly be converted into cash.

Pledges receivable   From the previous discussion, on the accrual basis, pledges are booked (recorded in the accounting records) as a receivable to the church, much like in business a receivable is booked when goods are sold on credit and the money is not yet collected. Pledges receivable for Church of the Holy Smoke™ represent all those pledges made by donors that have been promised but still have not been received. The presence of pledges receivable on the Statement of Financial Position indicates that the church is following accrual (GAAP) accounting in addition to the title of the statement.

Let's look again at the example in chapter 4 of the $70,000 donated for the youth building. At December 31, 20XX, six pledges of $10,000 had been made; two of them paid. There is the anticipation of four $10,000 donations that have been pledged but not yet received for the purpose of building the youth building. A seventh pledge was made after the new year began. While the last donor had made an oral intention known before year's end, the other four donors had actually signed pledge cards with their intentions to donate $10,000 each. Because there is recognition of the four signed cards, but nothing binding on the part of the oral intention, only the $40,000 is recorded for pledges receivable. The $20,000 already received is represented by the item "special deposits."

Special deposits   Sometimes there are donations made for special purposes that warrant their own account. If there is a significant amount of money, it will warrant showing it separately on the financial statements. In this case, "special deposits" represents the initial two $10,000 donations for the youth building and the interest earned thereon.

Endowments   The endowments line item represents the corpus and the investments of the endowments. Some financial statements will list the corpus and investment results thereon separately:

Endowments	
Permanent corpus	$1,000,000
Investment results at fair value	397,042
Total Endowments	$1,397,042

Or, they may include the schedule above in the Notes to the Financial Statements.

Capital campaign   Many organizations will have capital campaigns to build or refurbish property. The capital campaign item represents what has been received. There is likely some amount that is being held as collateral for a construction loan or invested short term. For the purposes of this financial statement for the Church of the Holy Smoke™, those details are not enumerated.

Property and equipment—net   The way to read this is "property and equipment that is net of depreciation." In other words, there is some information that is left out. How much is the total property and equipment on the books of Church of the Holy Smoke™ excluding the depreciation? Another way this could have been shown is:

Property and equipment

Land		$ 50,000
Building	$ 500,000	
Equipment	250,000	
Furnishings	500,000	
Total depreciable assets	1,250,000	
Accumulated depreciation	568,373	
Property and equipment		681,327
Total Property and Equipment		$731,327

Since the total gross amount of the assets and also the amount of depreciation are shown, there is no need to use the "—net" designation. Using the above detail, we can see the total amount of assets and the total amount of depreciation. Notice that land is never depreciated. If the "—net" designation is used as in the statement, then the preceding more detailed schedule would most likely appear in the Notes to the Financial Statements, which is covered later in this chapter.

Current and non-current assets For the accountants, sometimes the assets section of the Statement of Financial Position is segmented into current and non-current assets. In the OCBOA statements we will review later, there are current and non-current assets and a more detailed discussion of the topic is located later in this chapter.

Total assets This concludes one side of the accounting equation.

$$Assets = Liabilities + Net\ Assets$$

This is the sum of all the assets of Church of the Holy Smoke™.

Liabilities and Net Assets

This is the other side of the accounting equation, that is

$$Assets = Liabilities + Net\ Assets$$

The financial statement is broken down into its logical components from there. First, we will examine the Liabilities and then the Net Assets.

Liabilities A liability is the amount the church owes and has not yet paid. The mortgage, payroll taxes, invoices from vendors, and the diocesan commitment are representative of liabilities that should be recorded in the books. What about future payrolls for next month? The employees' wages should not be recorded until they are earned. That is, one should not "recognize" the liability until it is real and payable.

The liabilities portion of the financial statements will most likely contain a current and non-current component. "Current" refers to anything that has a timeframe of one year or less. For example, invoices that have been received that are expected to be paid in less than a year. "Non-current" means anything that is expected to be paid in more than one year.

Current liabilities: accounts payable Accounts payable usually means normal trade invoices—such as electricity bill, salary, payroll taxes, cleaning service, and florist's bill. These are invoices that have been actually received but not yet paid.

Current liabilities: accrued expenses Accrued expenses are usually payables that have been recorded in the books in anticipation of owing money, but the church has received no invoice. An example of an invoice not yet presented is accruing a portion monthly for some unpaid obligation, such as clergy pension. The church usually pays the pension quarterly, but the obligated amount is known and calculable each pay period, even though there is not an invoice right away to accompany the liability. As each payroll is prepared, the amount of the pension payable thereon should be calculated and recorded as a liability.

Payroll taxes are an example of the kind of accrued payable where the amount is known and for which there will never be an invoice. However, each time the payroll is run, the amount of payroll taxes due is known and should be recorded as an accrued payable. A federal government Form 941 will be filed with the U.S. Department of the Treasury and the amount of payroll taxes owed will be calculated on the form. Some churches have a large enough payroll that the form is filed more frequently than quarterly. States also have their own filing requirements, and these payroll taxes would also be accrued.

Current portion mortgage payable The proper way to show a mortgage on financial statements is to show the amount that is due within one year or less as the current amount. This is the principal amount due, not the total of twelve payment amounts that would include interest. Since the mortgage theoretically could be paid off at any time, the amount of interest is not included in the debt obligation. Interest is an expense item and only shows, when paid, on the Statement of Activities.

Non-current liabilities Since the upcoming twelve months' principal payments are shown as current portion mortgage payable, the remaining part of the mortgage is shown as non-current because it is due and payable greater than one year. The Notes to the Financial Statements explain the breakdown further and include additional information about the loan.

Total liabilities This is the sum of the current and long-term liabilities and is the liabilities portion of the accounting equation

Assets = *Liabilities* + Net Assets.

Net assets This is one of the most misunderstood parts of all the financial statements, even by CPAs if they are not familiar with NFP accounting. Not all CPAs are created equal, just as not all doctors or lawyers are created equal. CPAs specialize in different industries or different parts of accounting. If you have questions about NFP accounting, seek out a CPA who specializes in, not just does work in, the NFP industry, and preferably specializes in churches. Otherwise, asking any CPA a fund balance question is likely to result in an interesting but incorrect answer. Moreover, do not ask your software vendor an accounting question. Do not ask your CPA a software question. If you do either, you are likely to get an equally inaccurate answer.

It is this portion of the financial statement, Net Assets, that takes the place of the commercial accounting section of Owner's Equity. NFP organizations do not sell and issue stock ownership shares. A NFP entity is a stand-alone company. There is no ownership of a NFP entity. Hence, there is no Owner's Equity. That portion is replaced with Net Assets. Exhibit 5-2 should help identify some differences.

However, there is much more to the distinction between Owner's Equity and Net Assets than a different title. The entire structure of Net Assets, what accounts are there and how it is constructed, is different from that of the commercial Owner's Equity.

Going back to chapter 4, "Parish Monies," and the discussions about unrestricted, temporarily restricted, and permanently restricted funds, this Net Assets section of the Statement of Financial Positions is where those are represented.

In addition to stock ownership in the commercial world, Owner's Equity also includes all the Retained Earnings (sum of all the annual net incomes or losses) of all the years of existence of the company. In the NFP organization, unrestricted fund balance includes all the changes in Net Assets (net increases and net decreases) since the inception of the church. In smaller churches, Net Assets should be fairly close to the cash that is available for operations.

There should be a reconciliation done every month of the fund balances in Net Assets. Churches get into trouble managing money when they unwittingly spend all of the money received for operating expenses. Not knowing those unrestricted funds are depleted, they then spend designated funds to pay operating expenses rather than strictly paying designated expenses with designated funds. When the audit is done, they discover that they are out of money to pay the next operating invoice, but have money in the checking account. The problem occurs when what remains as cash and cash equivalents is solely in restricted funds.

This can happen for one or more reasons:

- The accounting system is not made specifically for churches.
- The accounting system is a commercial accounting system and not a NFP fund accounting system.
- The accounting system purports to be a fund accounting system but isn't.
- The person setting up the accounting system was not trained in fund accounting.
- Commercial accounting rules and practices are applied to fund accounting.
- The software user is not trained in fund accounting.
- The software user is not trained in how to use the software to accomplish fund accounting.
- There are too many users with no one being in complete charge of the general ledger.
- Multiple bank accounts are used to keep unrestricted and restricted funds separate, but transfers are done outside the computer system and not recorded in the computer system.
- Multiple checking accounts are used to keep unrestricted and restricted funds separate, but transfers are done inside the computer system among the checking accounts and the physical transfers of monies are not made among the bank accounts.
- A single checking account co-mingles unrestricted and restricted funds without having or using the proper accounting system to keep track of the net assets correctly.
- Journal entries are used to fix balances.

If you or someone in your church can identify with any of these possibilities, then your accounting may be somewhere between puzzling to frustrating to agonizingly painful.

For the purposes of reading the financial statements at the moment, we are going to assume that Church of the Holy Smoke™ does not have any of those issues and that the unrestricted, temporarily restricted, and permanently restricted fund balances are all correct.

Unrestricted "Unrestricted," also seen sometimes as "Unrestricted Fund Balance," represents <u>the net assets of the church not encumbered by donors or the vestry</u>. This is also the location of all the Changes in Net Assets that have occurred since the inception of the church. You must remember that the Statement of Financial Position is as of a moment in time, much like a photograph is a snapshot of a moment in time. What has gone on in the past is the complete accumulation of events that got us to this Statement of Financial Position.

Temporarily restricted "Temporarily restricted," also seen sometimes as "Temporarily Restricted Fund Balance," represents <u>that portion of net assets that have been designated by donors or allocated by the vestry for restricted usage</u>. One obvious portion of the temporarily restricted amounts are the donations made for designated purposes, such as for the altar guild or flower guild. Less obvious are the earnings on endowments that are designated for a particular purpose. And less obvious still are the property and equipment assets, net of depreciation, less any loans using those assets as collateral.

Permanently restricted "Permanently restricted," sometimes also seen as "Permanently Restricted Fund Balance," <u>generally includes endowment corpuses</u>. Remember, <u>the corpus is the amount given that can never be spent</u>. Only the earnings of corpuses can be spent, and the earnings are temporarily restricted, as previously mentioned.

This concludes our discussion of the Net Assets section of the Statement of Financial Position. Thus, we now have gone through all of the accounting equation:

$$\text{Assets} = \text{Liabilities} + \textit{Net Assets}.$$

Statement of Activities

The Statement of Activities is the second required financial statement for not-for-profit entities. In commercial accounting, this is the Income Statement. However, the Statement of Activities contains accounts and classifications that are not found in commercial accounting. The church is a NFP entity, so unlike its commercial counterpart, the Income Statement, it does not seek to report Net Income but rather the <u>Change in Net Assets as a result of its activities for the year.</u>

Refer to Exhibits 5-3 and 5-4 during the discussion below concerning the Statement of Activities.

Heading

Notice the date of the statement. It is not a single date as in the Statement of Financial Position. The date says, "For the Year Ended December 31, 20XX." This implies that <u>the statement is as of a</u> *period* <u>in time, not</u> *point* <u>in time as is the Statement of Financial Position</u>. Since Canon 7 (Title I, Canon 7.1.j: *The fiscal year shall begin January 1*) requires all financial church years to end on December 31, <u>the period of time for the financial year is the same as the cal-endar year</u>, January 1–December 31. We have already discussed in chapter 2, "Church Canons and Financial Matters," that all organizations of the church must use the calendar year as their financial reporting period. While many related church organizations want to use a different fiscal year because of their business cycle (church schools, preschools, and some camp and confer-ence centers, for example) that is not allowed by canon.

The argument has been made that teachers are hired and budgets pre-pared according to the school year. You are free to prepare and manage all the budgets you want that span calendar years, but the required financial re-porting is on a calendar-year basis. This means that the books are kept open from January 1–December 31. It also means that audits are conducted on the calendar-year basis, reports to the diocese are on the calendar-year basis, and if they are not stand-alone corporations but rather a part of the parish, the financial statements are consolidated as a church subsidiary with those of the church. The same is true for any other church organizations, such as thrift stores. Now we know that the Statement of Activities is always going to be "For the Year Ended December 31, 20XX".

Column Headings

Spread across the top of the page are four columns. The activities of the church are divided into three sets of activities (an accounting term) and then totaled. The activities are: Unrestricted, Temporarily Restricted, and Perma-nently Restricted. The reason these appear this way is found in the account-ing equation. But to see it more clearly, we have to expand the not-for-profit accounting equation.

$$\text{Assets} = \text{Liabilities} + \text{Net Assets}$$
$$\text{or}$$
$$\text{Assets} = \text{Liabilities} + (\text{Support} - \text{Expenses})$$

In commercial accounting, it is similar.

$$\text{Assets} = \text{Liabilities} + (\text{Owner's Equity} + \text{Net Income for the Year})$$

or

$$\text{Assets} = \text{Liabilities} + (\text{Owner's Equity} + (\text{Revenue} - \text{Expenses}))$$

Thus, the culmination of all the year's activity is summarized in one number, the Change in Net Assets. For this particular year, the church had an increase in Net Assets. Sometimes there will be a decrease in Net Assets if the church spent more than they took in. If there are comparative years on the same statement with an increase in one year and a decrease in another, it will be indicated as an Increase (Decrease) in Net Assets.

Support

The Statement of Activities does not use the word *income*. Instead, it is called *support*. Support can come from a myriad of sources. It can come from pledge and plate, investments (even if only on paper in the brokerage account, and conversely any paper losses—called "unrealized" gains or losses), interest on bank accounts, Wednesday night suppers, Lobster Hoopla fund-raising, Vacation Bible School tuition, and rental of the building. All these are support, and all support is recorded in the general ledger accounts of the church.

Plate and pledge In the statement we see an entry for Plate and Pledge Support in both the Unrestricted and Temporarily Restricted columns. This is because there were some pledges that were made strictly for designated purposes. Checks came into the church designated for something other than the regular unrestricted pledge.

Special gifts Special gifts do not have to be designated (temporarily restricted). In this case, a church member passed away. She was one of the pillars of the community and the family asked that a donation to the church be made in her honor instead of flowers for the funeral. Even though the donations were made in her honor, they were for no specific purpose; hence they are unrestricted rather than temporarily restricted. When that sort of thing happens, it is a good idea to keep the donations accounted for separately in Support. This way the budget committee for next year will know that, while they are undesignated, the support did not come from normal pledging and should not be counted on in the future. That is why it is listed under Special Gifts and unrestricted as opposed to Special Gifts that might have been given for some specific purpose. Regardless, when there is unexpected one-time support of significant amount, it is a good idea to account for it separately.

Capital fund campaign   Church of the Holy Smoke™ is in need of funds to build a youth building and a larger parking lot. Rather than borrow the funds, the church decided to conduct a capital campaign. The checks and marketable securities that came in were clearly designated as being for the capital campaign. Those monies were given for and are to be used for a special purpose: the youth building and the parking lot. Therefore, the amount is listed under the Temporarily Restricted Net Assets column.

Bequests   Ma Barker, a long-time parishioner who passed away, left a bequest in two parts. She left $25,000 for the maintenance of the church to be "spent as the vestry sees fit." That amount is in the Temporarily Restricted Net Assets column. The other part she left as a permanent corpus to be invested, with the support from the investments to be used for a scholarship fund for the church. The corpus is listed under the Permanently Restricted Net Assets column.

Investment income   Investment income is divided into its component parts, depending upon whether the support was derived from investments that had no designated purpose or from those that did. The church made a large amount of investment income from endowments, the majority of which had no specific designated purpose. The $300 is the amount earned the last few days of the year, as the corpus donation from Ma Barker's estate was not received and invested by the church until sometime in December.

Special events   The church held two fund-raising activities, the Spring Fashion Show and Tea, and the Hootenanny Hoopla Auction and Hayride for Halloween. (You can probably guess which one was sponsored by ECW and which one was sponsored by the men's club.) The money received from the two events is listed in Support. It is not netted against the expenses. The expenses are listed in the expense area of the statement. Because the events raised money for the general coffers of the church and not for outreach or some other special purpose, the money is listed in the Unrestricted column.

Other income   Usually, small amounts of support are received from various miscellaneous sources, but most likely from interest earned on certificates of deposit, savings accounts, money market accounts, and the like. Other miscellaneous income is also added to this line item.

Total   The support is totaled by column (known as footed in the accounting lexicon) and totaled by row (known as cross-footed in the accounting lexicon) to arrive at the Total Support by source, restriction, and in total for the church.

Net Assets Added to or (Released from) Restriction

The next thing we see on the Statement of Activities is something called "Net assets added to or released from restriction." This is a way of identifying, and balancing, the amount of money from temporarily restricted that was used for designated purposes. As an example: When money is given for Easter flowers, it is accumulated until the day the bill is paid to the florist after Easter. The accumulated donations are considered temporarily restricted since the donations were given specifically for the purpose of the Easter flowers. However, once the bill arrives, the funds held in the Easter flower fund are released from their temporary restriction to the unrestricted (operating) fund, and the bill is actually paid by the unrestricted operating account.

It seems like a merry-go-round, but that is what makes not-for-profit fund accounting work by segregating designated (temporarily restricted) funds and operating funds. This is uniquely fund accounting. The theory is that restricted funds are never spent, but are released from restriction to operating for expenditure. This is one way to make sure you always have your unrestricted and temporarily restricted net assets properly segregated and reconciled. There will be a corresponding change in Temporarily Restricted Net Assets as there is a change in Unrestricted Net Assets. This is how funds that were carried over from a prior year in a designated (temporarily restricted) account, such as the flower fund, get released and spent in a different year. If this seems too complicated, leave it to the bookkeeper and the software to keep it straight, and the auditor to make sure there are no lingering issues. However, this does not relieve the vestry from monthly oversight and the reconciliation of unrestricted with temporarily restricted and permanently restricted.

Expenses

Operating There are many different ways to divide the expenses. One of the most common is to show operating expenses separately from program expenses. Some financial statements will go into more detail in operating expenses, but remember this is the annual audited year-end statement. Usually, the detail is summarized so that the statement fits on one page. If additional detail is needed, it will be found in supplementary schedules later in the audit report or in the Notes to the Financial Statements, both of which we will see later in this chapter. What is separated are the general and administrative from the fund-raising expenses. This allows for an understanding of how effective the fund-raising was (or was not) by looking at the funds generated in the Support section and the corresponding expenditures in the Expense section.

Operating expenses are all the checks written that are categorized by purpose. Payroll, payroll taxes, pension contributions, electricity, water, music, formation supplies, and sexton services are all examples of expenses for which a check would be written and considered a general and administrative expense.

Notice I did not include mortgage payment. Paying the mortgage each month is not an expense—at least not in its entirety. A *portion* of the payment is used to reduce the loan (liability) principal balance outstanding. The other portion of the mortgage payment is for interest, and that part is an expense.

A recent audit I conducted had the Change in Net Assets drastically understated. The church thought they were in the hole and in dire straits when, in fact, they were doing well. They had expensed all of the mortgage payment, which drastically overstated their expenses and left them with a large negative Change in Net Assets for the year. Yet, they could not understand why they were not making headway on reducing the mortgage.

Once that was corrected, the amount of the loan outstanding on the Statement of Financial Position came down to match what the bank said was the remaining amount owed, and the Change in Net Assets on the Statement of Activities went positive because of a corresponding reduction in the amount charged to Interest Expense. Part of the oversight required by the vestry is to make sure mortgage payments are split properly between a principal reduction, a Statement of Financial Position item, and Interest Expense, a Statement of Activities item.

Program If you have organized the vestry so that its members also serve as commission chairs with underlying committees and have assigned general ledger account codes to the commission chairs for oversight in their areas, then it makes sense to summarize those expenditures by commission. In the case of Church of the Holy Smoke™, the summarization occurred according to program. I have previously recommended that activities (and their account codes) be aligned with the commission chairs on the vestry so that oversight responsibility is clearly defined. Had Church of the Holy Smoke™ done that, then the items within Program would be the Commissions, i.e. Worship, Youth, Buildings and Grounds, Outreach, Formation, Healing, Stewardship, etc.

Change in Net Assets

In this example for Church of the Holy Smoke™, the church had more support than expenses for the year. Increase in Net Assets shows an excess of total unrestricted support over unrestricted expenses of $38,858. However, a closer analysis would provide some additional insight. Of the $38,858 of increase in net assets, $30,725 of that came from expenses being offset by a release from temporary restrictions. In other words, of the expenses, $30,725 was donated specifically for designated purposes and the remaining ($392,147 − $30,725 = $361,422) amount of expenses were supported by undesignated support. When budgeting, it is important to be clear what funds will come from unrestricted pledge and plate and what is anticipated from temporarily restricted funds. See chapter 12 for more on budgeting.

Net Assets

The Change in Net Assets for the year is added to last year's ending Net Assets balance to give the current year's ending Net Assets balance. This is done for each column and for the total (footed and cross-footed). Notice that the Unrestricted Net Assets column total matches the Statement of Financial Position's Unrestricted Net Assets of $26,106. Notice that the other column totals match on the Statement of Financial Position as well. We go back to our accounting equation:

$$\text{Assets} = \text{Liabilities} + (\text{Support} - \text{Expenses})$$
$$\text{or}$$
$$\text{Assets} = \text{Liabilities} + \text{Net Assets}$$

How are the Statement of Activities and the Statement of Financial Position related? If you remember that the Statement of Financial Position is as of a certain date, then it must be the representation of all transactions since the inception of the church until the date of that statement. It would be most difficult to try to process or even understand the detail of every one of those transactions in determining their current balance. That is where the Statement of Activities comes in. We use the Statement of Activities to help us understand logically what the summations of the transactions are for a given year and then add them to the opening balance to get the ending balance, knowing that all the transactions are represented in the Statement of Activities. We manage the church on an annual basis, as proscribed by canon, January 1 through December 31.

The relationship between the two statements is in the Net Assets portion of the Statement of Financial Position. Thus, the Statement of Financial Position's previous balance is adjusted by adding all support and subtracting all expenses giving the final Net Assets for the end of the year.

You may have heard the term "close the books." At the end of the year, after all transactions for the year have been recorded, there is one last entry into the books called the closing entry. It is a series of debits and credits that cause all the support and expense for the year to be reset to zero so the new year (Jan. 1) can open showing no money spent or received. If statements are prepared monthly, then the books are "closed" monthly, and this process occurs monthly to get to Net Assets.

Without getting into a lot of detail, the monthly closing does not zero the annual amounts. It only resets the monthly amounts so management can see the comparison of statements on a monthly basis in addition to annually. The next financial statement reconciles the difference between the Net Assets on the Statement of Activities and cash on the Statement of Financial Position.

Statement of Cash Flows

The purpose of the Statement of Cash Flows is to reconcile cash and cash equivalents on the Statement of Financial Position with the Change in Net Assets on the Statement of Activities. There are some entries in the general ledger that do not involve cash, such as depreciation. There are others that use cash for varying purposes, such as the purchase of investments or assets. There are still other activities that create cash, such as the sale of an asset for cash or the collection of pledges receivable.

One of the confusing things for both small business owners and vestries is indicated by this comment: "The statement says we made money this year, but the cash is not in the bank. Why isn't the change in net assets (commercially, net income) the same as the cash I have available in the bank?" This statement reconciles and answers that question by showing what activities generated cash and which ones used cash since the Change in Net Assets does not represent solely cash. In the commercial accounting world, the Statement of Cash Flows is the same.

Refer to Exhibits 5-5 and 5-6 during the discussion below concerning the Statement of Cash Flows.

Heading

The Statement of Cash Flows is dated the same as the Statement of Activities. The reason is that it is reconciling at the last day of the year all the transactions that made for the change in assets from the beginning of the year.[20]

---

20. It may sound odd to use "at" in this context. However, the reconciliation does not occur on the last day. It cannot because the last day's transactions are not potentially completed until midnight. Therefore, the reconciliation is "as of" December 31. In the accounting profession, and in audited financial statements, it is written "at December 31, 20XX."

In other words, it is using only the transactions from the "Year Ended December 31, 20XX," to reconcile the opening balance of cash on January 1, 20XX to the closing balance of cash on December 31, 20XX using all the transactions in that calendar year.

Cash Flows from Operating Activities

The Statement of Cash Flows starts with the Increase in Net Assets. Of course, had there actually been a decrease in net assets, the appropriate title would be Decrease in Net Assets. This is followed by "Adjustments to reconcile the change in net assets to cash used by operating activities."

Depreciation   The issue with depreciation is that it has no effect on cash. When depreciation is recorded, there are two components. The first is "Accumulated Depreciation" that appears on the Statement of Financial Position. The corresponding amount is added to operating expenses thus reducing the Change in Net Assets on the Statement of Activities. These are only entries made in the general ledger, not in the checkbook. In order to reconcile the Change in Net Assets on the Statement of Activities with Cash and Cash Equivalents on the Statement of Financial Position, we have to add the Depreciation Expense back to the Change in Net Assets. The items in this first section of the Statement of Cash Flows are usually the ones that have no cash effect, such as depreciation. When depreciation is applied to the assets on the Statement of Financial Position, thereby decreasing the net book value of the assets, and the resulting expense for depreciation is taken on the Statement of Activities (an operating expense), it has no effect on cash, but does reduce the Change in Net Assets (Net Income, in commercial accounting terms).

Net unrealized gains and losses on investments   The accounting profession is going through a metamorphosis as the nature of business is becoming blurred with financial matters that are more related to Wall Street than main street. Because of actions by The Securities and Exchange Commission, the accounting profession and the essential nature of accounting are being revised at an ever-increasing rate.

One of the areas where this change is most evident is in fair value. Note I did not say fair market value. This is evident by the inclusion of the item "Net unrealized gains and losses on investments." As more financial statements are being presented at fair value, more of them include the value of investments on the day of the financial statements, as opposed to the historical cost of the investments. With sizable amounts invested in securities and subject to market fluctuations, historical cost may actually show an overly optimistic financial picture in this economy. If the economy takes off again, the converse will be true. The only real value that should be reported is historical cost—that is, what was paid for the asset. Regardless, the operative word here is *unrealized*. This represents a market fluctuation and not really a gain or loss in cash as if the investment had actually been sold. For that reason, it has no effect on cash, and it should be added or subtracted depending on its effect.

Asset and liability changes   The rest of the items in the Cash Flows from Operating Activities are cash-related and based on whether the activities generated or used cash. For example, an increase in Pledges Receivable would mean that Support was increased, but cash was not. (Pledges were increased but the cash to back them up did not come in.) Therefore, it is subtracted from the Increase in Net Assets. This may sound like a shell game, but I assure you it is not. I will not bore you with explanations of all the rest of the items in this category, but if you are bitten by the accounting bug and really want to know, you may refer to a not-for-profit or fund accounting textbook for more information.

Net cash provided by operating activities   The adjustments discussed above are listed and totaled. In essence, this is the cash that was either generated or used by operations. Since most support for a church is pledge and plate, the vast amount of cash would be provided here.

Cash Flows from Investing Activities

This section identifies anything, usually assets, the church may have bought or sold for cash. In the example above, cash was used to purchase a van and investments. Remember, this statement is not about assets, but rather about cash. Therefore, while Total Assets would be the same on the Statement of Financial Position, cash would be decreased and Property increased, indicating the use of cash to make a purchase.

Cash Flows from Financing Activities

The church paid part of the mortgage principal. Remember, only the interest portion of the monthly mortgage payment is expensed, so only the interest portion had an impact on the Increase in Net Assets of the Statement of Activities. But there was more cash expended than just the interest, so it has to be accounted for somewhere. Financing activities would also include a positive amount if there had been a new loan initiated. The proceeds from that loan would have appeared here.

The cash flow totals are summed with the Increase in Net Assets to give a total that indicates the Church of the Holy Smoke™ had a decrease in cash and cash equivalents for the year. This is then added to the cash and cash equivalents balance at the beginning of the year. That total should equal the amount of cash and cash equivalents at December 31 at the end of the year, and it does.

Now we know which activities provided cash and which ones used cash. So, we have answered the question, Why isn't the Change in Net Assets the same as the cash I have available in the bank? Answer: It was not strictly a set of checkbook transactions all year long.

Summary of GAAP (Accrual Basis) Financial Accounting Statements

The preceding three statements (the Statement of Financial Position, Statement of Activities, and Statement of Cash Flows) are all examples. Your actual financial statements will likely contain some different items or even be formatted slightly differently. All of the preceding financial statements are according to GAAP and not an OCBOA method. If your statements look significantly different, are not titled the same, and/or have no accruals, then your statements are likely OCBOA and not GAAP.

The Statement of Financial Position is as of a moment in time. It contains the assets, liabilities, and fund balance as its three main components. The fund balance is further broken down into unrestricted, temporarily restricted, and permanently restricted net assets. Not all entities will have permanently restricted net assets, but most church-based entities will have unrestricted and temporarily restricted net assets within their total net assets. The purpose of this statement is to determine the financial health and sustainability of the entity. Are there enough assets to cover the liabilities of the organization if the organization were to liquidate? A positive amount in Net Assets indicates that there are.

The Statement of Activities in commercial companies is known as the Income Statement. It represents the accumulation of all the transactions for a specific period of time. For the annual Statement of Activities, it will be dated "For the Year Ended December 31, 20XX" which means the statement represents the accumulation of all the transactions for revenues and expenses for the period of January 1, 20XX through December 31, 20XX. GAAP does not permit the inclusion of any other transactions occurring outside that time frame for any reason. Commercial income statements end with an amount of Net Income or Net Loss. Not-for-profit entities simply end with an amount that is called Change in Net Assets instead. The purpose of this statement is to determine if the operations for the period of time covered by the statement indicate an improvement in net assets or not.

The Statement of Cash Flows is titled the same as in commercial entities. Because some items in the Statement of Financial Position do not involve cash (depreciation, for example), there is a need to reconcile from the total cash on hand in the Statement of Financial Position to the Statement of Activities change in net assets. This statement is broken down into three parts: cash used or provided by operations; cash used or provided by investing activities; cash used or provided by financing activities. The purpose of this statement is to help the reader of the financial statements to understand how cash was used or gained in the organization throughout the year and what activities provided or used it. To where did the cash go, or from whence did it come? We can get more specific than Alice in Wonderland's "somewhere."

OCBOA (Other Cash Basis of Accounting) Financial Statements

Churches infrequently use purely cash basis statements. Usually, the statements will be modified cash basis. Church of the Holy Smoke™, like most churches, uses the OCBOA basis of accounting. The area in which that makes the most significant difference for churches and their accounting practices is in pledges receivable. A church rarely books pledges as support and a corresponding receivable for each pledge given. It is unrealistic for a parish to take the time to enter each pledge into the system as a receivable, especially as the pledge may or may not be fulfilled. However, it does make sense for the diocese to book each church's diocesan commitment as a receivable because the diocese does intend to hold the parish to it. Sometimes adjustments are made, but the diocese is fairly adamant about getting the congregation's commitment. Without the commitments being paid, most dioceses do not have adequate support to operate. You now see that Canon 7 appears to have been more thoughtfully crafted than may have initially appeared.

Statement of Assets, Liabilities, and Net Assets— Modified Cash Basis

Refer to Exhibit 5-7 for the discussion concerning the Statement of Assets, Liabilities, and Net Assets—Modified Cash Basis.

At first glance, the Statement of Assets, Liabilities, and Net Assets— Modified Cash Basis looks like the Statement of Financial Position. There are two differences in this example. There may be many differences in your financial statements. If you are just beginning to follow along with your financial statements and anticipating some high degree of difference between the GAAP (accrual) basis vs. the OCBOA basis, then you are about to be underwhelmed. The two differences in our examples are the heading and pledges receivable.

Heading

Remember, GAAP prescribes the exact name that must be used for GAAP-based statements—Statement of Financial Position—to indicate that the reader should assume that the entire financial statement and all the underlying transactions have been prepared according to GAAP. In our example, we know that is not the case because the title of the statement is different. I have chosen a title that leaves nothing to the imagination about the church's method of accounting—OCBOA—or its contents. I could have chosen some other name. All that is required is that the name be descriptive enough and different enough to indicate that the statements are not GAAP statements.

Pledges Receivable

There is no "Pledges receivable" item in these statements. Like the huge majority of churches, the Church of the Holy Smoke™ does not record in the financial accounting books the pledges as a receivable. They wait until the money is actually given and then record the pledge received as revenue.

Those two items are the extent of the differences for our examples. However, there are some other items you may see on your financial statements. Sometimes assets will be broken down into current and non-current assets, similarly to current and non-current liabilities. I have included some examples, in the event you may see that breakdown in your financial statements.

Current and Non-Current Assets

Refer to Exhibit 5-8 for the discussion regarding current and non-current assets.

Current Assets

While accounting policies can differ from church to church, GAAP defines *current* as anything that is able to be readily converted into cash (cash and cash equivalents), expenses paid in advance of their use (prepaid), receivables that are due within a year (receivables), and investments held for sale or intended for sale shortly, and a lot of other things we will not address here.

Prepaid insurance To illustrate prepaid expenses, I will use insurance as an example. The insurance bill is usually paid annually. However, to charge insurance to expense for the year when it is paid in June, for example, is not accurately matching (an accounting principle) the expense with the time in which the insurance is used. In essence, the church only uses the expense one-twelfth at a time, every month.

At any point in time, the church could cancel the policy and get a refund of the remaining premium unused, hence an asset for the unused portion. What will happen is that the bookkeeper will enter a (vestry approved) journal entry at the end of each month, reducing the amount of the prepaid insurance by one-twelfth and increasing insurance expense by the same amount. Do not confuse cash flow when the check is paid for the full amount, and accounting treatment by recording an asset rather than the entire amount as expense at the time of payment. When we get to budgeting, we will discuss the implication for cash management.

Endowment earnings Notice that Endowments include a current portion and a non-current portion. This is not based on which part is corpus and which parts are earnings. It is based on which parts of the earnings are expected to be used in the coming year. The entire amount is currently invested conservatively for the long term in a brokerage account, but it is anticipated that $45,000 will be converted from the investments into cash to be used in the first quarter of the coming year. For that reason, it would be misleading to show the $45,000 portion as long-term when the intention is to convert it into cash and spend it.

Non-current Assets

Non-current assets are those assets that are not intended to be converted into cash within a year or not readily convertible into cash. Since the remaining endowment is not intended to be converted into cash for the foreseeable future, it is considered to be a non-current asset. In addition, property and equipment are also considered non-current unless for some reason some are intended to be disposed of in less than a year. Those would be considered current assets in that case.

Statement of Revenues, Expenses, and Changes in Net Assets—Modified Cash Basis

Refer to Exhibit 5-9 for the discussion regarding the Statement of Revenues, Expenses, and Changes in Net Assets—Modified Cash Basis.

You should know by now that the GAAP accrual basis of accounting prescribes the name and contents of the Statement of Activities. One way to tell that a financial statement is not GAAP is by its name. In this case, I have chosen to call the OCBOA statement the Statement of Revenues, Expenses, and Changes in Net Assets—Modified Cash Basis.

OCBOA statements are not required to show the changes in the three classes of net assets—unrestricted, temporarily restricted, and permanently restricted. One of the differences you will notice between this statement and the GAAP version is the lack of multiple columns, since the three classes are not required to be considered in OCBOA statements. What is required is that the information be somewhere in the financial statements, which could be in the Notes to the Financial Statements or contained in a supplementary schedule. It could even be disclosed by percentages rather than by actual dollar amounts. I hope you are beginning to see why GAAP statements are preferable to OCBOA statements. GAAP statements are generally more inclusive of information in the statements that are OCBOA. However, churches are not required to report using GAAP per Canon 7.

Revenues

Since the Church of the Holy Smoke™ does not record pledges as a receivable on the OCBOA basis, there was not a corresponding entry recording Pledge Revenue. You will notice that Pledge and Plate is $40,000 less than in the GAAP statements, because a receivable causes revenue to be recognized when the receivable is booked. For example, a department store records a sale (revenue) when you make a purchase using your credit card. However, they do not have the cash. The sale is revenue and the corresponding entry is to Accounts Receivable. Hence, if GAAP accounting records pledges as receivables, then the corresponding entry is to Revenue. In OCBOA, no revenue is recorded until the cash is physically received. Thus, the $40,000 difference. Numerically, that is the only difference between this statement and the Statement of Activities prepared according to GAAP.

Expenses

Expenses are recorded when the check is written. At the end of the year, any checks mailed before midnight, December 31, are considered to be expenses of the year. If the checks were written, but not mailed until after the first of the next year, then the expenses should be posted to the next year. The idea is one of constructive use of the money. Until the check is mailed or otherwise tendered to the payee, the church still has the use of the funds. It does no good to write the check to get the expenses into this year and wait until January 15 to mail them. Auditors look for these things.

Statement of Cash Flows

The OCBOA Statement of Cash Flows looks similar to the one for accrual accounting. While there may be a difference in the Change in Net Assets because of the accounting method used, the calculation methods to arrive at cash are fundamentally the same. Refer to Exhibit 5-10 for an example.

Supplemental Schedule

Often, I will include a supplemental schedule that helps an organization reconcile its Net Assets into the three classifications of net assets—unrestricted, temporarily restricted, and permanently restricted—as these classifications often are not reflected on the Statement of Financial Position. Many times the designation will not even be Net Assets, but will be Fund Balance—a designation I find misleading. About forty percent of the time I find that the parish is incorrect in their representation of the amount available as operating cash. Often, they are vastly different amounts. Most of the time, the church—unintentionally—will have spent or currently be spending designated funds for operating purposes because the software did not report the separate balances in the three classifications of Net Assets.

Reconciliation of Net Assets

Refer to Exhibits 5-11 and 5-12 for the discussion regarding reconciliation of Net Assets.

These exhibits show what items go into the three classifications of Net Assets. The two reconciliations are fundamentally the same except the GAAP version contains Pledges Receivable while the OCBOA one does not. Current items of assets and liabilities are netted to give unrestricted net assets. Logically, these are presumably the operating assets and liabilities that are unencumbered by restrictions. Assets that have been designated by the donor or set aside by the vestry are classified temporarily restricted. All of these should be fairly obvious except "Property and equipment—net" and "Mortgage payable."

"Property and equipment—net" represents the fixed assets of the organization. They are temporarily restricted because the vestry chose to purchase them (or some may have been donated as fixed assets, such as a refrigerator) by converting cash into fixed assets. In essence, the vestry designated the cash used to purchase the asset for the purpose of the asset, and unless the asset is sold or otherwise disposed of, it remains temporarily restricted through that designation and use of cash. The depreciation causes the asset to decline in value over time (except for land). Since the recording of accumulated depreciation causes a corresponding recording of depreciation expense, which causes Net Assets to decline, the amount shown should be presented as net of depreciation.

Finally, we consider the mortgage. "Property and equipment—net" contains the full value of the land and buildings, but Church of the Holy Smoke™ does not own the land and buildings completely. The bank owns part of them via the outstanding balance of the mortgage. Therefore, the mortgage must be subtracted from the temporarily restricted net assets.

Permanently Restricted

Permanently restricted is usually fairly easy. Either you have permanent corpuses of endowments or you do not. There is not much else that would go here.

However, there is a reality in the Episcopal Church that may modify the previous comment. The land and buildings are held in trust for the diocese. Canon 7 says:

> **Title 1, Canon 7 Sec. 3**. No Vestry, Trustee, or other Body, authorized by Civil or Canon law to hold, manage, or administer real property for any Parish, Mission, Congregation, or Institution, shall encumber or alienate the same or any part thereof without the written consent of the Bishop and Standing Committee of the Diocese of which the Parish, Mission, Congregation, or Institution is a part, except under such regulations as may be prescribed by Canon of the Diocese.[21]

Because the local parish cannot get a loan or sell real property (land and buildings) without written permission from the diocese, I am of the guarded opinion that land and buildings could be classified as permanently restricted. Without taking sides, I am going by what the canon says. There is no professional literature of which I am aware that would support my position, and there is that which would support the contrary position. However, given the intent of the canon, I believe real property to be permanently restricted, at least on the financial statements of a church. That being said, until there is professional guidance, or until I or someone else can raise this issue with FASB, then I will defer to putting real property in temporarily restricted net assets.

---

21. *Constitution and Canons for the Government of the Episcopal Church* (New York: Church Publishing Inc., 2009), pp. 40–41.

Notes to the Financial Statements

Not everything can be contained in the numbers in the financial statements. The annual audit report from the CPA will contain notes that further explain what is behind some of the numbers. These disclosures are required by the Statements on Auditing Standards (SAS) as issued by the Accounting Standards Board of the AICPA. They are known as Generally Accepted Auditing Standards (GAAS). Much more than the promulgation of required notes are contained in GAAS, including the high standard of ethics required by a CPA auditor. Incidentally, only a CPA who is a member in good standing with the AICPA should issue audit opinions.

Below are Notes to the Financial Statements for Church of the Holy Smoke™. Please refer to the previous financial statements when reviewing the Notes.

NOTE A—ORGANIZATION AND SUMMARY OF SIGNIFICANT ACCOUNTING PRINCIPLES

Nature of Business

Church of the Holy Smoke™ (Church) is a not-for-profit organization incorporated February 8, 1916 under the laws of the State of Agape and operates as a religious organization. The Church is a member of the Episcopal Diocese of Agape, Inc. The Church is supported primarily by donations from the congregation.

Basis of Accounting

The accompanying financial statements have been prepared on the modified cash basis of accounting, which is a comprehensive basis of accounting other than generally accepted accounting principles. Under the modified cash basis of accounting, revenue is recognized when received and expenses are recognized when paid except for certain accrued assets and liabilities.

Pledges of Support

Revenue is recognized in the period in which received, unless received with a donor designation for a future pledge. Prepaid pledges are recorded as liabilities and recognized as income when the conditions are met or restrictions removed by the donor. Promises to give are not recorded as receivables. Conditional promises to give are only recognized when the conditions of which they depend are substantially met and the promises become unconditional.

Cash and Cash Equivalents

Cash and cash equivalents represent funds without legal restrictions on hand or on deposit with financial institutions available for use within a thirty-day period subject to donor restrictions, if any. In addition, cash and cash equivalents include funds with donor imposed or Vestry imposed restrictions.

Property and Equipment

The Church does not maintain accounting records for all property and equipment. The amounts represent management's subjective estimate of the value and are not independently determinable.

Contributions

Contributions received are recorded as unrestricted, temporarily restricted, or permanently restricted support depending on the existence and nature of any donor restrictions. Temporarily restricted net assets are reclassified to unrestricted net assets upon satisfaction of the time and purpose of the restrictions. The Church has permanently restricted net assets at December 31, 20XX.

In-Kind Transactions

Gifts in-kind are recorded at the fair market value of the gift on the date received.

Estimates

The preparation of financial statements in conformity with the modified cash basis of accounting may require management to make estimates and assumptions that affect certain reported amounts and disclosures. Accordingly, actual results could differ from those estimates. The Church has estimated the value of fixed assets in a manner that is not determinable by independent means.

Tax Status

Church of the Holy Smoke™ is a not-for-profit organization incorporated February 8, 1916. The Church operates under a 501(c)3 group determination letter from the Internal Revenue Service dated November 13, 1972 to the Episcopal Diocese of Agape, Inc. Accordingly, no provision for income taxes has been made.

NOTE B—RECLASSIFICATION

The accounting classification of various accounts has been made in the financial statements to provide consistent statements. The effect on the overall amounts is unchanged.

NOTE C—CASH AND CASH EQUIVALENTS

The Church maintains cash and cash equivalent balances in banks and brokerage firms. Brokerage holdings include stocks, corporate bonds, mutual funds, and money market funds. At December 31, 20XX, no balances were comprised of derivatives.

		20XX
Operating Checking	$	26,106
Designated Checking		76,413
Total	$	102,519

NOTE D—PERMANENTLY RESTRICTED DONOR-DESIGNATED ENDOWMENT

The Church received a donation of $150,000 on April 15, 20XX to establish a permanent endowment fund known as the Ma Barker Scholarship Fund to provide scholarships for high school graduating seniors of good report to further their studies at the college level. Terms of the donation require the funds to be segregated from other Church funds and invested. Only investment income received is to be used for the scholarships as the corpus is to be preserved permanently. The donor-designated endowment corpus is reported as permanently restricted net assets and the investment earnings are reported as temporarily restricted net assets. The amounts in the fund at December 31, 20XX are as follows:

		20XX
Temporarily Restricted	$	350
Permanently Restricted		150,000
Total	$	150,350

NOTE E—NONCOMPLIANCE WITH DONOR RESTRICTIONS

During 20XX, the Church utilized designated funds to pay for operating expenses. No designated program expenses failed to be paid from designated funds due to a surplus of designated funds from prior years. However, the Church has comingled some designated funds in the operating checking account.

Designated funds kept in operating cash at December 31, 20XX are as follows:

	20XX
Total temporarily restricted designated fund balance	$ 84,142.00
Less Designated checking account balance	76,413.00
Designated funds kept in operating checking	$ 7,729.00

	20XX
Operating checking account balance	$ 26,106.00
Less: Designated funds kept in operating checking	7,729.00
Net cash available for operations in operating checking	$ 18,377.00

NOTE F—SIGNIFICANT ESTIMATES OF FIXED ASSETS

The Church does not maintain adequate fixed asset records. Accordingly, accumulated depreciation and related depreciation expense are management's subjective estimate and are not independently determinable. The amounts in the financial statements are not substantiated by documentation or appraisals.

NOTE G—DIOCESAN COMMITMENT

The Church made a commitment in 20XX to the Episcopal Diocese of Agape, Inc. in the amount of $36,000 to be paid in 20XY.

NOTE H—LOANS

On May 22, 20XU, the Church entered into a loan agreement with Bank of Koinonia. The original amount of the loan was $475,000, payable $3,000 monthly over 240 months, at the rate of 4.5 percent interest. The first payment of principal and interest was due June 25, 20XU. The note represents the closure of the line of credit obtained April 19, 20XO in the amount of $500,000, and the original principal is the remainder of the line of credit converted to conventional monthly principal and interest payments. The loan is collateralized by a general lien upon security interests in pledges. Principal amounts due in future years are as follows:

Due	20XX Principal
20XY	$ 16,098
20XZ	16,837
20YA	17,611
20YB	18,420
20YC	19,266
20YD-20YW	361,768
Total	$ 450,000

On August 15, 20XQ the Church entered into a loan agreement with the Diocesan Foundation of the Episcopal Diocese of Agape, Inc. The original amount of the loan was $200,000 payable monthly for 180 months, at the rate of 5.0 percent interest. The first payment was due October 1, 20XQ. There is no collateral pledged for the note. Principal amounts due in future years are as follows:

	Diocesan Foundation Loan	
	20XX	
Due		Principal
20XY	$	11,938
20XZ		12,550
20YA		13,192
20YB		13,867
20YC		14,576
20YD-20YG		80,097
Total	$	146,221

Interest expense for the Bank of Koinonia loan for the year ended December 31, 20XX, is $20,670. Interest expense for the Agape Diocesan Foundation loan for the year ended December 31, 20XX, is $7,573.69.

NOTE I—UNRESTRICTED FUNDS

Unrestricted funds at December 31, 20XX are:

		20XX
Unrestricted Fund Balance		
Cash in operating account	$	26,106.00
Total Unrestricted Fund Balance	$	26,106.00

NOTE J—TEMPORARILY RESTRICTED FUNDS

Temporarily restricted funds at December 31, 20XX are:

	Temporarily Restricted Designated Funds		
			20XX
800010	Memorial Fund	$	26,780
800100	Outreach Programs		9,692
800310	Special Offerings		8,544
800015	Building/Designated Fund		1,835
800210	St.Christopher's Guild		3,737
800240	Wednesday Night Supper		4,823
800265	Holy Smoke™'s Discretionary Fund		1,767
800041	Children's Ministry		2,911
800215	Men's Group		1,576
800045	Youth Golf Tournament		1,084
800135	Holiday Flower and Music Fund		1,293
800275	Children's Choir		1,691
800180	Choir/Organist/Musicians		451
800040	Youth Group		539
800066	Labyrinth Fund		1,046
800080	Episcopal Church Women		576
800130	Altar Flowers/Weekly		2,287
800090	Garden Guild		683
800120	Advent Wreath		152
800200	Gift Fund		67
800195	Community Lenten Service		241
800205	Christian Education		-
800105	Daughters of the King		168
800185	Altar Guild		40
800055	Arts and Gifts		34
800050	Memorial Garden Fund		500
800070	Prepaid Pledges		8,000
800270	Vacation Bible School		436
800290	Haiti Fund		372
800341	Lobster Hoopla		2,818
800315	Vestry Retreat		-
	Total Temporarily Restricted Designated Funds	$	84,142

NOTE K—PERMANENTLY RESTRICTED FUNDS

The Church received a donation of $150,000 on April 15, 20XX, to establish a permanent endowment fund known as the Ma Barker Scholarship Fund. The donor-designated endowment corpus is reported as permanently restricted net assets. The amount in permanently restricted funds at December 31, 20XX, is $1,000,000. Earnings on the endowments are represented as temporarily restricted funds.

	20XX
Building Maintenance	$ 500,000
Outreach	350,000
Ma Barker Scholarship	150,000
Total	$ 1,000,000

NOTE L—FAIR VALUE MEASUREMENTS

Fair values of assets measured on a recurring basis are as follows:

		Fair Value Measurements at Reporting Date Using		
	Fair Value	Quoted Prices In Active Markets for Identical Assets (Level 1)	Significant Other Observable Inputs (Level 2)	Significant Unobservable Inputs (Level 3)
December 31, 20XX				
Cash and Cash Equivalents	$ 102,519	$ 23,993	$ -	$ -
Domestic Mutual Funds	397,042	80,540	-	-
Total	$ 499,561	$ 104,533	$ -	$ -

NOTE M—PENSIONS AND ANNUITIES

The Church contributes 18 percent for salaried clergy and 9 percent for staff working 32 or more hours per week, or 1,000 hours or more per year, to a defined contribution plan based as a percentage of salary. For the year ended December 31, 20XX, the amounts contributed were $21,500 and $24,000 respectively.

NOTE N—SUPPORT WITHDRAWN

During the year, three families withdrew from the church. Each family had traditionally contributed support of $25,000 each as undesignated pledged support to Church of the Holy Smoke™. The loss of $75,000, representing 20 percent of support, is significant and will have an impact on operations in the coming years.

There are notes that will be generated each time a set of audited financial statements are presented. Should the bank, a vendor, a parishioner, the diocese, or anyone want a copy of the financial statements, the Notes to the Financial Statements must accompany them. The audited financial statements are not complete unless all the Notes to the Financial Statements are attached.

Regardless of organization, NOTE A always explains various policies about the way the accounting was conducted, such as basis of accounting, tax status, and revenue and expense recognition.

The remaining Notes explain in more detail many of the major items in the financial statements. Notice that the order of the Notes is somewhat in sequence with the statements. Also notice that there are some Notes that explain more about what is going on in the church and its impact on the finances. (See NOTE E and NOTE M.)

You should see that there is much more to the financial statements than just numbers. In order to properly provide oversight of the finances of the church, you must understand the underlying transactions and the other activities in and around the church. As clergy, employees, vestry, and volunteers, it is everyone's obligation to conduct financial matters in an ethical and prudent manner.

In the next chapter on audits, we will again briefly visit these financial statements and notes as part of the larger set of audit reports and letters to and from management.

Church of the Holy Smoke™
Statement of Financial Position
December 31, 20XX

ASSETS

Cash and cash equivalents	$	102,519
Pledges receivable		40,000
Endowments		1,397,042
Capital campaign		985,000
Special deposits		20,300
Property and equipment - net		731,327
TOTAL ASSETS	$	3,276,188

LIABILITIES AND NET ASSETS

Liabilities:

Current Liabilities:

Accounts payable	$	4,013
Accrued expenses		12,000
Current portion mortgage payable		60,400
Total Current Liabilities		76,413

Non-Current Liabilities:

Mortgage payable	485,000
Total Liabilities	561,413

Net Assets:

Unrestricted	26,106
Temporarily restricted	1,688,669
Permanently restricted	1,000,000
Total Net Assets	2,714,775

TOTAL LIABILITIES AND NET ASSETS	$	3,276,188

EXHIBIT 5-1 Statement of Financial Position

Not-for-Profit Fund Accounting is Different from Commercial Accounting

Not-for-Profit Fund Accounting

- Statement of Financial Position
  - Assets
  - Liabilities
  - Net Assets
    - Unrestricted Fund Balance
    - Temporarily Restricted Fund Balance
    - Permanently Restricted Fund Balance

Commercial Accounting

- Balance Sheet

  - Assets
  - Liabilities
  - Owner's Equity
    - Common Stock
    - Retained Earnings

Accounting Equation

Assets – Liabilities = Net Assets

Accounting Equation

Assets – Liabilities = Owner's Equity

EXHIBIT 5-2 Not-for-Profit Fund Accounting Is Different from Commercial Accounting

Not-for-Profit Fund Accounting is Different from Commercial Accounting
Statement of Activities

Not-for-Profit Fund Accounting

- Support
- Net Assets Added to or Released From Restriction
  - Transfers from/to Temporarily Restricted and Unrestricted Net Assets
- Expenses
- Increase/Decrease in Net Assets

Commercial Accounting

- Income
- (Absolutely nothing like this on the commercial side)

- Expenses
- Net Income

Exhibit 5-3 Statement of Activities Differences

Church of the Holy Smoke ™
Statement of Activities
For the Year Ended December 31, 20XX

	Unrestricted Net Assets	Temporarily Restricted Net Assets	Permanently Restricted Net Assets	Total
Support:				
Plate and pledge	$ 336,427	$ 13,512	$ -	$ 349,939
Special gifts	14,924	-	-	14,924
Capital fund campaign	-	104,030	-	104,030
Bequests	-	25,000	625,000	650,000
Investments	40,938	300	-	41,238
Fund raising	6,904	-	-	6,904
Other	1,087	-	-	1,087
Total Support	400,280	142,842	625,000	1,168,122
Net Assets added to or (released from) restriction				
For programs	30,725	(30,725)		
Total Net Assets added to or (released from) restriction	30,725	(30,725)		
Expenses:				
Operating:				
General and administrative	243,319			243,319
Fund raising	14,455			14,455
Total Operating	257,774			257,774
Program:				
Worship	99,439			99,439
Vacation Bible School	7,413			7,413
Choir and Music	4,302			4,302
Missions	14,000			14,000
Youth	9,219			9,219
Total Program	134,373			134,373
Total Expenses	392,147			392,147
Increase in Net Assets	38,858	112,117	625,000	775,975
Net assets December 31, 20X1	(12,752)	1,576,552	375,000	1,938,800
Net Assets December 31, 20X2	$ 26,106	$ 1,688,669	$ 1,000,000	$ 2,714,775

Exhibit 5-4 Statement of Activities

Not-for-Profit Statement of Cash Flows is the Same as Commercial Accounting

Not-for-Profit Fund Accounting	Commercial Accounting
• Cash Flows from Operating Activities	• Cash Flows from Operating Activities
• Cash Flows from Investing Activities	• Cash Flows from Investing Activities
• Cash Flows from Financing Activities	• Cash Flows from Financing Activities

EXHIBIT 5-5 Cash Flow Differences

Church of the Holy Smoke™
Statement of Cash Flows
For the Year Ended December 31, 20XX

Cash Flows From Operating Activities

Increase in Net Assets	$ 775,975

Adjustments to reconcile change in net assets to
cash used by operating activities:

Depreciation	12,225
Net unrealized gains and losses on investments	19,077
Increase in pledges receivable	(40,000)
Decrease in accounts payable	(5,468)
Increase in special deposits	(20,300)
Net cash provided by operating activities	741,509

Cash Flows From Investing Activities

Purchase of van	(21,400)
Purchase of investments	(725,000)
Net cash used by investing activities	(746,400)

Cash Flows From Financing Activities

Decrease in mortgage payable	(29,600)
Net cash used by financing activities	(29,600)
Decrease in cash and cash equivalents	(34,491)
Cash and cash equivalents at Beginning of Year	137,010
Cash and cash equivalents at End of Year	$ 102,519

Exhibit 5-6 Statement of Cash Flows

Church of the Holy Smoke™
Statement of Assets, Liabilities, and Net Assets - Modified Cash Basis
December 31, 20XX

ASSETS

Cash and cash equivalents	$	102,519
Endowments		1,397,042
Capital campaign		985,000
Special deposits		20,300
Property and equipment - net		731,327
	$	3,236,188

LIABILITIES AND NET ASSETS

Liabilities:

Current Liabilities:

Accounts payable	$	4,013
Accrued expenses		12,000
Current portion mortgage payable		60,400
Total Current Liabilities		76,413

Non-Current Liabilities:

Mortgage payable	485,000
Total Liabilities	561,413

Net Assets:

Unrestricted	26,106
Temporarily restricted	1,648,669
Permanently restricted	1,000,000
Total Net Assets	2,674,775

TOTAL LIABILITIES AND NET ASSETS	$	3,236,188

Exhibit 5-7 Statement of Assets, Liabilities, and Net Assets—Modified Cash Basis

ASSETS
Current Assets:

Cash and cash equivalents	$	102,519
Capital campaign		985,000
Special deposits		20,300
Prepaid insurance*		3,400
Pledges receivable		40,000
Endowment earnings**		46,600
Total Current Assets		1,197,819
Non-Current Assets		
Endowments		1,347,042
Property and equipment - net		731,327
Total Non-Current Assets		2,078,369
TOTAL ASSETS	$	3,276,188

* Added for illustration purposes
** Adjusted for illustration purposes to allow TOTAL ASSETS to balance

Exhibit 5-8 Current and Non-Current Assets Example

Church of the Holy Smoke ™
Statement of Revenues, Expenses, and Changes in Net Assets - Modified Cash Basis
For the Year Ended December 31, 20XX

Revenues:		
Plate and pledge	$	309,939
Special gifts		14,924
Capital fund campaign		104,030
Bequests		650,000
Investments		41,238
Fund raising		6,904
Other		1,087
Total Support		1,128,122
Expenses:		
Operating:		
General and administrative		243,319
Fund raising		14,455
Total Operating		257,774
Program:		
Worship		99,439
Vacation Bible School		7,413
Choir and Music		4,302
Missions		14,000
Youth		9,219
Total Program		134,373
Total Expenses		392,147
Increase in Net Assets		735,975
Net assets December 31, 20X1		1,938,800
Net Assets December 31, 20X2	$	2,674,775

Exhibit 5-9 Statement of Revenues, Expenses, and Changes in Net Assets—
Modified Cash Basis

Church of the Holy Smoke™
Statement of Cash Flows
For the Year Ended December 31, 20XX

Cash Flows From Operating Activities

Increase in Net Assets	$ 735,975

Adjustments to reconcile change in net assets to
cash used by operating activities:

Depreciation	12,225
Net unrealized gains and losses on investments	19,077
Decrease in accounts payable	(5,468)
Increase in special deposits	(20,300)
Net cash provided by operating activities	741,509

Cash Flows From Investing Activities

Purchase of van	(21,400)
Purchase of investments	(725,000)
Net cash used by investing activities	(746,400)

Cash Flows From Financing Activities

Decrease in mortgage payable	(29,600)
Net cash used by financing activities	(29,600)
Decrease in cash and cash equivalents	(34,491)
Cash and cash equivalents at Beginning of Year	137,010
Cash and cash equivalents at End of Year	$ 102,519

EXHIBIT 5-10 OCBOA Statement of Cash Flows

```
                    Church of the Holy Smoke™
                    Reconciliation of Net Assets
                       December 31, 20XX


    NET ASSETS
      Unrestricted
        Cash and cash equivalents        $       102,519
        Current liabilities                      (76,413)
            Total Unrestricted                    26,106

      Temporarily Restricted
        Pledges Receivable                        40,000
        Special deposits                          20,300
        Earned portion of endowments             397,042
        Capital campaign                         985,000
        Property and equipment - net             731,327
                                               2,173,669
        Mortgage Payable                        (485,000)
            Total Temporarily Restricted       1,688,669

      Permanently Restricted
        Endowments                             1,000,000
            Total Permanently Restricted       1,000,000


            TOTAL NET ASSETS             $     2,714,775
```

Exhibit 5-11 GAAP Reconciliation of Net Assets

```
                    Church of the Holy Smoke™
                    Reconciliation of Net Assets
                       December 31, 20XX


    NET ASSETS
      Unrestricted
        Cash and cash equivalents        $       102,519
        Current liabilities                      (76,413)
            Total Unrestricted                    26,106

      Temporarily Restricted
        Special deposits                          20,300
        Earned portion of endowments             397,042
        Capital campaign                         985,000
        Property and equipment - net             731,327
                                               2,133,669
        Mortgage Payable                        (485,000)
            Total Temporarily Restricted       1,648,669

      Permanently Restricted
        Endowments                             1,000,000
            Total Permanently Restricted       1,000,000


            TOTAL NET ASSETS             $     2,674,775
```

Exhibit 5-12 OCBOA Reconciliation of Net Assets

6

Audits

All accounts of the Diocese shall be audited annually by an independent Certified Public Accountant. All accounts of Parishes, Missions or other institutions shall be audited annually by an independent Certified Public Accountant, or independent Licensed Public Accountant, or such audit committee as shall be authorized by the Finance Committee, Department of Finance, or other appropriate diocesan authority.

—**Title I, Canon 7, Section 1, (f)**

This paragraph tells us two things: Every part of the church is subject to audit annually, and that audit is to be conducted in one of two ways. But, please note two things:

1. Nothing short of an audit is acceptable.
2. The canon uses the word audit and none other to represent an examination of the financial records.

Often, the distinctions among the terms *audit, review,* and *compilation* are misunderstood, but each is different in the level of services performed. While the outcome may look similar to the uninitiated, it is important to know the difference, because the level of assurance ranges from reliance (audit), to limited (review), to none (compilation), yet they all produce financial statements.

An *audit* gives reasonable assurance that the financial statements fairly represent the financial condition of the entity audited. The financial statements and their underlying records have been subjected to a series of tests by a CPA following professional standards.

A *compilation* is basically what the church's bookkeeper does every month, but may be done by an outside accounting or bookkeeping service. There are no tests of the transactions or the financial statements. There is no assurance that the books of the church are correct.

Why the distinction? The common usage of the word *audit* is often incorrect. The three words—*audit, review,* and *compilation*—are often incorrectly used interchangeably. To call the work performed in a review (and the resulting financial statements) an audit is wrong and misleading. However, there are many churches that think they are getting an audit when they are not. I believe the language allowing an audit by committee in Canon 7 can only be properly interpreted as an audit by a committee of unpaid CPAs who can legitimately sign the audit opinion letter. The term *independent audit* axiomatically means a CPA must perform it. There are others who are internal auditors for banks, for example, who have many of the skills, but if not a CPA, do not share the requirement to adhere to the standards, procedures, and ethics of the profession as members of the AICPA must.

There can be no audit by anyone who has any connection with the financial records, including oversight. However, churches and dioceses allow non-CPA committees to use the Manual for Business in Church Affairs checklist for an audit, and that is just wrong per Canon 7. At best, it is a quasi-review. The likelihood of a review uncovering a fraud scheme is remote. Audits are not designed to uncover fraudulent activity, but because of the more extensive nature of the required tests, the likelihood is much higher that a fraud may be detected during an audit than in a review.

It is important to note that the canons do not permit anything but an audit. Because of cost, many congregations instead get someone to "look over" their books, or may even have a review done, but neither provides the assurance called for in the canon. I believe the canon was carefully crafted with full knowledge of the proper use of the word *audit*. Because of the prevalence of fraud in churches, this requirement must not be changed (see chapter 7 on fraud).

External independent audits cost nearly the same for a small mission as for a medium-sized church. The steps involved in conducting the audit are dictated by the Statements on Auditing Standards from the AICPA. There are no shortcuts or steps that can be eliminated in performing the audit regardless of the size of the church. With the addition of the complexity of the types of investments, endowments, loans, or the addition of a thrift store, preschool, school, or bookstore, the price of the audit will be higher due to the additional work that has to be done.

Even more work has to be done when it is the first audit conducted in over a year, or if the books have never been audited. The issue is that an auditor is providing reasonable assurance that the opening balances on January 1 of the year being audited are reasonably correct in all material respects. That is difficult to do if there were no audited financial statements for the year ending December 31, 20XW, the day before the opening of the books on January 1, 20XX.

The intent is clearly that the performance of the audit be done in the order presented, that being first and foremost by a Certified Public Accountant. Certified Public Accountants are the professionals of the accounting industry. CPAs must meet strenuous educational requirements—a minimum of five years of university courses, followed by thousands of hours of supervised experience by a CPA who personally signs and attests to the experience-hours requirements, and a passing grade on a uniform CPA exam given nationally. Finally, auditing standards require the auditor CPA to be knowledgeable in the industry in which the audit is done.

A second option mentioned in performing an audit is the Licensed Public Accountant (LPA). At the risk of stating the obvious, an LPA is not a CPA. As already mentioned, LPA is a holdover designation from those who began practicing accounting before there was a uniform CPA exam, and were grandfathered in by secretaries of states as a license designation. Most LPAs perform bookkeeping services or tax services and do not perform audits.

Finally, we arrive at the last and least-preferred method of examining the record keeping. We should pay attention to some key words—*diocesan authority*. This specifically states that the diocese is directly involved and charged with the oversight of the examination of the books if that examination is not performed by an independent CPA.

You should not have an audit performed unless the CPA is a member of the AICPA. This is the body that holds the independent auditor to the highest of professional and ethical standards. There is no audit unless performed according to the Statements on Auditing Standards and other bodies of professional work and practice of the American Institute of Certified Public Accountants. Likewise, there is no audit unless there is an audit opinion letter rendered. There is no one who can legally sign a properly prepared audit opinion letter other than a CPA. No CPA would risk his or her license by signing such a letter without having performed the work. A CPA who volunteers to perform an audit is not relieved of professional requirements or professional liability because he or she is not being paid for the audit work.

There is no shortcut to getting an audit. There also is no substitute for an audit. Reviews are not acceptable, regardless of method used or who performs them. The canon is explicit—an audit is required annually. Hence, the ECU-SA Manual of Business Methods in Church Affairs is not an acceptable replacement for an audit, according to canon. The checklist is a good guideline of the kinds of documents that need to be available and a good indication of the kinds of questions that will be asked, but should never be used as a substitute for an audit.

Diocesan Override of Canonically-required Audits

I was working with a church when I discovered a fraud committed by the bookkeeper. The church did not have insurance from Church Insurance Companies, but from a large independent commercial insurance company. The corporate adjuster happened to be an Episcopalian and familiar with TEC canons and the canons of that particular diocese. The diocesan canons stated that an audit was only required once every three years, overriding the TEC canon. Further, the diocesan canons only required audits of churches with revenue in excess of $500,000. It allowed reviews for the smaller churches once every three years. There was no oversight or approval by the diocese of any committees.

The claim was for $50,000 for theft by an employee. In the conversation, the adjuster said, "The national canons require an *audit* every year. This church claims it did not have one because the diocese did not require it (by overriding the TEC canon). Why should I pay this claim? It seems to me *the diocese was complicit in allowing the fraud to occur.*" I have to agree with the adjuster. Why would a diocese ever enact a canon that attempts to override a denomination-wide requirement regarding money? Being an Episcopalian, she paid the claim. I doubt it would have been paid if a non-Episcopalian had made the same observation.

Cost of an Audit

An audit of a church should cost approximately one percent of the budget. As a caveat, there is a floor below which the cost cannot go unless the auditor is giving away the work, and a cost it should not exceed regardless of the size of the church. As mentioned earlier, there can be situations that add to the cost of an audit, such as a preschool or thrift store being included. These should add approximately .25–.50 percent of the budget to the cost, depending on complexity. If there has not been an audit in recent memory, then expect the audit costs to be .10–.25 percent of the budget higher. The auditor's out-of-pocket travel costs are usually added as a reimbursement of expenses. The floor for an audit depends on the auditor.

The ceiling for audits is reached because auditors used statistical inference for sampling techniques. Eventually the population size gets so large that the sample size does not change. Ever wonder why a poll of 1,500 people could in some way indicate the preference of the population of the United States plus or minus three percent? Statistically, it can and does. The same is true of sampling transactions in a church. It does not matter whether the church has ten thousand transactions or a million. The sample size will be practically the same. Other complicating factors for large churches may involve the presence of multiple locations, and expanded service times. These can add time to the process as the auditor seeks to understand and test the processes and procedures of the church.

To get a reasonably priced audit, it takes an auditor who is dedicated to the safeguarding of the church's money and is committed to more than just the dollar amount of fees that can be gained. An experienced church auditor will likely take less time than one who has never before done this type of audit.

In negotiating audit fees, the church should attempt to secure a fixed price. If an auditor charges a billable rate per hour, fees can spiral surprisingly high. Make sure the vestry understands the resulting deliverables. I have included some of the deliverables—the Statements, Notes, letters to and from management and others—so you would know how the proper deliverables should look. Hire only auditors who are members of the AICPA, which should ensure a professional audit according to industry standards. Membership in a state society is not a substitute for membership in the AICPA.

Preparation for an Audit

One way to lower the cost of an audit is to have all documentation available and organized when the auditor arrives. The more trips to the church the auditor has to make, the more time it takes to conduct the audit, and the more the cost of the audit will be. While small churches may not understand that there are no short cuts in audit procedures because of their size, auditors may not want to audit small churches, presuming disorganized records or missing information.

At minimum, gather these materials before the auditor arrives:

Initial Assistance for Annual Audit
(for each year being audited)

Upon initial visit, the auditor may use your ACS system to generate the financial statements and details in electronic form needed for the audit. If you are not using ACS, the auditor will need the following in electronic and paper form.

1. Prior year Working Trial Balance, General Ledger detail (in ACS, this is the detailed Posting Journal), and Financial Statements (audited)
2. Current year Working Trial Balance and General Ledger detail
3. Balance Sheet
4. Statement of Activities (Income Statement)
5. Sources and Uses of Funds
6. Temporarily Restricted Funds
7. Permanently Restricted Funds
8. Contribution records (Contributions/People module in ACS)
9. Fixed Assets and depreciation
10. Loans and loan amortization schedules
11. List of all financial institution accounts of any kind, including brokerage accounts and loans (Daughters of the King accounts are not needed); Institution name, address, account name, account number, balance at end of year being audited.
12. List of Vestry members and their roles
13. List of Clergy and employees, and their roles
14. Name and address of attorney
15. Name and address of parties for any in force leases, and rents receivable and payable, even if only partly in force during the year being audited.

Available at Time of Auditor's Arrival

1. All Endowment fund documents, bequests, and by-laws, and minutes
2. Vestry minutes for the year being audited and to date
3. Approved budget—should be included in the vestry minutes of the month in which the vestry approved the budget
4. 941s and W-3s, W-2s and 1099s for the year
5. All financial institution account statements, including endowments and rector's discretionary funds of the year being audited, plus the subsequent year's first month's statements
6. Insurance policies' declaration pages

Once the Audit Begins
1. Confirmation letters on your letterhead to financial institutions, attorney(s), lenders, lessees, lessors, and renters. An authorized signature will need to be affixed to the letter. At that point, the auditor will mail the confirmation letters and receive the replies.
2. Full access to all receipts, documents, and accounting systems.
3. A workplace with Internet access, either wired or wireless.

Some documents from prior years will need to be found, for example, a mortgage. These documents contain information that is required to be included in the Notes to the Financial Statements.

Understanding of Internal Control

The auditor is required to document his or her understanding of internal processes of the church. This means gathering information about the processes and conducting a walkthrough of sample transactions to see how well the process works. For example, the counting process is very important, and the auditor will inquire how the process is supposed to work in sufficient detail to be able to document the process in the work papers. Then, to make sure it is operating the way it is described (two people at all times with the money, counted behind locked doors, etc.), the auditor will observe the process of collection, counting, depositing, and reconciling of the deposits. This walkthrough will go on for as many processes as the auditor feels necessary. This is a requirement of auditing standards and is not a procedure found in a review or a compilation.

Verification of Financial Institution Account Balances

Once the auditor arrives, he or she will ask the church to prepare, on church letterhead, a request to every financial institution and for every account, a letter to the financial institution asking they confirm directly to the auditor the balances at year end and any other information the auditor may include in the letter.

This is called "independent verification." The auditor will mail the letter and receive the reply from the financial institution directly. The auditor uses this independent verification to compare the balance at the bank with the

Church of the Holy Smoke™
123 Elm Street
Paxville, Agape 12345

ORIGINAL
To be mailed to
**The Bank of
Smokeville
PO Box 123
Smokeville,
Agape 12399**

We have provided to our accountants the following information as of the close of business on December 31, 20XW, regarding our deposit and loan balances. Please confirm the accuracy of the information, noting any exceptions to the information provided. If the balances have been left blank, please complete this form by furnishing the balance in the appropriate space below.* Although we do not request nor expect you to conduct a comprehensive, detailed search of your records, if during the process of completing this confirmation additional information about other deposit and loan accounts we may have with you comes to your attention, please include such information below. Please use the enclosed envelope to return the form directly to our accountants.

At the close of business on the date listed above, our records indicated the following deposit balances:

ACCOUNT NAME	ACCOUNT NO.	BALANCE at December 31, 20XW
General	1234	
Designated	5678	
Discretionary	91011	

_____
Sis Barker, Parish Administrator

January 12, 20XX

The information presented above by the customer is in agreement with our records. Although we have not conducted a comprehensive, detailed search of our records, no other deposit or loan accounts have come to our attention except as noted below.

_____
(Financial Institution Authorized Signature)

_____
(Date)

_____
(Title)

EXCEPTIONS AND/OR COMMENTS

Please return this form directly to our accountants:

Findem, Trackem & Down, LLC
Corner Wall & Fraud Streets
Paxville, Agape 12345

Approved 1990 by American Bankers Association, American Institute of Certified Public Accountants, and Bank Administration Institute.

Bank Confirmation Letter

balance on the books at year end, and if different, reconciles the discrepancy. If the discrepancy cannot be easily reconciled, this indicates there may be a problem with the amount shown in the books. The auditor must receive the reply directly, or the process will need to be repeated; that is why it is called independent verification. This is one of the procedures performed only in an audit and not in a review or compilation.

Attorney's Representation Letter

The auditor will also ask for a letter authorizing the church's attorney to reveal information about any current, pending, or suspected litigation. Based upon the lawyer's reply, there may actually be entries made in the books (a lawsuit has been lost by the church, is unpaid, and may be on appeal) to record the liability in the Notes to the Financial Statements. Or, if the lawsuit is ongoing, and the attorney thinks there is likely liability on the part of the church, then the auditor may include only a note in the financial statements of a contingent liability and not record an entry in the books themselves. This is another of the many steps included in an audit not found in a review or compilation.

Management Representation Letter

Once the audit is finished, the auditor will require the Management Representation Letter. In this letter, the senior warden and treasurer, presumably the legal representatives of the church corporation registered with the Secretary of State, make assurances to the auditor. This is a fairly standard letter, but an audit will not be issued without both signatures on the letter. Read this carefully, because it indicates the information needed to be provided to the auditor throughout the audit. If you don't see this letter before the presentation of the audited financial statements, you did not have an audit at your church.

Church of the Holy Smoke™
123 Elm Street
Paxville, Agape 12345

January 15, 20XX

Willum, Soakem, and Down, Attorneys at Law
1 Ambulance Drive
Paxville, Agape 12345

Our auditors, Findem, Trackem & Down, are conducting an audit of our financial statements at December 31, 20XW and for the year then ended. Please furnish to him the information requested below involving matters with respect to which you have been engaged and to which you have devoted substantive attention on behalf of Church of the Holy Smoke™ in the form of legal consultation or representation.

<u>Pending or Threatened Litigation, Claims, and Assessments (excluding unasserted claims and assessments)</u>

Please prepare a description of all material litigation, claims, and assessments (excluding unasserted claims and assessments). Materiality for purposes of this letter includes items involving amounts exceeding $10,000 individually or in the aggregate. The description of each case should include:

1) the nature of the litigation;

2) the progress of the case to date;

3) how management of Church of the Holy Smoke™ is responding or intends to respond to the litigation (e.g., to contest the case vigorously or to seek an out-of-court settlement); and

4) an evaluation of the likelihood of an unfavorable outcome and an estimate, if one can be made, of the amount or range of potential loss.

Also, please identify any pending or threatened litigation, claims, and assessments with respect to which you have been engaged but as to which you have not yet devoted substantive attention.

<u>Unasserted Claims and Assessments</u>

We understand that whenever, in the course of performing legal services for us with respect to a matter recognized to involve an unasserted possible claim or assessment that may call for financial statement disclosure, if you have formed a professional conclusion that we should disclose or consider disclosure concerning such possible claim or assessment, as a matter of professional responsibility to us, you will so advise us and will consult with us concerning the question of such disclosure and the applicable requirements of *FASB Accounting Standards Codification 450, Contingencies* (formerly Statement of Financial Accounting Standards No. 5) (excerpts of which can be found in the ABA's *Auditor's Letter Handbook*). Please specifically confirm to our auditors that our understanding is correct.

We have represented to our auditors that there are no unasserted possible claims or assessments that you have advised us are probable of assertion and must be disclosed in accordance with *FASB Accounting Standards Codification 450, Contingencies*

Lawyer Representation Letter, page 1

Church of the Holy Smoke™
123 Elm Street
Paxville, Agape 12345

Response

Your response should include matters that existed as of December 31, 20XW and during the period from that date to the effective date of your response. Please specify the effective date of your response if it is other than the date of reply.

Please specifically identify the nature of, and reasons for, any limitations on your response.

Our auditors would appreciate receiving your reply by July 31, 20XX with a specified effective date as close as possible to that date. You may also be requested to provide verbal updates to your written response at a later date. We appreciate your timely response to such requests.

Other Matters

Please also indicate the amount we were indebted to you for services and expenses (billed and unbilled) on December 31, 20XW.

Very truly yours,

Senior Warden

Church of the Holy Smoke™

Lawyer Representation Letter, page 2

Church of the Holy Smoke
123 Elm Street
Paxville, Agape 12345

July 31, 20XX

To Findem, Trackem & Down, LLC

We are providing this letter in connection with your audit of the statement of financial position of Church of the Holy Smoke™ as of December 31, 20XW and the related statements of activities and cash flows for the year then ended for the purpose of expressing an opinion as to whether the financial statements present fairly, in all material respects, the financial position, changes in net assets, and cash flows of Church of the Holy Smoke in conformity with U.S. generally accepted accounting principles. We confirm that we are responsible for the fair presentation in the financial statements of financial position, changes in net assets, and cash flows in conformity with generally accepted accounting principles. We are also responsible for adopting sound accounting policies, establishing and maintaining effective internal control over financial reporting, and preventing and detecting fraud.

We confirm, to the best of our knowledge and belief, as of July 31, 20XX, the following representations made to you during your audit.

The financial statements referred to above are fairly presented in conformity with U.S. generally accepted accounting principles and include all assets and liabilities under the Church's control.

1) We have made available to you all—

   a) Financial records and related data.

   b) Minutes of the meetings of the Vestry or summaries of actions of recent meetings for which minutes have not yet been prepared.

2) There have been no communications from regulatory agencies concerning noncompliance with, or deficiencies in, financial reporting practices.

3) There are no material transactions that have not been properly recorded in the accounting records underlying the financial statements.

4) We believe the effects of the uncorrected financial statement misstatements summarized in the attached schedule are immaterial, both individually and in the aggregate, to the financial statements taken as a whole.

5) We acknowledge our responsibility for the design and implementation of programs and controls to prevent and detect fraud.

6) We have no knowledge of any fraud or suspected fraud affecting the Church involving—

   a) Management,

   b) Employees and volunteers who have significant roles in internal control, or

   c) Others where the fraud could have a material effect on the financial statements.

Management Representation Letter Holy Smoke, page 1

Church of the Holy Smoke
123 Elm Street
Paxville, Agape 12345

7) We have no knowledge of any allegations of fraud or suspected fraud affecting the Church received in communications from employees, former employees, grantors, regulators, or others.

8) The Church has no plans or intentions that may materially affect the carrying value or classification of assets, liabilities, or net asset balances.

9) The following, if any, have been properly recorded or disclosed in the financial statements:

   a) Related party transactions, including revenues, expenses, loans, transfers, leasing arrangements, and guarantees, and amounts receivable from or payable to related parties.

   b) Guarantees, whether written or oral, under which the Church is contingently liable.

   c) Significant estimates and material concentrations known to management that are required to be disclosed in accordance with FASB Accounting Standards Codification 275, *Risks and Uncertainties*.

10) We are responsible for compliance with the laws, regulations, and provisions of contracts and grant agreements applicable to us; and we have identified and disclosed to you all laws, regulations and provisions of contracts and grant agreements that we believe have a direct and material effect on the determination of financial statement amounts or other financial data significant to the audit objectives.

11) Church of the Holy Smoke™ is an exempt Church under Section 501c(3) of the Internal Revenue Code. Any activities of which we are aware that would jeopardize the Church's tax-exempt status, and all activities subject to tax on unrelated business income or excise or other tax, have been disclosed to you. All required filings with tax authorities are up-to-date.

12) There are no—

   a) Violations or possible violations of laws and regulations and provisions of contracts and grant agreements whose effects should be considered for disclosure in the financial statements, as a basis for recording a loss contingency, or for reporting on noncompliance.

   b) Unasserted claims or assessments that our lawyer has advised us are probable of assertion and must be disclosed in accordance with *FASB Accounting Standards Codification 450, Contingencies* (formerly *Statement of Financial Accounting Standards No. 5, Accounting for Contingencies*.

   c) Other liabilities or gain or loss contingencies that are required to be accrued or disclosed by *FASB Accounting Standards Codification 450, Contingencies* (formerly *Statement of Financial Accounting Standards No. 5*.

   d) Designations of net assets disclosed to you that were not properly authorized and approved, or reclassifications of net assets that have not been properly reflected in the financial statements.

Page 2 of 3

Management Representation Letter Holy Smoke, page 2

Church of the Holy Smoke
123 Elm Street
Paxville, Agape 12345

13) The Church has satisfactory title to all owned assets, and there are no liens or encumbrances on such assets nor has any asset been pledged as collateral.

14) We have complied with all restrictions on resources (including donor restrictions) and all aspects of contractual agreements that would have a material effect on the financial statements in the event of noncompliance. This includes complying with donor requirements to maintain a specific asset composition necessary to satisfy their restrictions.

No events have occurred subsequent to the statement of financial position date and through the date of this letter that would require adjustment to, or disclosure in, the financial statements.

Signed: _____   Signed: _____

Title: <u>Senior Warden</u>   Title: <u>Treasurer</u>

Date: _____   Date: _____

Management Representation Letter Holy Smoke, page 3

The Audit Report

An audit report contains a number of documents sequenced as required by the AICPA. The audit report will contain something similar to this:

- Title page
- Table of Contents
- Auditor's opinion letter
- Statement of Financial Position (or, if OCBOA, some other form of a balance sheet)
- Statement of Activities (or, if OCBOA, some other form of an income statement)
- Statement of Cash Flows
- Statement of Change in Net Assets
- Notes to the Financial Statements
- Supplemental Schedules (and auditor's comments), if any

For detailed information regarding financial statements, notes, and supplemental schedules, see chapter 5, "How to Read Church Financial Statements." I will cover only the auditor's opinion letter here.

Auditor's Opinion Letter

The auditor's opinion letter, on the auditor's letterhead, is prominently displayed in the annual audit report directly behind the Table of Contents and before any financial information. An auditor has several kinds of opinions they can issue in their auditor's letter.

Unqualified opinion An unqualified, or "clean" opinion is one where there are no material misstatements anywhere in the financial statements. My experience with churches has been that a clean opinion is the case only ten to fifteen percent of the time. While this is the normal opinion for commercial companies, it is not for churches. There is usually something in the auditing process or in the financial statements that causes one of the other opinions to be rendered.

Here is an example of an unqualified opinion report:

INDEPENDENT AUDITOR'S REPORT
To the Vestry of Church of the Holy Smoke™

We have audited the accompanying statement of financial position of Church of the Holy Smoke™ (a nonprofit organization) as of December 31, 20XW, and the related statements of activities and cash flows for the year then ended. These financial statements are the responsibility of the Church's management.

Our responsibility is to express an opinion on these financial statements based on our audit.

We conducted our audit in accordance with auditing standards generally accepted in the United States of America. Those standards require that we plan and perform the audit to obtain reasonable assurance about whether the financial statements are free of material misstatement. An audit includes examining, on a test basis, evidence supporting the amounts and disclosures in the financial statements. An audit also includes assessing the accounting principles used and significant estimates made by management, as well as evaluating the overall financial statement presentation. We believe that our audit provides a reasonable basis for our opinion.

In our opinion, the financial statements referred to above present fairly, in all material respects, the financial position of Church of the Holy Smoke™ as of December 31, 20XW, and the changes in its net assets and its cash flows for the year then ended in conformity with accounting principles generally accepted in the United States of America.

Firm's signature
City, State
July 31, 20XX

Qualified opinion   A qualified opinion is one that finds some part of the financial statements to be problematic. One of the most frequent examples that cause church financial statement opinions to be qualified is the lack of fixed assets being recorded. GAAP and OCBOA both require that fixed assets be recorded, as does Canon 7: "Books of account shall be kept so as to provide the basis for satisfactory accounting." If fixed assets are not recorded, that is not satisfactory accounting by definition of generally accepted accounting principles (GAAP). Notice the third paragraph below. This is part of what makes this a qualified opinion. We know now that this is not acceptable under any method of accounting, because it distorts the financial picture of the church by not having fixed assets. Remember our accounting equation? There are also corresponding Net Assets that are not properly recorded either. An example of a qualified opinion letter:

INDEPENDENT AUDITOR'S REPORT
To the Vestry of Church of the Holy Smoke™

We have audited the accompanying statement of financial position of Church of the Holy Smoke™ (a nonprofit organization) as of December 31, 20XW, and the related statements of activities and cash flows for the year then ended. These financial statements are the responsibility of the Church's management. Our responsibility is to express an opinion on these financial statements based on our audit.

We conducted our audit in accordance with auditing standards generally accepted in the United States of America. Those standards require that we plan and perform the audit to obtain reasonable assurance about whether the financial statements are free of material misstatement. An audit includes examining, on a test basis, evidence supporting the amounts and disclosures in the financial statements. An audit also includes assessing the accounting principles used and significant estimates made by management, as well as evaluating the overall financial statement presentation. We believe that our audit provides a reasonable basis for our opinion.

The Church does not record fixed assets, accumulated depreciation, or depreciation expense. The amounts are not determinable.

In our opinion, except for the effects of not recording fixed assets, accumulated depreciation, or depreciation expense, the financial statements referred to in the first paragraph present fairly, in all material respects, the financial position of Church of the Holy Smoke™ as of December 31, 20XW, and the changes in its net assets and its cash flows for the year then ended in conformity with accounting principles generally accepted in the United States of America.

Firm's signature
City, State
July 31, 20XX

Disclaimer opinion   A disclaimer of opinion is more disconcerting, as this means there was not enough evidence of good accounting to be able to render an opinion at all. Sometimes a church will keep such bad records, having no financial statements in existence (or consisting of Excel spreadsheets from checkbooks), that no manner of auditing will suffice to render an opinion. There are other reasons for a disclaimer, but in a church this is the most common. The auditor's letter would thus say:

INDEPENDENT AUDITOR'S REPORT
To the Vestry of Church of the Holy Smoke™

We were engaged to audit the accompanying statement of financial position of Church of the Holy Smoke™ (a nonprofit organization) as of December 31, 20XW, and the related statements of activities and cash flows for the year then ended. These financial statements are the responsibility of the Church's management. Our responsibility is to express an opinion on these financial statements based on our audit.

No accounting controls are exercised over plate-to-bank cash collections prior to the initial entry of such contributions in the accounting records. Accordingly, it was not practicable for us to extend our audit of such receipts beyond the amounts recorded.

Because we were unable to satisfy ourselves concerning the amount of cash contributions, as explained in the preceding paragraph, the scope of our work was not sufficient to enable us to express, and we do not express, an opinion on the financial statements referred to in the first paragraph.

Firm's signature
City, State
July 31, 20XX

Adverse opinion An adverse opinion is not what anyone wants. This means that the financial statements are materially wrong, and the church is unwilling to change them to make them right. This could also mean that the auditor and management had a major disagreement in the treatment of something in the books.

Consider this: the treasurer insists that the mortgage should not be recorded in the books if the related mortgaged asset is not also recorded. Failure to record the assets will result in a qualified opinion because that situation is not as severe as the failure to record a significant debt. The implication is that all the transactions associated with the mortgage payments are not recorded. Thus, the Statement of Financial Position is misleading for not containing the liability for the mortgage, and the Statement of Activities does not contain the interest expense. There is no way to reconcile the Statement of Cash Flows as a result. The opinion letter would look something like this:

INDEPENDENT AUDITOR'S REPORT
To the Vestry of Church of the Holy Smoke™

We have audited the accompanying statement of financial position of Church of the Holy Smoke™ (a nonprofit organization) as of December 31, 20XW, and the related statements of activities and cash flows for the year then ended. These financial statements are the responsibility of the Church's management. Our responsibility is to express an opinion on these financial statements based on our audit.

We conducted our audit in accordance with auditing standards generally accepted in the United States of America. Those standards require that we plan and perform the audit to obtain reasonable assurance about whether the financial statements are free of material misstatement. An audit includes examining, on a test basis, evidence supporting the amounts and disclosures in the financial statements. An audit also includes assessing the accounting principles used and significant estimates made by management, as well as evaluating the overall financial statement presentation. We believe that our audit provides a reasonable basis for our opinion.

The Church's financial statements do not disclose the existence of a mortgage on real estate owned by the church. In addition, the church does not maintain fixed asset records. In our opinion, disclosure of that information is required to conform with accounting principles generally accepted in the United States of America.

In our opinion, because of the significance of the omission of information discussed in the preceding paragraph, the financial statements referred to in the first paragraph do not present fairly, in conformity with accounting principles generally accepted in the United States of America, the financial position of Church of the Holy Smoke™ as of December 31, 20XW, or the results of its operations or its cash flows for the year then ended.

Firm's signature
City, State
July 31, 20XX

Notice that in all letters, the actual opinion is in the last paragraph.

Letters to Management

Now we get to the letters to management that accompany the audit report. There is a required letter the CPA must issue, and one that the CPA must issue as the conditions warrant—SAS114, The Auditor's Communication With Those Charged With Governance (AU 380) and SAS115, Communicating Internal Control Related Matters Identified in an Audit (AU 325). These two letters plus the Letter to Management are the ones to which Canon 7, Sec. 1 refers here:

> **(g)** All reports of such audits, including any memorandum issued by the auditors or audit committee regarding internal controls or other accounting matters, together with a summary of action taken or proposed to be taken to correct deficiencies or implement recommendations contained in any such memorandum, shall be filed with the Bishop or Ecclesiastical Authority not later than 30 days following the date of such report, and in no event, not later than September 1 of each year, covering the financial reports of the previous calendar year.[22]

The real value in an audit is not the resulting auditor's opinion or the financial statements; it is the examination of the internal policies and procedures, and their compliance with good internal control best practices. The resulting summary of the auditor's observations is called the Letter to Management.

SAS114. The SAS114 letter is required of a CPA when conducting an independent audit. SAS is an acronym for Statements on Auditing Standards

---

22. *Constitution and Canons for the Government of the Episcopal Church* (New York: Church Publishing Inc., 2009), p. 40.

and 114 comes from pronouncement number 114 requiring the letter and its contents accompany the delivery of an audit. An example:

July 31, 20XX
To the Vestry and Wardens of Church
of the Holy Smoke™
We have audited the financial statements of Church of the Holy Smoke™ for the year ended December 31, 20XW, and have issued our report thereon dated July 31, 20XX. Professional standards require that we provide you with information about our responsibilities under generally accepted auditing standards as well as certain information related to the planned scope and timing of our audit. We have communicated such information in our letter to you dated July 31, 20XX. Professional standards also require that we communicate to you the following information related to our audit.

Significant Audit Findings
Qualitative Aspects of Accounting Practices
The Vestry is responsible for the selection and use of appropriate accounting policies. The significant accounting policies used by Church of the Holy Smoke™ are described in Note A to the financial statements. The Church adopted accounting policies related to the inclusion of estimated fixed assets and loan liabilities beginning with the year ended December 31, 20XW. Accordingly, the accounting change has been retrospectively applied to prior periods presented as if the policy had always been used.

We noted no transactions entered into by the Church during the years for which there is a lack of authoritative guidance or consensus with the exception of fixed assets which are not recorded by any generally accepted accounting method or other comprehensive basis method of accounting, including the lack of accumulated depreciation and lack of depreciation expense as described in Notes A and G.

Accounting estimates are an integral part of the financial statements prepared by management and are based on management's knowledge and experience about past and current events and assumptions about future events. Certain accounting estimates are particularly sensitive because of their significance to the financial statements and because of the possibility that future events affecting them may differ significantly from those expected. The most sensitive estimate affecting the financial statements was:

Management made subjective estimates of the value of fixed assets. We evaluated the key factors and assumptions used to develop the estimates of value in determining that it is not reasonable in relation to the financial statements taken as a whole.

Certain financial statement disclosures are particularly sensitive because of their significance to financial statement users. The most sensitive disclosures affecting the financial statements were:

The disclosure of Noncompliance with Donor Restrictions in Note E and Significant Estimates of Fixed Assets in Note G in the Notes to the Financial Statements.

Difficulties Encountered in Performing the Audit
We encountered significant difficulties and delays in the audit for the year ended 20XW due to the lack of reconciliation and refusal by the Treasurer to reconcile the bank statements necessitating a change in Treasurers. Once a new Treasurer was installed, the audits were further delayed in 20XW by the near immediate discovery of fraudulent activity in the accounts and subsequent efforts in the recovery of the funds from insurance companies.

Corrected and Uncorrected Misstatements
Professional standards require us to accumulate all known and likely misstatements identified during the audit, other than those that are trivial, and communicate them to the appropriate level of management. The attached schedule summarizes uncorrected misstatements of the financial statements. Management has agreed to make the attached changes in the general ledger to match the financial statements reflected in our audit.

Disagreements with Management
For purposes of this letter, professional standards define a disagreement with management as a financial accounting, reporting, or auditing matter, whether or not resolved to our satisfaction, that could be significant to the financial statements or the auditor's report. We are pleased to report that no such disagreements arose during the course of our audit.

Management Representations
We have requested certain representations from management that are included in the management representation letter dated July 31, 20XX.

Other Audit Findings or Issues
We generally discuss a variety of matters, including the application of accounting principles and auditing standards, with management each year. However, these discussions occurred in the normal course of our professional relationship and our responses were not a condition to our retention.

This information is intended solely for the use of the Vestry and management of Church of the Holy Smoke™ and is not intended to be and should not be used by anyone other than these specified parties.

Very truly yours,
Findem, Takeum & Down, LLC

SAS115. Uh-oh. The SAS115 letter is only issued if there are real problems with the internal controls of the church. I like to explain this letter as, "I found fraud, and this is what caused it," or "It is amazing to me that you have not been stolen blind yet, and here is why." Church of the Holy Smoke™

has some real problems. This letter never goes away, year after year, until the conditions that generated it are corrected. Of course, other conditions than the ones listed can cause this letter to be generated, or added to it from a prior year if the conditions have not been corrected. If you get a SAS115 letter, fix the problems identified—now. Most likely it will be the result of the violation of the Three-Legged Stool™ of internal control. A SAS115 example for the Church of the Holy Smoke™:

> **To the Vestry and Wardens of**
> **Church of the Holy Smoke™**
> In planning and performing our audit of the financial statements of Church of the Holy Smoke™ as of and for the years ended December 31, 20XW, in accordance with auditing standards generally accepted in the United States of America, we considered Church of the Holy Smoke's ™ internal control over financial reporting (internal control) as a basis for designing our auditing procedures for the purpose of expressing our opinion on the financial statements, but not for the purpose of expressing an opinion on the effectiveness of the Church's internal control. Accordingly, we do not express an opinion on the effectiveness of the Church's internal control.
>
> Our consideration of internal control was for the limited purpose described in the preceding paragraph and was not designed to identify all deficiencies in internal control that might be significant deficiencies or material weaknesses and therefore there can be no assurance that all such deficiencies have been identified. In addition, because of inherent limitations in internal control, including the possibility of management override of controls, misstatements due to error or fraud may occur and not be detected by such controls. However, as discussed below, we identified certain deficiencies in internal control that we consider to be material weaknesses and other deficiencies that we consider to be significant deficiencies.
>
> A deficiency in internal control exists when the design or operation of a control does not allow management or employees, in the normal course of performing their assigned functions, to prevent, or detect and correct misstatements on a timely basis. A material weakness is a deficiency or combination of deficiencies in internal control, such that there is a reasonable possibility that a material misstatement of the entity's financial statements will not be prevented, or detected and corrected on a timely basis. We consider the following deficiencies in Church of the Holy Smoke's™ internal control to be a material weakness:
> - The process of counting, depositing, posting, and reconciling of cash receipts lacks sufficient internal control to the degree of a material weakness.
> - The process of check writing and bank reconciliation lacks sufficient internal control to the degree of material weakness.

A significant deficiency is a deficiency, or a combination of deficiencies, in internal control that is less severe than a material weakness, yet important enough to merit attention by those charged with governance. We consider the following deficiencies in Church of the Holy Smoke's ™ internal control to be significant deficiencies:

- Reconciliation of donor restricted accounts with cash in bank
- Lack of policy and records for fixed assets

This communication is intended solely for the information and use of the Vestry, Wardens, clergy, and others within the Church, and is not intended to be and should not be used by anyone other than these specified parties.·

Church of the Holy Smoke's ™ written response to the Bishop and Diocese of the significant deficiencies and material weaknesses identified in our audit has not been subjected to the audit procedures applied in the audit of the financial statements and, accordingly, we express no opinion on it.

Findem, Takeum & Down, LLC
July 31, 20XX

Letter to management   In my opinion this is the real value of an audit. This still does not go into all the detail of every step needed; it only hits the high spots. The auditor should be consulted at a minimum, or hired, to design and document the corrected processes for vestry approval and subsequent implementation. Your church may identify with some of these common issues and find the recommendations to Church of the Holy Smoke™ generally useful, too.

To the Wardens and Vestry of
Church of the Holy Smoke™
In planning and performing our audit of the financial statements of Church of the Holy Smoke™ (Church) for the year ended December 31, 20XW, we considered the Church's internal control in order to determine our auditing procedures for the purpose of expressing an opinion on the financial statements and not to provide assurance on internal control.

However, during our audit, we became aware of several matters that are opportunities for strengthening internal controls and operating efficiency. This letter does not affect our reports dated July 31, 20XX, on the financial statements of Church of the Holy Smoke™.

We will review the status of these comments during our next audit. We have already discussed many of these comments and suggestions with various Church personnel, and we will be pleased to discuss these comments in further detail at your convenience, to perform any additional study of these matters, or to assist you in implementing the recommendations.

Our comments are summarized as follows:

Strengthen Cash Counting Internal Control Procedures

During our observation and documentation of the cash counting, depositing, and posting process, we noted several critical deficiencies regarding the protection of the cash, staff, volunteers, and the Church. There are currently multiple opportunities in the process that allow for the money to go missing and be undetected prior to deposit in the bank. Specifically we observed:

- The Vestry Person of the Day (VPoD) is not usually at the 8 a.m. service to oversee the collection of the cash from the chancel to the sacristy to the safe. Often a single person, not always a vestry member, is left to carry the offering plates to the sacristy.
- The money is left in an unlocked drawer in the sacristy in a bag marked as a bank bag. The sacristy is left unattended between services.
- At the 10:30 a.m. service, often only one person takes the offering plates from the chancel to the sacristy. Sometimes only one person is with the money in the sacristy.
- The 8 a.m. service cash is not recounted to verify its completeness.
- Only one person takes the money from the sacristy and deposits it in the safe.
- The door to the finance office was unlocked.
- The parish administrator opens the safe and takes the money to her office where she counts the cash, prepares the bank deposits, posts the contributions, and takes the cash to the bank. All parts of this step are done solely by the parish administrator.
- The parish administrator posts contributions records that are not reconciled independently.

Our recommendations are based on the need for separation of duties and duality in the presence of the cash.

- Two adult persons of no common kinship should be in the presence of the cash at all times. This means at 8 and 10:30 a.m. services, from the chancel, to the sacristy, to the safe. It is highly recommended these two persons be vestry members only as the vestry members are the only ones fiduciarily liable.
- The money should not be kept in the sacristy between services. Rather, it should be counted and put in the safe after the 8 a.m. service.
- Counting should not occur in the sacristy after either service. The counting should occur in the finance office in the undercroft with the door locked at any time prior to putting in the safe.
- Two adult persons of unrelated kinship should count the money, prepare the bank deposit, and take the bank deposit to the bank. The deposit ticket should be returned to the treasurer in a sealed, signed envelope for the treasurer's use at the time of bank account reconciliation.

- The parish administrator should receive the pledge envelopes (with the written amount of currency previously inside, if any), photocopies of all checks, and a photocopy of the count sheet. Because the parish administrator posts the contributions to the system, under no circumstances should she handle the physical cash or checks in any manner.
- The original, signed count sheet should be put in an envelope, sealed, and signed by the two counters and left for the treasurer for use at the time of bank account reconciliation.
- Only the treasurer should open any and all correspondence from the bank or other financial institutions where accounts are held.
- Wednesday night suppers, men's club, and any other function where cash is collected should follow the same procedures as those recommendations for Sundays.

Implement Internal Control Measures for Cash Disbursements

During our audit, we observed the following:
- Checks are written by the parish bookkeeper.
- Checks are left in full view for signature in the finance office, which was left unlocked.
- Checks are given back to the parish bookkeeper for mailing.
- Bank statements are given to the parish bookkeeper for opening and reconciliation.
- The rector's discretionary account was never reconciled.
- The 20XV bank statements were not reconciled.
- There are problems with the 20XW reconciliations.

Our recommendations are based on the need for separation of duties.
- Approvals for expenditures are made by the person receiving the funds.
- Approvals are missing or lack appropriate approval for some expenditures.
- Only the treasurer should open and reconcile all bank accounts every month prior to the vestry meeting.
- The Ma Barker Scholarship Fund and the rector's discretionary account should be recorded in the general ledger and reconciled monthly.
- Checks should be secured in the safe prior to signing and returned to the safe in a sealed, signed envelope once signed.
- The parish bookkeeper should never have access to signed checks. The parish administrator or other person should mail the checks, giving a copy of the signed checks and stubs, and supporting documentation back to the parish bookkeeper to file in check number sequence.
- The vestry should approve the financial statements in the minutes of the meeting as the treasurer is not a member of the vestry.
- No employee or volunteer should be allowed to approve his or her own expenses. The parish bookkeeper should be directed to not pay any invoices not properly approved.

- The vestry should clearly document the approval process and, when inspecting documentation attached to checks for signature, should not sign any checks that do not have proper documentation and proper approvals.

File Receipts in Check Number Order

Receipts with check stubs attached should be filed in check number sequence. Voided checks should be marked void across the face of the check and the signature area removed and discarded. These voided checks should also be filed in check number sequence. Only authorized persons should have access to these receipts. If retrieval is needed, the ACS system will quickly identify the proper check, which can be quickly found. Additionally, this provides for the quick determination of any missing checks from the sequence, adding an additional internal control.

Establish a Fixed Asset Capitalization Policy

We noted that the Church does not have a policy for capitalization of fixed assets for recording in the fixed asset accounts. Consequently, purchases and significant repairs made by the church that are valid fixed assets are being expensed that should be capitalized as fixed assets. The Church's records reflect a number of material items that should have been capitalized in the past. The Church should document the capitalization policy and communicate it to those who code invoices to ensure the policy is consistently followed. The treasurer should examine the detailed transaction journal monthly for items that have been improperly recorded in the general ledger. In addition, a policy should be established regarding any repairs made that would extend the useful life of fixed assets. Such repairs or replacements, such as HVAC, roof, or carpeting, should be separately identified and separately depreciated.

Maintain a Schedule of Property Additions

A schedule of additions should be maintained as assets are purchased to simplify the process of capitalizing property and equipment additions. The schedule should include the date the asset is acquired, a description of the asset, the vendor or donor name, and the amount. Invoices for asset acquisition and invoices for all other disbursements should be kept on file in a manner that allows retrieval of the original invoice for review and verification as needed by management and auditors.

Detailed Property Records

The Church should embark on a task, with urgency, of accurately establishing a detailed fixed asset schedule utilizing historical records, computer records, inventory methods, and certified appraisals. The insurance company will conduct appraisals to some extent at no charge, if they are the Church's insurance carrier. At a minimum, the detailed property records should include the following information:

- Description, asset number, and location.
- Acquisition cost, manufacturer name, donor name, and date of acquisition.

- Assigned life and method of depreciation per fixed asset policy.
- Depreciation should be calculated monthly and appropriate accumulated depreciation and depreciation expense should be recorded in the financial records monthly.
- ACS Fixed Asset Module should be used with integration to the Financial Module.
- When disposed—date of disposal, sales proceeds, and cost of sale, if any.

The fixed asset schedule should be examined monthly by the building and grounds commission chair and junior warden. The finance committee and treasurer should examine the fixed asset records and advise the stewardship committee and budget preparation committee of any necessary capital or maintenance needs in the coming year. Appropriate provisions for reserves should be made.

Policy and Procedures Manual

The Church does not have a complete policy and procedures manual documenting the church's policies and procedures for fiscal operations. A written manual is necessary to ensure that transactions are consistently treated in a standardized manner and that proper internal controls exist in the processes. Should employees or volunteers have a question regarding the proper handling of a transaction in accordance with management's authorization, such information is not available in writing. We recommend that operating guidelines for fiscal activities be prepared including a description of each fiscal procedure, such as paying of invoices, counting, depositing, and reconciling contributions. In addition, an expense allocation methodology should be incorporated into the accounting manual. We are happy to provide a template for your use, should you desire.

Single Checking Account

The Church should utilize ACS to keep monies separate between unrestricted and temporarily restricted assets, and should consolidate the monies into a single checking account. Two checking accounts complicate the accounting process, and create additional work on the bookkeeper and treasurer.

Reconcile Net Assets Monthly

Consistently, the designated accounts are not in balance with the allocation of cash between operating and designated checking accounts. The net asset categories—unrestricted, temporarily restricted, and permanently restricted—should be reconciled with the assets monthly to ensure proper alignment with the funds and allow for proper oversight. Particular attention should be paid to the designated accounts.

Record All Cash and Cash Equivalent Monies in the General Ledger and Reconcile Monthly

The rector's discretionary bank account and the Ma Barker Scholarship Fund are not recorded in the ACS system. The canons call for *all* assets of the Church to be recorded and reconciled. This should be done monthly to provide oversight and accountability for the funds. The resolution establishing the procedures for the Ma Barker Scholarship Fund requires this, in addition to canon.

Rector's Discretionary Account

- All accounts, including the rector's discretionary account, are subject to oversight and accountability by the vestry, and all are subject to the audit. They are also to be recorded in the general ledger and reconciled monthly by the treasurer.
- Checks should never be written from the discretionary account to an individual, the rector, other clergy, or staff.
- The vestry should establish a policy of inclusion of the discretionary money as an integral part of a single process of oversight, accountability, recording in the general ledger, and reconciliation. Most parishes that adopt a single checking account for all church matters include discretionary funds in that single account.
- The discretionary account should not be used to supplement the operating or designated funds of the church. By canon, they are for pastoral purposes only.

We wish to thank the vestry, treasurer, former and current parish administrators, clergy and staff for their support and assistance during our audit.

A copy of the audit report and all letters to management along with actions taken or planned to be taken regarding the auditors letters are due to the bishop within 30 days of delivery to the vestry, but no later than September 1, 20XX, regardless, per canon.

This report is intended solely for the information and use of the vestry, management, and others within the Church and is not intended to be and should not be used by anyone other than these specified parties.

Findem, Takeum & Down, LLC
Paxtown, Agape
July 31, 20XX

When I deliver an audit report to a vestry, the presentation ranges from 1.5 to 2.5 hours. Over two-thirds of the time is spent on the letters—SAS114, SAS115, and the Letter to Management—and less than a third on the audit report itself. The issues discussed in this book are the accumulation of the items discovered in those audits, the resulting long discussions with vestries, and best practices within the industry. Some of those discussions were the result of fraud being discovered. Some involved having to allow the adoption of the notion of personal liability for the financial matters of the church by virtue of being on the vestry. Interestingly, none of those discussions resulted in disagreement with the information or concepts presented.

CHAPTER
7
Fraud

One topic that no one wants to address is fraud in the church. However, the problem is far more prevalent and pervasive than anyone will admit. The Association of Certified Fraud Examiners (ACFE) has conducted surveys of its members for almost two decades.[23] The survey asks detailed questions regarding cases engaged by the examiners. Consistently, the not-for-profit industry exhibits sixteen percent fraud in its organizations year after year in the United States and globally. While more than just churches or religious organizations comprise the not-for-profit industry, it is an indicator of the pervasiveness of the problem. Who would steal from the Salvation Army, Red Cross, United Way, or our hometown church? Answer: Anyone with access to the money.

We want to believe that persons we know and trust would not commit fraud. Invariably, though, persons who commit fraud are those put in a position of trust, because they have access to the money. They are put in that position of access because they are clergy, a staff member, or a volunteer who has been asked to perform some function with the money.

From my experience in auditing churches I know that fraud exists. In just one diocese, I discovered fraud in thirty-three percent of the churches I audited, which represented forty percent of the churches in the diocese. There are a couple of ways to view these statistics: either one in three churches in the diocese currently is experiencing fraud, or fraud occurs once out of every three years in every church. I believe the latter is more likely the case.

The statistics are overwhelming. Whether it is one in six churches as the ACFE survey suggests, or one in three as my experience in a diocese suggests,

---

23. Information from the ACFE is used with express permission. All ACFE charts are from: *Report to the Nations on Occupational Fraud and Abuse 2012* (Austin, TX: Association of Certified Fraud Examiners, 2012), www.acfe.com

the amount of loss is staggering and the incidence of fraud is far more frequent than generally acknowledged. Either way, this does not bode well for the church or its donors. Usually, once fraud is discovered donors either leave the parish altogether or the loose plate donations decline. The special needs and other designated donations are not as forthcoming, as people no longer trust that their gift is going where they intended.

I recovered over $250,000 for the diocese's parishes, but much more was unrecoverable. Earlier in the book I quoted the canon to the ordinary, who proclaimed the frauds "a catastrophe of preponderous proportions." That means that donors were betrayed. I cannot help but think of the parable of the widow's mites and wonder how many similar sacrificial gifts are included in what was stolen.

Who is liable for replenishing the money stolen from the church? The sitting vestry at the time of discovery is liable, not the vestry under which the fraud occurred, unless collusion with a prior vestry member can be proven. (Collusion in this example is when the perpetrator and a vestry member collaborated to steal the money.) I would not rely on this defense. Once fraud is discovered, a new vestry should not be elected or seated until the fraud investigation is complete, and the funds returned to the church. My preferred order for who should reimburse the money: the perpetrator, the church's insurance company, the congregation, and then the vestry members.

Fraud has a devastating effect on a parish. It shakes our faith in humanity itself. "Billy was such a kind man." "How could Susie do that?" "How can I go back to church and listen to a sermon of his?" It affects the church's reputation in the community. And it is personally devastating to the perpetrator.

How Fraud Is Committed and by Whom

Before addressing the details of how to guard against fraud, we must first understand how the fraud is committed and by whom. I will use a combination of material from ACFE to examine the perpetrators, and examples from the Church of the Holy Smoke™ to illustrate how some frauds can occur.

Since some of the data in ACFE's survey is not broken down by industry or sector, interpretation of some data needs to be tempered with experience and common sense. For example, according to the survey the primary way to determine if someone is committing fraud is related to living beyond one's means. However, in an Episcopal church, personal financial difficulties are a more likely cause for committing fraud. I found that to be the case more than sixty percent of the time.

These financial difficulties can come in a variety of forms. The motivations for committing fraud are as varied as the individual and the opportunity. Here are a few examples:

Motivation for Committing Fraud

Greed "I will win the lottery and pay back the money plus a ten percent tithe." In a rural farming community of about 13,500, the two staff members of the local Episcopal church were the rector and parish administrator. After much debate, the citizens of the state finally passed a lottery. A person could buy a ticket for $1 for a chance toward a jackpot that sometimes reached into the several millions. The parish administrator was convinced that God wanted her to win the lottery so she could help the struggling parish. Since she was the one who counted the money, deposited it, posted the contributions, and reconciled the bank account, no one would know if she took money from the church with which to play the lottery.

Besides, when she won the lottery, she would pay back what she took, plus give the church ten percent of the winnings. Of course, she was convinced that God wanted her to have the other ninety percent, less the "borrowed" money. This went on for some time. Sometimes she would buy twenty or fifty tickets; it all depended on the contributions in the plate on a given Sunday. Finally, the diocese ordered an audit since the church had not had one in recent years. That is when it was discovered that the administrator had bought 100,000 lottery tickets, $1 at a time. It took her ten years at nine percent interest to pay the money back.

Analysis The problem with this situation is that there really is nothing else to tell about the story. There were no audits. No one was inspecting the books. No one was inspecting the deposits, the bank balance, or the bank statements. There was a complete and total void of oversight that was nonexistent for years. It makes one wonder how the church functioned or if there were budgets at all.

Need "The lawyer wanted more money to defend me in the divorce." Sometimes forces not in our control create a need. The church preschool director was on top of the world. Her last child was on her way to college, and now she would have time for other things. That is, until she was presented with divorce papers the day after her daughter left for college. She was embarrassed and devastated. She quietly went to an attorney who charged her a $1,500 retainer to contact her husband's attorney to find out if things could be reconciled. She did not want to upset her children, especially the one who just left for the university. Her husband had moved out while she was at the preschool, taking most everything. Maybe the attorney could do something. The lawyer called her in a couple of days to say there was no chance of reconciliation, and if she wanted him to continue, it would cost another $10,000. She could drop off the check in a day or two.

She was too embarrassed to ask anyone for help, and she just wanted the nightmare to end. However, other than her meager preschool salary, she had no other income and no way to pay the attorney. She borrowed $8,000 from her aging, retired father and used some of the tuition checks from the preschool to pay the rest. At least that was taken care of—until her daughter called to tell her she needed $4,500 for housing and meals—by tomorrow! Where was that kind of money to be found overnight?

It was Monday and most of the tuition checks had arrived with the morning drop-off of children. There was enough cash to meet the payroll this week and buy anything else needed. That is when the preschool director opened a shadow bank account in the preschool's name at another bank and deposited some of the tuition checks there. She then wrote a check to herself and deposited it into her personal bank account. This shadow bank account existed for over two years. In all, with fraudulent credit card use thrown in, she took $82,000 until she was caught by the audit. Since she was the only one who had access to the preschool bank account, had her own bank accounts for the preschool, since she reconciled the preschool and her own bank statements, and since no one else ever looked at the preschool books but her—it was easy for her to perpetrate the fraud.

Analysis   Life for the preschool director probably felt like wave after wave of endless monetary and personal problems. The difference is that this was not an issue created by internal desires as in the previous example, but by external forces which were thrust upon her unforeseen.

The problem with this situation is similar to the previous, but more complex than the previous. Even though the church had oversight responsibility of the preschool, the vestry did not ask for anything other than an annual financial statement which the preschool director prepared. There was no audit of the church or the preschool.

Since she was depositing some of the tuition checks into her own shadow account, there was never a record of the tuition being deposited in the preschool account. Money can't go missing that is never counted in the first place. She collected all the tuition, made all the enrollments, and kept the weekly tuition log on a spreadsheet. It was very easy for her to not show several children as registered, collect the tuition checks, and deposit them into her shadow bank account.

Nobody ever bothered to inspect the preschool records. Even a count of the children's noses compared to the enrollment spreadsheet would have identified a discrepancy. She had been there 10 years, and the fraud continued for at least four.

When the fraud was discovered, the rector, senior warden, and auditor went to the branch of the shadow bank where the account was opened. Because no one other than the preschool director was on the signature card, the shadow bank would not release any information about the accounts, even though they were in the name of the church preschool.

The church ultimately lost dozens of families and the bishop had to install a priest-in-charge to rebuild the church.

Perceived need "I need that operation." The parish administrator and the rector were the only staff members of a small church in a small, rural town. Parishioners were mostly manufacturing or retail employees. The surgeon in town was the senior warden and a major contributor to the church. Unbeknownst to everyone but the surgeon and the rector, the parish administrator needed an operation. The insurance company would not cover the $3,500 cost since the procedure was elective. Yet, the operation must go on.

Here is how the parish administrator got the money. She used an inexpensive printer and simple, easy-to-obtain software to commit the fraud. An innocuous printer costing $99 led to the fraud of $11,500.

The parish administrator searched church files from five years prior. She found invoices from vendors that were frequently used or related to the church. She used the all-in-one printer to scan an image of the old invoice. Then she modified the date to a more current one and printed it. She was careful to choose original invoices that contained no color so her inkjet printer would only need to print black and white. She chose invoices over five years old because no one currently on the vestry was serving then, and when she put the invoice through for payment, no one remembered it.

With the new invoice, she attached an approval form and forged signatures of approval for payment. She cut the check made payable to the vendor and sent the package of invoice, approval form, and check to the vestry for two signatures. The appropriate vestry members signed them and gave them back to the parish administrator.

The parish administrator scanned the signed checks into the computer. Now she had an image of the check made payable to the vendor and signed by vestry members. She took the signed check and taped over the name of the payee to cover it up. She wrote her name as the payee on the check.

She took the check to the bank and deposited it in the ATM. Her bank account was at the same bank as the church's, so this check became what is known in the banking industry as an "on us" check. In other words, it got processed by the bank internally and did not have to go through the Federal Reserve System to another bank where there might be additional scrutiny of the check. When a check is deposited through an ATM and it is "on us," it receives little to no visual inspection.

When the bank statement arrived at the church, the parish administrator opened it. She found the page where the image of the check was located, and it clearly showed that she was the payee. She scanned the page into the computer. Remember, she had an image of the check that was properly made payable to the vendor, not her. She used the software to replace the image of the check payable to her with the one she originally scanned made payable to the vendor, and printed out the page of the bank statement. She put the bank statement page she falsified back into the bank statement and then into the treasurer's box for reconciliation. Everything balanced, all the documentation matched, no one was the wiser.

One day, the music minister noticed a printout of the budget indicating the available music budget was much lower than she believed it to be. Apparently, the reaction by the parish administrator to the inquiry was enough to cause suspicion by the music minister, who reported it to the rector. The parish administrator said she would "fix" the problem with a new budget printout. She said, she "must have charged the wrong budget line item, but that will be fixed before the vestry meeting."

I was called on a Saturday afternoon to investigate. The next day, I was in the parish hall waiting for the 10:30 a.m. service to end when I noticed the financial statements on the bulletin board. The fund balances were off by $11,500 and did not match the change in net assets. That was how much the parish administrator had stolen in ninety days. It was in plain view, but no one knew how to read the financial statements to identify it.

This was right before Thanksgiving. The parish administrator pleaded guilty and confessed to each instance. She had never been in trouble with the law before. Since she confessed, the judge, a childhood classmate, sent her home for the holidays with sentencing in January. He hinted it would probably be probation.

But she went to work for another business in town sometime between Thanksgiving and Christmas. That business owner suspected fraud and called the State Bureau of Investigation, who put her in jail until the trial in which she was sentenced to five years with possible parole in twenty-seven months. It was no longer a magistrate court and a solicitor, but a district attorney and a state court judge who sentenced her. Fraud has human consequences in addition to monetary ones.

There is more to this story. The church was so small that the loss of $11,500 was devastating. The diocese could not help, "It's the holidays and all but $5,000 is already identified where it is going." The rector and senior warden had the unenviable task of standing in front of the congregation and essentially saying, "I know you gave it once, but we lost it (due to our lack of internal controls and oversight). Would you mind giving it again?" That did not work at all. There was no insurance to cover the loss. The vestry meeting was short and to the point. All vestry members announced to the senior warden that they were mill folk, she was a medical doctor, and she could reimburse the church. Then they walked out. The Senior Warden wrote a check for $11,500 to the church to reimburse the church for the theft—not because she wanted to, but because each individual vestry member is liable for the entire loss singularly as well as collectively.

Analysis Sometimes we create a perceived need within ourselves that we ultimately could control. This was an elective operation of a cosmetic nature—a fabricated need and not a real one.

There are multiple problems with this situation. The vestry had no one looking closely at the financial statements. No one knew how to read the financial statements. The fraud had been in plain sight on the bulletin board for three months had anyone looked at the Change in Net Assets on the Statement of Activities and the Net Assets on the Statement of Financial Position. They did not total correctly.

No one understood accounting—except the parish administrator who was also the bookkeeper. The vestry meetings consisted of less than five minutes allocated to finance. This case cries out for an independent auditor to educate the vestry.

The major problem is that the signed checks were given back to the bookkeeper who also posted the books. The second problem was the software was QuickBooks, and she manipulated the numbers to be what she wanted them to be with no audit trail of her altering transactions (cooking the books). The third problem is she opened the bank statements rather than the treasurer. Had the treasurer opened them, he would have immediately seen the checks made payable to her on the check image. Another problem was that the vestry was more of a coffee klatch than a fiduciarily liable and responsible party. Overarching this all was a rector that did not provide leadership for the church, vestry, staff, and volunteers. She held no one accountable and did no inspection of process. She was moved to an assistant rector position and is still in that role five years later.

Beyond belief, once the fraud was discovered, the parish administrator was not released from the church for two weeks. (The rector was worried about who would write the checks). During that time, she still had her key to the church and had access to the computer and files. She destroyed all the altered invoices and discarded the files from prior years from which she had taken the invoices to copy. All the paper evidence of her defalcation was destroyed. If fraud is discovered, the perpetrator must be removed from access to the church, church files, and church computers *immediately*.

Veil of authority "She worked for an accountant in town. We thought she was trustworthy." Sometimes things are not as they appear. The church bookkeeper kept the books at the accounting office where she worked. She wrote all the checks, the vestry signed them, and the parish administrator mailed them. The financial statements were always on time for the vestry meetings and were presented by the treasurer. When an audit was finally done, it was discovered that there was no one examining the transactions or the books. The bookkeeper did all the bank reconciliations. The bookkeeper also made up the deposits every Monday and kept the donor records. The church and vestry did not have to concern themselves with the accounting. It all balanced and, although the reports were not as useful as desired, they were there nonetheless.

Offsite books. No oversight. No independent reconciliation. No inspection of the books. Stealing the money was easy. Of course, she meant to pay it back, but never got around to it. The auditor demanded the electronic records and that was when the fraud was uncovered. The bookkeeper had cooked the books to make them look right to the auditor in the year being audited. What she did not realize is that the data file contained all the transactions for several years.

One of the audit steps is to do a comparison of current year to prior years for reasonableness. It was not even close. It was obvious that she had been making journal entries to change balances to be what people expected them to be. The prior years were a mess because she had made entries that crossed years, among other things. She skimmed money for several years before she was caught. An annual audit would have saved the church over $50,000—the amount not covered by the meager fraud insurance maximum of $5,000.

Analysis Having someone perform the bookkeeping for the church who is not a church member is common. What is not acceptable, church member or not, is for the church records—bank bags of money, deposit book, computer records, check requests, and bank statements to be delivered anywhere outside the church premises. All accounting and records must be kept on the church's property. They are the church's property. Oversight cannot be provided when there is nothing at the church to inspect. Accountability cannot occur if there is no one there to question.

This was a case of the vestry abdicating its fiduciary responsibility to a third party offsite bookkeeper. There was no count sheet that could have been used to verify the deposits. There was nothing but blind trust.

The vestry thought it would be okay since the bookkeeper worked for a local accounting firm. However, it was known to the vestry that she was using the firm's equipment and software in off-hours, and was billing the church independently of the firm. The agreement was with her, not the accounting firm. The firm had no knowledge of the arrangement.

Since all the deposits, bookkeeping, and reconciliation was done by her, the fraud was easy to perpetrate. Since the vestry provided for no internal controls or oversight, getting away with it was easy.

This is a case that all too often has a common thread of trust. Ronald Reagan had a saying, "trust, but verify." That is accountability. There is nothing wrong with trust, but trust is unfounded if in the person solely. Who steals the money? Anyone with access. Trust the process—the checks and balances, the independent reconciliations, the absolute separation of duties, the inspection of actions by people, oversight by approval signatures, etc.—do not trust the person explicitly. Continuously verify the process and checks and balances work.

Real human need "I just found out I have multiple sclerosis. My mom is in late stage Alzheimer's, and I am the only relative. Neither of us has medical insurance." Sometimes the need created is only in God's hands to resolve. What a contrast there is between "greed or need" and "real human need." The church bookkeeper worked odd jobs, mostly contract work for medium-sized companies who needed fill-in technology or accounting work. The church bookkeeping job at $400 per month was the only consistent job she had. With a key to the church office, she would come in at night after her other jobs to enter the invoices and print the checks.

The new treasurer, a banker, refused to reconcile the bank accounts. There was a meeting of the interim rector, treasurer, bookkeeper, parish administrator, auditor, and Senior Warden. Since no one else in the church would reconcile them either, there was no audit for two years.

Since no one reconciled the bank account, the bookkeeper knew there was no close scrutiny. She wrote her monthly paycheck. Then she wrote another one in three weeks, not four. That second check made it through with two signatures with no problem. She did this for several months, writing paychecks to herself every three weeks.

The vestry rotated its duties weekly. Vestry-persons-of-the-day changed every week. The checks, their vouchers, and their receipts would be put in the sacristy in a drawer for them to affix their two signatures and return to the bookkeeper. When a new vestry was installed, she began writing checks every week. The problem was that she had to do something with the extra expense. The comparative budget vs. actual would quickly show her salary as over budget.

That is when she started posting the expense to 20YC, six years out, instead of the current year. Now she could write the checks, cash them, and only allow the ones that needed to show on the current year's books to show each month. The rest of them were in a budget year so far in the future that she would be gone by then. Since no one was reconciling the bank statements, this would be no problem. (Do you see a lack of leadership on the part of the interim rector and senior warden through inaction to replace the treasurer?)

She got away with it for two-and-a-half years, until a new rector came and he got a new treasurer who reconciled the bank statements. The fraud was discovered three and a half *hours* into the reconciliation of the last three years' bank statements. The church had just raised their fraud coverage from $2,500 to $10,000 the year before. Luckily, the coverage matched the theft and the church was made whole. The church now has $100,000 in coverage. The bookkeeper was not prosecuted.

Analysis   Another perfect storm of multiple things lead to fraud. Lack of leadership is a key ingredient in this failure. Lack of pastoral care for the bookkeeper was probably complicit, too.

The role of the treasurer (see chapter 3, "Roles and Responsibilities") is not fulfilled by a lack of reconciling the bank accounts. The vestry did not do what they were supposed to do when signing checks—look for proper authorization and documentation for the expenditure—including payroll—which included time sheets for hourly paid staff.

In addition, the new vestry did not take the time to understand contracts in force at the beginning of the new year. Had they done so, each would have known that the bookkeeper was paid monthly and not weekly.

Because the VPoDs who signed checks rotated weekly, it gave an opportunity for checks to be written without knowledge of prior payment.

The reason the canon requires two signatures on a check is not for signatures; it is for inspection. Every time a vestry person signs a check, the accompanying documentation should be thoroughly inspected for proper authorization and a standard of documents that meet church policy, such as original receipts or time cards.

Opportunity "No one ever looks at the discretionary fund . . . and the beach is great R&R," so thought the rector of an old, established parish. The parish had millions in endowments and millions in income each year. It was a plum parish in the diocese, located in the ritzy part of the state capital. Previous years' "audits" had been done by a committee comprised of the same small group of individuals, because the diocese did not require them to have a real audit by a CPA. The committee was comprised of a banker, a stock broker, and a parishioner who could not even balance her own checkbook but was a big donor—none of whom had any experience as a CPA or any idea of what a real audit was about. They followed the checklist in the *Manual for Business Methods for Congregations* published by The Episcopal Church's Finance Office.[24] The checklist is a woefully inadequate method of "audit" that will not examine the internal controls properly and will almost never find fraud.[25]

The church explained the inadequate audit this way: "It was easier and less expensive." Who would suspect such a large church would have the largest fraud committed to date in the diocese—and perpetrated by the rector? However, the audit committee had not audited the rector's discretionary fund because the rector insisted it was private and not subject to an audit.

No report was ever made to the vestry or anyone regarding the balance of the rector's discretionary fund. The bank statement was sent to the rector's home, and the checking account was in the rector's name. With all that money, it was too much of a temptation. The rector, son of a well-known and loved retired rector, had grown up going to the beach frequently. He really missed being able to do that. Given that there was no one else looking at the account, he bought a condo in Florida, never told anyone, and paid for it out of the discretionary fund. He told his family a vague story regarding its use.

---

24. *The Episcopal Church Manual of Business Methods in Church Affairs* (New York: The Domestic and Foreign Missionary Society of the Protestant Episcopal Church in the USA, 2007, 2009, 2012). Online: http://www.episcopalchurch.org/sites/default/files/downloads/full_manual_spring_2012.pdf.

25. Well intentioned as it might be, the *Manual* gives churches and dioceses a false sense of security and fails to identify or perform critical elements of the true audit process that potentially would identify fraud. Fundamental to all audits performed by CPAs are the documentation of the processes, examination for checks and balances, independent confirmations, existence of audit trail, analytical methods, and testing methods—none of which are included in the *Manual's* checklist.

He was nearing retirement and would make up some excuse about a gift, or buying the condo, or something when the time came.

The new vestry had heard about the extent of fraud in churches and hired an independent auditor, a CPA. When the new auditor arrived, the fraud was quickly discovered when the rector was asked for the records. When he refused, the auditor appealed to the diocese who forced the records to be given to the auditor. (Do you see the leadership in not only the tone set by the diocese, but also the insistence of canonical compliance?) The rector had not bothered to conceal the payments for the condo. The fraud was discovered in minutes. The canon to the ordinary and the bishop were dismayed. The story spread all over the diocese like wildfire. It was a dark day. Even rectors are susceptible when the access to the funds is left without oversight and internal controls. The loss was over $125,000.

Analysis   In the ACFE study below, notice that those in a position of authority cause the most dollar amount of fraud. Enron, AIG, Madoff, MCI, MF Global are massive scandals because they were perpetrated by the top leaders in charge. A rector in a parish is no different position than being in control at the top. It is one thing when leaders fail to lead; it is another when leaders fail their fiduciary responsibility.

There is an old school still in the church where the rector's discretionary account is allowed to be as secret as Mother Teresa's diary. This is not according to canon and is simply wrong. I devote time to this topic throughout this book because of the potential damage that can be done by a rector, not only financially, but to the vitality of the parish.

No one in the church is above the inspection, oversight, and accountability. This means, the rector's discretionary account should be examined monthly by at least the senior warden and reconciled monthly by the treasurer. All accounts, including the rector's discretionary account are to appear monthly on the Statement of Financial Position.

The opportunity was there, and the rector took advantage of it. No one is above accountability for funds.

Indifference   "This church does not get much cash on Sundays." One Sunday morning, I showed up unannounced at a parish I was working with to observe the cash process from the collection plate to the bank or other safekeeping. This particular church had an average plate and pledge budget of $650,000 per year. The rector had said several times in conversation and preparation for the audit that the church did not get much cash (currency) on Sundays. He felt that electronic giving, the high use of envelopes, and a seemingly large quantity of checks was explanation for that.

The particular Sunday I attended, I observed the collection during the 8 a.m. service. It is my practice during an audit that the money never leaves my sight, even if I have to observe from another room through an open door. It's not my intention to be sneaky, but people tend to not do what they normally do when they think someone is watching.

After the service this Sunday, a single individual took the contributions from the plate and put them in a zippered bank bag. The person, unaccompanied, took the bag and put it in the top drawer of the unlocked parish administrator's desk in the unlocked parish office and left. Between the services, there were many people coming and going out of the office, sometimes when no one else was there. As the 10:30 service began, everyone vacated the offices and left the desk and the office doors unlocked. I stayed behind to collect information from the computer in another room, but with full view of the desk drawer. After a half hour, an individual came in and went to the drawer. I discovered she was the kitchen worker who prepared breakfast for the church every Sunday, and she came to deposit the cash (all currency) in the bank bag—alone. No one had helped her count it and there was no count sheet.

During the middle of the 10:30 a.m. service, the treasurer came in and took the bank bag back to the service with her—alone. I followed. After the service, the treasurer and another person counted the money in plain sight on the altar rail. The church had not yet emptied of parishioners. They were interrupted numerous times by people coming up and handing them donations, asking questions, and chatting.

There was no double counting. One counted the checks and that was it. There was no addition of the amounts, no adding machine tape made—nothing. The other person did not even count behind the first. That was because she was busy counting the cash and being interrupted. The person counting the checks did not count the cash. There was no count sheet to record anything. Both just announced to the other what they counted, and that was it.

All the money was put back into the bank bag, and the treasurer put it under her arm and walked off. I followed her out of the nave into the parish hall and down a corridor away from the offices. She turned and said, "Do you need anything else?"

"No, I am just following the money," I replied.

"Well, I have a meeting to go to," she said as she turned to walk away. I followed. "I said, I have a meeting to go to," she said, stopping and confronting me.

"Well, I guess I am going, too. I am not letting that money out of my sight until it is in the bank or in a safe," I said as I stood my ground.

"Okay, fine. I will put it in the safe. That is what I always do every Sunday and count it on Monday," she said. About face and back to her locked office we went. She had to get the combination for the safe in her desk . . . no, in her purse . . . maybe in her wallet . . . ah, there it was—a tightly folded small piece of paper stuck under a photo in her wallet.

Since I had been all over most of the church by now, I was interested to see where the safe was kept. I had not discovered it on my own. Off we went to a back staircase leading up to the second floor of the education building. She stopped at the base of the stairs. "See, there it is," she said.

"Where?" I said.

"Right there," she said pointing under the stairs. She started to turn to walk away.

"Aren't you going to put the money in the safe?" I asked. Huffily, she whirled around and began moving the six dust-covered music stands that had been blocking my view of, and her access to, the safe. It was an old safe, easily weighing a ton or more. It had a heavy steel casing of six inches. The dial and handle were dusty. In the process, she could not remember which way was left and which was right on the combination. All she had written down were the numbers to the combination. She had to read from the paper—the same three numbers she purportedly had been using at least twice weekly for several years.

After several failed attempts at opening the purported "finicky" safe, she finally got it open. There was absolutely nothing inside the safe. She put the money bag in, shut the door, spun the dial, and stalked off without a word. I told the rector about my experience, and he still insisted it was not a big deal since they don't get much cash on Sundays, no more than a couple hundred dollars at best. I informed him that it was July and the stack of bills was two inches high. His eyes widened and jaw dropped. The church's annual revenue was $650,000, a medium-sized church.

Analysis The rector and vestry need to pay attention to the warning signs. There was something in the process that did not sound right or look right, and parishioners were complaining.

First, there are best practices about counting money—two people at all times with the money, in a locked room, with count sheets, cross-counted by the two. (See chapter 9, "Support Internal Control" for a detailed list and flow chart.) The counting process violated all of these and more.

Second, the money was left unattended in the parish office where everyone knew where it was. Anyone in the church could have come by to help themselves during the service. The church office was also ten feet from an exterior door to the parish hall that was unlocked on Sundays.

Third, the hired breakfast worker had free access to the uncounted early service offering in the drawer. In addition, the money was not counted and a count sheet not prepared for the breakfast money. It was whatever she decided to bring forth after taking money out for her expenses for which she had no receipts and for which no one else was involved.

Fourth, the money was not deposited into the safe or the bank immediately after counting. It was being taken home by the treasurer. Her excuse was that she needed it to post the contributions to the system. By now, you should have flares going off when you see handling the money and posting the books being done by the same person. A concern should be whether the money that comes into the church ever gets counted or deposited.

Fifth, the rector showed a lack of leadership through a tone of indifference to the complaints and an acceptance of "that is the way we have always done it." If the rector does not care, why should anyone else?

The treasurer resigned the next week after five years in the position. It is undeterminable if anything was being skimmed from the church, but donations in cash approximately doubled immediately upon her departure and the implementation of internal control.

Who Commits Fraud?

The long-standing, trusted church member "Emma Bea is always here helping with the altar guild on Sunday. She is so dependable." When I took over as auditor of a large $1.4M annual revenue church founded in 1857, I did my usual follow-the-money routine. But I also asked each of the clergy and staff, wardens, and treasurer—individually—if they knew of, had heard of, had rumors of, had suspicions of any problems with the money. Usually, the answers go like this, "Nobody else knows this, but . . ."

Everyone else knows it, and the guilty party is the one who says everything is fine. Why would they admit their own guilt to me?

Emma Bea had been a member of the church all her life. She had been a proud member of the altar guild for fifty-two years, and the church had recognized her with a celebration in her fiftieth year of service. One Sunday, when the bishop came, the congregation gave all non-designated, non-pledge donations to the bishop for her discretionary fund. That following Tuesday as I was conducting some field work, the assistant rector came into the finance director's office and remarked how well the bishop had done in the loose offering that past Sunday.

"Why?" asked the finance director.

"Because of all the twenty dollar bills I saw as I took the offering plates from the ushers on Sunday. There must have been six or eight," the assistant rector replied. The finance director pulled out the count sheet that had been prepared by the counters on Sunday. There were no twenty dollar bills indicated as having been included in the count and deposit. The senior warden and rector were notified. The next Sunday, a marked twenty was put in the offering. By the time the money was counted, there were no twenties at all, or tens for that matter. Now we knew something was up.

The counters on Sundays were the ushers. This large church had about sixty ushers on the roster and most were active. They would be at the doors at the back of the church shaking hands and talking with people after each service. After about fifteen to twenty minutes when most people had left the church, they would go into the sacristy behind the altar and count the money. The money would be in the offering plates waiting for them when they arrived—right where Emma Bea had put them.

Emma Bea never missed church. At Easter, Thanksgiving, Christmas—any service really—she was always there. If other members of the altar guild wanted to go out of town or had other reasons not to be on the altar guild schedule for any Sunday, she was always the one to call. She sat up front in her pew and after the service, swiftly took the linens, hosts, and the offering plates into the sacristy and began cleaning. Most Sundays, she was the only one.

There were two doors into the sacristy, one from the sanctuary and one from a corridor in the office area. The next Sunday, the senior and junior wardens positioned themselves in view of either door to the sacristy. There were marked bills in the offering plates. After fifteen minutes, when the ushers arrived to count the money, they were told that the wardens would be doing the counting. The ushers were dismissed and the wardens entered the sacristy from the two doors. No one had entered the room since the service ended except Emma Bea. The wardens went to the offering plates and found the marked bills were not there. No twenty dollar bills were there at all.

The rector called Emma Bea into his office. She was told she was permanently off the altar guild and permanently banned from the sacristy. If she did not comply, the rector would ask the bishop to excommunicate her. The best estimate was that she got at least $10,000 per year or more. She would not admit to it and would not say how long it had been going on. She was not in need of the money. Perhaps it was the thrill of seeing how much she could take.

Those who have access to the books and money "Our treasurer does all our bookkeeping on QuickBooks[26]." Here is the first clue—treasurers should not do bookkeeping. The second *big* clue is QuickBooks. The treasurer was a retired bookkeeper in a small town. He was not a CPA, but did keep books for various small businesses. For whatever reason, he decided the church needed to start doing business with another bank closer to his house, and the vestry went along. He spent the next seventeen months transferring funds from an account at the old bank to the new. There is clue number three.

In the audit, it was discovered that the deposit slips (he did the deposits, too) indicated cash back. He would, for example, write a check out of the old bank for $8,000 and deposit the $8,000 check, but get $2,700 back in cash at the time of deposit. In the seventeen months, he stole over $21,000. Since he prepared the financial statements and reconciled the bank statements, it was easy for him to go into QuickBooks and change the amounts in the transaction to show a complete $8,000 deposit with no cash back. In order to determine exactly how much he had stolen, the senior warden had to rekey into a new dataset all the transactions and reconcile every month, one month at a time, for three years' data. As he did, the fraud became apparent in the old dataset. However, this was the only way to determine the fraud because the QuickBooks files had been altered—and in typical QuickBooks fashion, without a trace of evidence of what had been done or by whom.

Those who are crafty and deliberate "Why did the budget not show the expenses?" The bookkeeper knew her accounting equation. A debit to expenses could be replaced by a debit to fixed assets. A credit to revenue could be replaced by a credit to accumulated depreciation. A debit and a credit, both, to revenue would leave revenue flat but hide the deposit and subsequent check to herself in the same amount. The journal entries were everywhere, yet no one provided oversight of the transactions or the financial statements. It was a rote exercise to have the financial statements presented each month at the vestry meeting where they were summarily approved in a matter of seconds and given no further thought.

It amazes me that vestries believe that because statements come out of the computer, they must not contain any errors—accidental or deliberate. Only a vestry can approve journal entries. Journal entries should be brought to the vestry for approval *before* they are made. Any journal entries not approved need exceptional scrutiny and explanation—and still need approval.

---

26. QuickBooks is a registered trademark of Intuit, Inc.

The operative word is *exceptional*. There should never be any exceptions to this rule. The books should be scanned monthly for journal entries that are not approved and/or not properly recorded, or in this case, downright fraudulent. That is what the treasurer does since the treasurer is an oversight position and not one of touching the books to make transactions. It is easy to cook the books with journal entries, particularly if no one is looking and providing oversight.

A Comment to the Clergy of the Church

Is there something wrong, pastorally, in a church when staff or members of the congregation who are hurting do not feel they can come into the clergy's office, shut the door, and pour out their plight? Is it because the employer/employee relationship stops us from seeing the human side of the business relationship? Whatever the reason, the clergy need to look for common signs of need and opportunity. Later in this chapter, common characteristics of the potential for fraud are presented. Being in the leadership role of staff and volunteers, it is especially important that the clergy become familiar with those signs.

A Comment to the Laity of the Church

No one wants to think of one of the Ten Commandments being broken within the confines of the church. But it happens every day. No one wants to think that a member of the clergy or vestry would commit fraud. However, no one is above the temptation, especially when there is a need or an opportunity. The fact is that clergy and others in positions of authority in the church need the same level of oversight as anyone else.

Findings of the Association of Certified Fraud Examiners (ACFE) Survey on Occupational Fraud and Abuse[27]

Since 1996, the ACFE has surveyed its members in the United States every two years. The purpose of the survey is to understand the nature of fraud, the perpetrators, and other conditions surrounding fraud. Since 2010, they have surveyed their 34,000 members worldwide. The results are amazingly consistent regardless of location or economic condition. I have previously

---

27. Information from the ACFE is used with express permission. All ACFE charts are from: *Report to the Nations on Occupational Fraud and Abuse 2012* (Austin, TX: Association of Certified Fraud Examiners, 2012). www.acfe.com

mentioned that the findings indicate on average sixteen percent of the fraud is committed in not-for-profit entities. My experience in auditing churches leans more to one in three. The data in the survey gives some insight into why, how, and by whom this is occurring. It is useful to examine the characteristics of fraudsters and the fraud crime itself because there are clear indicators that will help identify potential fraud situations.

Some of the findings from the executive summary of the survey:

- "Survey participants estimated that the typical organization loses 5% of its revenues to fraud each year."[28] This is probably accurate when thinking of churches because whether the fraud occurs every year or occurs every several years, the loss is usually cumulative when thinking of the amount of the loss in total.

- "The frauds reported to us [ACFE] lasted a median of 18 months before being detected."[29] That has been my experience, too, on average. Some were discovered within ninety days. Others were discovered after several years, but thinking of the three-year vestry life cycle, it is not hard to discern that eighteen months is about right.

- "As in our previous studies, asset misappropriation schemes were by far the most common type of occupational fraud, comprising 87% of the cases reported to us; they were also the least costly form of fraud, with a median loss of $120,000."[30] Asset misappropriation means stealing the money or other assets of the church. Since the chalice would be readily missed, it really means the money. The average for the survey is higher than my experience, but in the range of the higher amounts stolen. My detected average was $60,000, which is usually beyond the amount of insurance carried by the church for such things.

- "Occupational fraud is a significant threat to small businesses. The smallest organizations in our study suffered the largest median losses. These organizations typically employ fewer anti-fraud controls than their larger counterparts, which increases their vulnerability to fraud."[31] Absolutely, the smaller churches are more susceptible, but

---

28. *Report to the Nations on Occupational Fraud and Abuse: 2012 Global Fraud Study* (Austin, TX: Association of Certified Fraud Examiners, 2012) p.4.

29. *Report to the Nations on Occupational Fraud and Abuse: 2012 Global Fraud Study* (Austin, TX: Association of Certified Fraud Examiners, 2012) p.4.

30. *Report to the Nations on Occupational Fraud and Abuse: 2012 Global Fraud Study* (Austin, TX: Association of Certified Fraud Examiners, 2012) p.4.

31. *Report to the Nations on Occupational Fraud and Abuse: 2012 Global Fraud Study* (Austin, TX: Association of Certified Fraud Examiners, 2012) p.4.

none are immune. In my experience, the largest churches experienced the largest dollar amount of fraud. Regardless the size of church, the amount was always over $25,000 except for two instances.

- "The presence of anti-fraud controls is notably correlated with significant decreases in the cost and duration of occupational fraud schemes. Victim organizations that had implemented any of 16 common anti-fraud controls experienced considerably lower losses and time-to-detection than organizations lacking these controls."[32] The operative word here is *any*. Any of sixteen common anti-fraud controls would have yielded considerably lower losses. It is a theme you may have noted running through this book. Trust the process not the person. Inspect, oversee, ask questions, demand accountability—add those to the inspection of the process and you will have a much better chance of thwarting fraudsters.

- "Perpetrators with higher levels of authority tend to cause much larger losses." [33]When someone in power in an organization has control or power over the money and is unchecked, the losses are staggering. To reiterate, the largest loss to date in one diocese was caused by the rector. The loss at the denominational level was staggering, but makes the point. Ellen F. Cooke was the treasurer of the Domestic and Foreign Missionary Society and of General Convention from 1986 until January 1995, when she was asked to resign by former Presiding Bishop Edmond L. Browning. The embezzlement was discovered one month later. She stole approximately $2 million.

- "The longer a perpetrator has worked for an organization, the higher fraud losses tend to be. Perpetrators with more than ten years of experience at the victim organization caused a median loss of $229,000. By comparison, the median loss caused by perpetrators who committed fraud in their first year on the job was only $25,000."[34] This makes sense, but also supports a couple of the other points. Even though there might have been a need that existed in someone's life that may have originally caused them to steal, once they begin it becomes harder to stop as they get used to that additional ill-gotten income. It also supports my experience of most frauds being over $25,000.

32. *Report to the Nations on Occupational Fraud and Abuse: 2012 Global Fraud Study* (Austin, TX: Association of Certified Fraud Examiners, 2012) p.4.

33. *Report to the Nations on Occupational Fraud and Abuse: 2012 Global Fraud Study* (Austin, TX: Association of Certified Fraud Examiners, 2012) p.4.

34. *Report to the Nations on Occupational Fraud and Abuse: 2012 Global Fraud Study* (Austin, TX: Association of Certified Fraud Examiners, 2012) p.4.

- "Most occupational fraudsters are first-time offenders with clean employment histories. Approximately 87% of occupational fraudsters had never been charged or convicted of a fraud related offense, and 84% had never been punished or terminated by an employer for fraud-related conduct."[35] This is an amazing statistic, but true. My experience is that the fraudsters I have encountered have all had clean records. Trust the process, not the person.

Other information found in the survey indicates that the median loss for a not-for-profit organization is $85,000. The number of cases reported was greatest in organizations with less than one hundred employees. Almost forty percent of all the cases were in small organizations. The median loss was greater in organizations with less than one hundred employees than in organizations with greater than ten thousand employees. The most prevalent methods of fraud that would be applicable to a church were:

1. Check tampering   22%
2. Skimming   21%
3. Expense reimbursement   17%
4. Cash-on-hand larceny   16%
5. Payroll   14%

There were others; usually the fraud constituted more than one offense. The primary internal control weaknesses involved with the crime were:

1. Lack of internal controls   45%
2. Override of internal controls   19%
3. Lack of management review (oversight)   19%
4. Poor tone at the top   9%
5. Other   5%
6. Lack of audit   3%

Notice that the audit was not a deterrent to the crime. However, over ninety percent of the weaknesses involving the fraud are ones that all vestries have in their control by simply following procedures and having annual audits.

Characteristics of the Perpetrator

Besides someone with access to the money, who would steal from the church? Some parts of the survey were not broken down to reflect data from

---

35. *Report to the Nations on Occupational Fraud and Abuse: 2012 Global Fraud Study* (Austin, TX: Association of Certified Fraud Examiners, 2012) p.4.

the not-for-profit industry, so the results will have to be tempered with good judgment for your church. The survey identified some fascinating characteristics of the perpetrator:

1. Duration of the fraud ranged from twelve months for an employee to twenty-four months for a person in management. This gives us the average of eighteen months per fraud case.

2. Two-thirds of the time the fraudster acted alone. Disturbingly, one-third of the time there was collusion—two or more people involved in the scheme. More than twice the amount of money is lost when there is collusion. My experience is that there is significantly less collusion in churches, partly because there are so few people who have access to the money. In larger organizations it will require more collusion to get around the more likely existence of internal controls and oversight.

3. Males accounted for fifty-five percent of the losses, and females for forty-five percent. My experience is that fraud is gender neutral; anyone who wants to can commit fraud.

4. The age of the perpetrators are:

a. Under 30	16%
b. 30–40	34%
c. 41–50	33%
d. Over 50	17%

5. Interestingly, age also contributed to the amount of loss:

a. Under 30	$ 25,000–$ 50,000
b. 30–40	$100,000–$150,000
c. 41–50	$183,000–$200,000
d. Over 50	over $250,000

6. Longevity of employment and amount of loss, respectively:

a. Less than 1 year	6%	$ 25,000
b. 1 year to 5 years	42%	$100,000
c. 6 years to 10 years	27%	$200,000
d. More than 10 years	25%	$230,000

7. Education level and amount of loss, respectively:

a. High school	25%	$ 75,000
b. Some college	21%	$125,000
c. College degree	37%	$200,000
d. Post-graduate degree	17%	$300,000

Clearly, the older, more educated, more stable employee is more damaging in terms of amount of loss. The most likely combination of characteristics is a fraud that occurs longer than twelve months, committed by a sole individual, who could be of either gender, is between the ages of thirty and fifty, has worked for the church more than a year, and is well educated. That sounds a lot like me. Does that sound like someone like you? Now do you see why there might be complacency in the church—the perpetrator has characteristics like you and me, and we both know we would never steal, so why would anyone like us steal? Because they have access to the money, they can, and they do. Notice that fraud was reported in every demographic area. Everyone is potentially culpable.

Behavioral Red Flags

The survey also identified behaviors exhibited by fraudsters that could have given an indication of fraud:

1.	Living beyond means	36%
2.	Financial difficulties	27%
3.	Control issues, unwillingness to share duties	18%
4.	Divorce, family problems	15%
5.	Wheeler-dealer attitude	15%
6.	Irritability, suspiciousness, or defensiveness	13%
7.	Addiction problems	8%
8.	Past employment-related problems	8%
9.	Complained about pay	8%
10.	Refused to take vacation	7%
11.	Excessive pressure from within the organization[36]	7%
12.	Past legal problems	5%
13.	Complaints about lack of authority	4%
14.	Family pressure to succeed	4%
15.	Instability of life circumstances	4%

These behaviors sum to more than one hundred percent because there was often more than one contributing factor. Go back to the scenarios presented

---

36. Excessive pressure means that in order to meet financial objectives, a department head might falsify their numbers to keep their job.

earlier in the chapter and see if you can identify the characteristics of the perpetrator in each situation. It is eye-opening. Do not assume that these characteristics are only found in employees. Volunteers with access to the money can be just as culpable as those on the payroll.

General Recommendations

Two People with the Money

This is simple. Only a lack of leadership and a lack of commitment keep this from being implemented. Remember the lady on the altar guild, the treasurer and the "finicky safe"? Even the smallest of gatherings can do this. Never—not even for a few seconds—leave the money in the presence of only one individual. This means that the offering is taken off the credence table, or wherever it may be, to the place where it is counted *by two people*. Just because it is done in plain sight is not good enough, particularly for uncounted cash. It means two people take the Wednesday night supper collection to its counting location. It means two people count the money together, never leaving the other alone with the money. It means counting all the money—cash, coins, and checks—totaling them and recording them on the count sheet before leaving the counting room to go to the restroom, if you must. It means counting it all again when you come back from the restroom. It means two people taking the money from the sacristy to the counting room. It means taking the deposit to the bank with two people. It means two people put it in the safe. It means the parish administrator does not count the offering on Monday by herself in the office and make up the deposit slip. No one counts the money alone.

"Two people" means two unrelated people who are rotated in their duty at least monthly. Unrelated means not married, no blood relation, and are not parent and child.

The number one time that money will be stolen with no hope of discovering it, with no record of it ever having been in existence, is before it can be counted and deposited into the bank. The altar guild lady most likely made off with thousands of dollars even before the ushers ever laid eyes on it. The treasurer of the church who could not find the combination to the safe was most likely taking the contribution home with her, but there was no count sheet or other written record of the offering, even though it was counted on the altar rail.

If people in your church are supposed to be participating in this process of counting and depositing the money, and they are not, do not hesitate to remove them from that position. They are putting the trust and faithful giving of the donors at extreme risk. The rector, senior warden, and vestry person-of-the-day should inspect for compliance of the two-person rule frequently throughout the year. Which would you rather have—one unhappy person who is removed or a congregation dumbstruck by fraud?

The church either creates the environment for fraud or takes the steps to prevent it. If there is a lack of interest or leadership on the part of the clergy or vestry, they have fostered a certain tone. In an environment of indifference the perpetrator has no real qualms about "borrowing" the money, just this once, with full intention to pay it back. However, rarely does this happen.

Financial Records on Premises

The accounting records of the church are as much the property of the church as the register and should never be taken off premises. How can you inspect what you do not know even exists?

One church I audited had a family who acted as if they owned the church. The matriarch of the family insisted on being the parish treasurer. She also insisted on taking the contribution records home. She felt "it was nobody's business who gave what to the church." The family had actually owned the entire county at one time as a plantation in the post-Revolutionary War period. It took a legal threat from the canon to the ordinary and the chancellor of the diocese to return the records to the parish. She had taken all the donor records she could out of the church and tried to get the rest. I had advised the rector to sequester the records because the treasurer had a key to the church office.

Financial Correspondence Sent to Church

As we noted earlier, all mail of a financial nature should come to the church. No one should be allowed to receive any correspondence regarding financial matters belonging to the church at their home, their business, or anywhere other than the church. That means the rector does not get the bank statement to the discretionary account sent anywhere other than the church office. It means that no endowment documents go anywhere other than the church office.

"All correspondence" means *all correspondence*. I have seen bank accounts that had overdrafts and no one knew except the perpetrator because the overdraft notices went to their home along with the bank statements. I have seen IRS notices for failure to pay payroll taxes go to the treasurer's home because the treasurer prepared the 941, wrote the check to the IRS, and took them to the post office to mail. He changed the address on the 941 to his home address before he mailed it and pocketed the check. The IRS sent delinquent notices for three years to the treasurer's home. It was discovered in the audit that the payroll tax checks had not been cashed by the IRS, and the payroll taxes were due. It cost the church $19,000 in penalties and interest to the Federal government, plus the actual payroll taxes. The state got their share, too. If someone has a strong will to have the statements and correspondence sent anywhere other than the church office, do not do it and find someone else to perform the task.

We have to remember we are dealing with frail humans, not saints. It is that recognition that allows us to understand that the environment must therefore protect the assets from the frailty of humans. Without the processes, without the inspection, without the recognition of the necessity of the protections, the environment is too tempting for a mortal soul in need, greed, or other self-justifying reason to resist.

Accountability means setting expectations of performance and holding a person to it. Praise and coaching are perfectly acceptable in a church as they are in business. People will do what is expected of them. However, if one does not provide boundaries, objectives, goals, or acceptable minimum levels of performance, then people will perform at a level of comfort and ease to them, but probably not to your expectations.

Leadership

Volumes have been written on this subject for centuries. Either one leads, or follows, or sometimes just gets out of the way. There are those who make things happen, watch what happens, or wonder what happened. Which one is a leader?

The flock needs to know its boundaries, directions, successes, failures, corrective action, and expected outcomes. The clergy and vestry set the tone and see that the tone permeates the life of the church. People most often do what is expected of them if it is clearly defined and inspected.

Leadership is about taking action, encouraging, setting boundaries, setting expectations, holding people accountable, and making decisions—sometimes even when they are not popular but are proper. In the examples told about parishes and in the survey data about fraud, it is obvious to me that there is a lack of leadership thread that runs through it all.

Without the tone of inspection and accountability being set at the top at the diocese and the parish—clergy, vestry, staff—then pervasive fraud will naturally occur. There is no substitute for active leadership. We may never know the results of any frauds deterred, but we can see the results of frauds perpetrated with the lack of leadership.

8

Introduction to Internal Control

We have covered a number of issues, all in preparation for this topic. To understand internal control, we must understand its basic principles. We begin by examining the term *internal control*.

Internal is defined as relating to, or occurring on the inside of an organized structure. For our purposes, this means that all processes in the church occur inside the church and are performed by clergy, employees, and volunteers of the church. These internal processes are not purchased or brought from the outside, but conceived by the vestry, implemented by the people of the church, and ingrained into the daily life of the church. It is as much a part of the parish as the ambo or the order of service.

Control is defined as power or authority to guide or manage. Control is an authorized technique for protecting and managing money within defined boundaries in the church, for example, the money that is given is deposited in the proper church account, and checks are written only for legitimate and prior-approved purposes.

Internal control involves the protection of the church's assets and the detection of thefts. It is a way of doing things that has value and is worth preserving. There are specific aspects of internal control established to accomplish each objective. The protection part is more important because, if designed correctly and implemented fully, it will deter all but the most determined—or foolhardy—thief. Detection provides for the identifiable and measurable checks and balances that allow for efficient inspection of the process, detection of deviation from the process, and detection of any defalcation. <u>Defalcation is the theft or misappropriation of money by those in whose care the money has been entrusted</u>.

Protection of Assets

Process

First, internal control is a system of processes. The processes are based on policies established by the vestry and implement the intent of the policies. For example, it may be a policy that two people will accompany the money at all times. The process would identify all the inputs of money and describe and illustrate how that should happen.

Policies and processes have no validity unless voted upon in the vestry, with minutes recorded and a copy of the policy and/or process attached to the minutes. Once a policy or process is thoroughly vetted and voted upon, there should be a high degree of resistance to changing that process unless the current policy or process violates internal control or the change will improve internal control.

A church operations manual should be created and logically organized to include all the policies and procedures. This manual should be given to each vestry member upon election with instructions to read, understand, and follow the procedures. How can you tell that a new vestry member is about to violate a properly defined and documented internal control? When they start a sentence with "But wouldn't it be easier if . . ." your internal control antennae should start tingling. "QuickBooks is so much easier. I already know how to use it. It costs less than ACS. I am the new bookkeeper, why not let me use what I know." NEVER!! Find a new bookkeeper if needed. "Once we sign the checks, it would be easier if we just leave them on the bookkeeper's desk since the parish administrator's office is always locked on Sundays." Never give signed checks back to the bookkeeper. "I have to go out of town a lot in my new job. Just give the bank statements to the bookkeeper to reconcile, and I will look over it when I come back to town. That way the financial statements will be ready for the vestry meetings, most of which I am probably going to miss." Get a new treasurer. Internal control has deliberate checks and balances; sometimes they are not the easiest way to get things done. If you begin to sympathize with the requests for "an easier way," and you are a member of the vestry, let me remind you of your fiduciary liability. Suddenly, the process does not appear to need changing to make it easier, does it? The Church of the Holy Smoke™ has a manual that is approximately 160 pages.

A copy of the policies and procedures manual should be made available to every member of the congregation. We are not trying to keep the policies and processes a secret. Rather, we are trying to change the culture in the church so that our practices regarding finances and money are more transparent. The more people are aware of the policies and processes, the more buy-in the vestry will have. The more comfortable people feel that their donations are going for the purposes intended, comfortable that the internal control is there to assure that, the more likely they are to give or participate in church activities involving money.

When properly designed, processes provide a system of checks and balances to provide a visible trail for the money. This trail is traceable by anyone with knowledge of business practices. Along the way, there are points at which the money is totaled and compared with another total prior to or in parallel with the current total. The process should be documented with a flow chart indicating the steps necessary for the financial transactions of the church. Examples follow when we get into specific processes.

If you think about all the processes—collecting, counting, depositing, reconciling, posting the contributions, approving invoices, writing checks, signing checks, posting the books, preparing financial statements, to name a few—you will realize they are all connected. It is one entire system of recording the events that take place in the financial matters of the church. There are no disconnected parts. While there are major subcomponents, cash in and cash out, for example, they are all connected to the financial statements by their individual transactions. Therefore, there is only one system of internal control comprised of the people, organization, process, and technology, and any breakage opens a window for fraud to occur.

People

The most critical elements of internal control are the people. If the people who execute the steps of the processes are not properly trained, then the processes will likely fail to safeguard the assets. If the people who are supposed to provide oversight are not properly trained, then detection of fraud likely will not occur. Even if trained, if the people executing the steps in the process do not approach their work seriously and with diligence, then apathy, complacency, and shortcuts taken will defeat the internal control. As I have said before, trust the process, not the people. Inspect the execution of the process by the people and the resulting documentation generated during the process. The inspection must reflect the highest degree of diligence of all because it will identify defalcations and weaknesses in performance of the process.

Organization

The process is not merely a series of boxes and arrows accompanied by instructions; it also includes the roles involved in performing the process. Using roles instead of people's names on the flow charts allows for the definition of a role that could be filled by anyone with the skills. The roles become an integral part of the process as they provide for the separation of duties that must be in place in any process of internal control. Specific skill and experience requirements should be assigned to roles. Just as a person may fill the roles of verger and usher, he or she does not fill them at the same time or with the same skill set or experience. With roles named and assigned, multiple roles may be filled by the same person at different times with a different set of requirements for successful completion of the tasks. Roles assist in implementing the oversight and accountability required in internal control and should be thoughtfully documented. Let's review material from chapter 3:

- Who is responsible for designing and approving the internal control processes? The vestry.
- Who is responsible for implementing the internal control processes? The rector, by directing staff and volunteers on a daily basis.
- Who is responsible for overseeing the internal control processes? Both the rector and the vestry.
- Who is responsible for periodically testing the internal control processes? Both the rector and the vestry at least monthly, and the auditor annually.
- Who is subject to the internal control structure, policies, and procedures? Everyone.

Without inspection and verification that the policies are being followed and the processes are functioning as designed, a lackadaisical attitude may creep into those who fulfill them. Since no one is looking, shortcuts will be taken. The system of internal control will begin to break down, and the probability that fraud will occur will increase.

Technology

The right technology—computers, networks, and software—can enhance internal control or defeat it. The hardware (computers and networks) is not as much a concern as the software.

The right accounting software can strengthen internal control, just as the wrong one weakens it. While I cannot determine the proper software for your situation, I do have requirements that all software must meet. I have found one vendor whose software meets all my requirements. No software is perfect, and all good vendors are constantly improving their software. I have my preference for one vendor for many good reasons. The requirements are explained below, but their order does not suggest prioritization. They are all equally important and must be present to select the software for use in your church.

The software must:

1. Be written for the not-for-profit industry and use fund accounting principles and accounting methods in its transactions.
2. Use the right nomenclature for churches in its financial statements, chart of accounts, user documentation, and training materials.
3. Be robust enough to easily allow for the initial set-up by church personnel (once properly trained).
4. Never allow a transaction to be altered or deleted. If a transaction is entered incorrectly, another must be entered to correct it. This creates an audit trail to follow all transactions, even errors and their corrections, within the system.
5. Provide user-specific access with password control at the function level. In other words, prevent the person who posts the contributions from also accessing the general ledger. Allow for an individual to print reports, but never touch the accounting transactions. Allow the rector to access the demographic data of parishioners, but not the financial giving data. All of this requires user-specific access with password control.
6. Provide for the retrieval of data to produce user-specific reports in addition to GAAP statements.
7. Provide for the proper accounting of unrestricted, temporarily restricted, and permanently restricted fund balances and identify if they should ever get out of balance.
8. Provide for GAAP accounting transactions of all types.
9. Provide for cash and accrual bases of accounting separately and intermixed to create a modified cash basis of accounting.
10. Contain all modules necessary to keep the financial records of the church. For example, a module for contributions, one for fixed assets and depreciation, a receipts journal, a disbursements journal, a record of all journal entries, and a check register. These are not only useful, but also required for internal control, audit trails, or reconciliation.
11. Process transactions as they normally occur in the daily life of the church. If you do not know how to process a particular transaction, the

software intuitively leads to where to start and follows a logical method because the software works like the church does. It may sound vague, but if you are using software that does not work like this, you know exactly to what I am referring.

12. The vendor has to be of sufficient size and longevity to provide proper customer service, prompt issue resolution, program fixes, clear and concise documentation, and detailed educational materials. These take lots of money. A small vendor has 2,000 churches using their software. An adequate number of churches using the software is 10,000. I prefer 20,000 churches.

In the interest of full disclosure, I have never received any remuneration from any software vendor. I do not sell any software, and I do not get any finder's fee, commission, or any kind of compensation for my opinions or services from a vendor. The church is my client and where my allegiance lies, not the vendor. At IBM, I was the originator of the consulting practice in software selection, and my small group wrote the methodology, many parts of which are still in use today. I offer my opinions regarding software and software selection based on my experience.

QuickBooks When I get a call from a church about a potential fraud being committed, the first question I ask is, "what software are you using for bookkeeping?" Despite being a former certified member of the QuickBooks Pro Advisor Team, I advise churches to never use QuickBooks (QB). There are many different commercial applications where QB is appropriate, but a church is not one of them. One, there is no audit trail automatically generated that cannot be defeated. Audit tracking is the automatic recording by the system of who performed the transaction on what machine at what time of day. The administrator of the program can turn tracking on and off at will. This means that in a small organization such as a parish, the administrator of the software is likely the person who first installed the program, probably on his or her own machine, so that the user of the software is also the administrator. Whether he or she is the individual who posts the contributions or the one who writes the checks, neither should be able to turn tracking off.

Two, QB allows for the direct modification of a transaction that is already recorded in the books, including the dollar amount. With tracking turned off, no one will ever know that it occurred. When QB is used, the difficulty in discovering fraud goes up exponentially. In some cases, the only way to prove the fraud is to rekey the entire set of transactions. Some churches actually have had to do that for three years' worth of contributions and checks, one transaction at a time, to discover the fraud because the bookkeeper turned tracking on and off at will, making the modifications necessary to hide the fraud. There is the argument that an individual other than the book-keeper can keep the administrator's password and not allow the tracking to be turned on and off, but there are ways around that.

Three, although QB purports to have a not-for-profit edition, it simply does not meet the criteria above. Originally designed for the distribution industry, QB is a far cry from not-for-profit fund accounting. The documentation and training require mental translations of the nomenclature. For example, think of customers as donors. There is no provision for tracking designated funds properly as an integral part of the chart of the accounts. That is a semi-manual process comprised of separate transactions that are unnecessary in a true fund accounting system, adds to the effort to process transactions, and requires a fair level of accounting knowledge to work correctly in the first place. My advice is to not use QB for the church or any organization related to the church. If you currently use QB, convert to another package that meets the criteria listed above.

Vendor X Vendor X is a smaller software vendor with a great looking website. At one of my client churches, the bookkeeper set up the system initially and entered a one-sided transaction. He entered a debit for fixed assets and no corresponding credit for net assets. (Remember the accounting equation: assets = liabilities + net assets.) The vendor's software let him save the transaction with no warning. It gave no indication of any problem when the financial statements were generated. The software did not flag the Statement of Financial Position as being out of balance, in this case by $900,000. According to the client, the vendor confirmed that was possible in their software. Be careful to thoroughly put software through its paces before selecting one for use. Save yourself the trouble and use the software requirements previously mentioned.

ACS Technologies Or, you could use ACS[37]. In the interest of disclosure, I was the IBM marketing representative in Florence, S.C., when Harris Rogers, who started ACS, came into my office in 1978 and announced he was forming a software company whose product was church software. The company was named Computer Dimensions originally and later changed to ACS, an acronym for Automated Church Systems. People tend to recommend what they know best, and I am no exception. I have known this company all these years and have nothing but high regard for their software, their

---

37. ACS Technologies can be contacted at http://www.acstechnologies.com

training, their support, and their people. They meet all the criteria outlined above and then some.

I have never received any compensation from them for their software sales and never will. It simply makes my life and the life of my client churches easier and safer, so I try to get it implemented wherever I can. I have not discovered a way to commit fraud with ACS software that could not be discovered in a short period of time. Some have tried it, but the discovery was made in hours or less upon inspection. ACS is integral and key to internal control as the technology component for some of my clients.

Others   There are other good software vendors out there. I have no problem with them unless they do not meet my criteria. You may have additional criteria. The key is to know what features and functions you are seeking in software *before* you go looking for software and then to compare vendor offerings to your requirements. Do not let vendors set the requirements for you.

Note that I am using the singular, internal control, not internal controls. In my view, there either is a working set of processes that provide internal control, or there is not. Any one part that breaks down breaks the entire process. Any one part—people, process, or technology—could be the link that breaks. Without the separation of duties (people) that follow the Three-Legged Stool™, the internal control is broken. Without the appropriate functions remaining with the role of treasurer, the process breaks internal control. Without technology that is adequately designed and programmed to prevent tampering (the computer system), the technology breaks internal control.

Process—The Three-Legged Stool™

In order to develop internal control, there must be a set of guiding principles—the simpler the better. I created the three-legged stool concept of internal control with this axiom:

> If you handle the money, you do not post the books. If you post the books, you do not handle the money. A third person, who does neither, reconciles. The three legs of the stool do not meet except on the common plane of internal control.

This axiom creates the key element of internal control—separation of duties. Note that the three legs remain separated at all times, never touching each other. The separation of duties is total and complete. The full separation of handling the money from the recording of the transaction involving the money will allow for the detection of fraud and deter the commission of

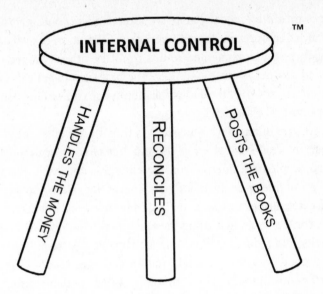

Three-Legged Stool™ of internal control

fraud, except for one instance. Should the person handling the money conspire with the person posting the books to steal the money, then collusion exists from a deliberate act designed to deceive. It is more difficult to detect fraud when there is collusion, but not impossible. However, collusion occurs infrequently in church fraud cases.

There is still hope. The third person that neither handles the money nor posts the books but does the reconciliation has the opportunity to detect the fraud with heightened sensitivity and diligence. Woe is to the church if all three are in collusion, although the likelihood of that is low.

What is considered money? Currency, checks received, checks written by the church with signatures affixed (thereby making the checks negotiable), stock certificates, certificates of deposit—anything that falls into the cash and cash equivalents definition is considered money. We saw in the scenario where the fraud was committed using a scanner that bank checks, once signed (money), should never be given back to the bookkeeper (who posts the books)—a clear violation of the axiom of internal control.

What is meant by posting the books? Any recording of a financial transaction in the accounting records or journals of the church is posting the books—recording donations in the contribution module of the software, entering the invoices for payment and writing the checks, and making journal entries are all examples of posting the books. Merely generating reports is not.

What is meant by reconciliation by someone who does neither posting nor counting? In order for there to be a clear separation of duties, the third person gathers the documented results from the other two persons in the process and reconciles any differences. The best example of this is reconciling the bank statement at the end of the month with the ending bank balance per the statement of financial position.

The best part of all about the axiom is that it only takes three people to implement internal control. Even the smallest of congregations or organizations can implement internal control using this approach. Examine your own process of internal control for violations of the axiom and fix them. The axiom also subscribes to the "keep it simple" method. It is likely that your processes can be simplified using the axiom, creating less work, increasing productivity, and reducing stress generated by needless steps.

Like all good consulting models, the Three-Legged Stool™ has the components of people, process, and technology. What is often missing from the discussion of the consulting model is the fourth element: organization, or roles. When we introduce the roles held by the individuals who perform the process, we add organization to the model. For example, the treasurer is a role (organization), held by an individual (people), who performs a process, often using technology. Now you know why roles and responsibilities are an integral part of the internal control of the church. Now you know why it is important we be clear about the role of the treasurer, for example. The treasurer is not a member of the vestry but reports to the rector and vestry equally, is appointed by the rector, receives the independent original documents from the other two legs of the stool, and is the one who reconciles. At this point, it may be useful for you to peruse again chapter 3, "Roles and Responsibilities." I was not being casual or suggestive in my description of the functions of those roles, but rather very deliberate and exacting regarding their participation in the internal control of the church.

Detection of Defalcations

Internal control deters but does not entirely prevent fraud. Internal control makes it far more difficult for the perpetrator to attempt the fraud. Usually, fraud involves getting one of the elements—people, organization, technology, or process—changed inconspicuously or cause it to fail to provide the opening.

Thus, internal control is a tool of management. It is a tool to ensure the smooth operations of the financial matters of the church. Properly designed and implemented, with accountability and diligent inspection, internal control can provide a lot more time to focus on the pastoral matters of the church.

Clergy Influence

The clergy play an important role in internal control. They cause the policies and processes to be implemented by the staff and volunteers. They can make it a priority or shrug it off. Either way, the staff and volunteers will follow that lead. As we have noted, the financial tone of the church is set by the clergy and vestry. But since the vestry is not represented at the church every day, clergy usually have a larger influence on internal control, for instance, by inspection, goal setting, and encouragement.

The best way to lead is by example, and the clergy's leadership is significant. Vestries by their very nature have a built-in potential total memory loss as the vestry turns over completely every three years. Once the initiative for deliberately instituted and documented internal control is started, various members of the vestry, staff, and volunteers will probably continue the momentum, but here is another opportunity for leadership by the clergy in financial matters by inspection, goal setting, and encouragement.

Inspection

Once implemented, internal control must be inspected to ensure it is operating effectively. If left uninspected, a perpetrator can commit fraud and remain undetected for a long time.

There are multiple ways to conduct inspections. The most overt and obvious is reconciling all financial institution accounts. Another method is management by walking around. Ask who will accompany a vestry person with the money to the safe after Wednesday night supper (so there are two people with the money at all times). Stop into the bookkeeper's office and observe. If checks are being printed, pick up the documentation and look at it. Does the invoice appear to be an original? Is the general ledger code to which the invoice is being charged reasonable? Is the authorization for the payment present and appropriate? If not, ask questions.

Inspection requires diligence. Complacency is a threat to internal control. If the vestry, staff, or volunteers are allowed to become complacent about the execution of the policies and processes as designed, then the opportunity for fraud will occur. Notice I did not include the clergy in that list. If the clergy become complacent—the game is over.

One threat to a well-designed and implemented internal control is turnover of people. If the clergy-in-charge leaves the congregation, who will perform the inspections of the staff? Who will set the tone for the church for internal control? Who will guide the vestry and resist their inclination to simplify things (violating internal control)? If the bookkeeper leaves, who will step into that role and preserve the separation of duties? Who will train the new bookkeeper? What documentation is there regarding the clear definition and boundaries of the bookkeeper's role?

As one-third of the vestry are replaced each year, is there a clearly-written set of church processes provided to the new members to help them understand the importance of their fiduciary liability, and the processes in place to protect them? If the treasurer leaves, who will reconcile next month? It cannot be someone who touches the books or the money, or is in a position of influence over the funds. Are there clear written procedures for the interim or new treasurer to follow? When volunteers who had a role at men's club, altar guild, Wednesday night suppers, or anywhere money is present leave that role, who will train the replacement in the proper internal control? Who will inspect?

I have provided some insight into the kinds of things that need to be considered and examples to use as a guide. Good design and good policies are not accomplished in a weekend, but a good start can be made. It will take time to develop good internal control, but with diligence and leadership, you will get there.

Now that we have the elements of internal control—people, organization, technology, and process, represented by the Three-Legged Stool—it is time to describe in some detail how to implement internal control in your church or organization.

9

Support
Internal Control

With the introduction to the Three-Legged Stool™ of internal control we will now get into some specific processes and procedures in the next several chapters. This is a major part of the "how to" section of the book and what is missing in most Episcopal churches and organizations—clearly documented internal controls designed to deter and detect defalcations. At times, you may feel that some of this is overkill for your situation. Always revert to the Three-Legged Stool™ in reviewing your own situation. If you are not able to separate the duties and properly reconcile with a full audit trail holding identified persons accountable along the way, adopt the process presented here. If you can, use your own as long as you:

1. Keep it simple.
2. Do not create a different process for the same type of transaction.
3. Are able to hold an individual or two accountable for the transaction.
4. Can reconcile with independent verification from alternate sources.

Ingathering of Support

The church receives support in a myriad of ways. With the influx of money, the financial wheels of the church begin to turn. The ingathering of support is the set of financial transactions that enable all the rest.

Sources

There are many sources of income for the church. Below are some categories and examples of each:

Collection plate   This includes anything in a collection plate at *all* services: Sunday morning, Saturday night, Wednesday healing, sunrise Easter and other special services, United Thank Offering (UTO), Sunday school, designated funds of any kind (flowers, music, etc.).

Events   Any non-fund-raising activity where money is present: youth mission trip, Vacation Bible School, women's retreat, Wednesday night supper, Sunday morning coffee and breakfast, men's club, mother's morning out. In some situations, money will be collected at the event; in others, money will have been collected in advance. Invariably, some people will wait until the day of the event and bring the money with them or wait and pay after the event, regardless of the announced method of collecting.

Fund-raising   Includes any activity that is designed to generate additional net revenue through sales of goods, outright donations, or sale of tickets: Cookbook sales, bake sales, art sales, goods from mission trip sales, Shrove Tuesday pancake supper, Valentine dinner dance, Lobster Hoopla, haunted house, raffles, bingo, flea market. Some fundraising events have a starting till amount to make change.

Online   any source of support that comes in via Internet: credit card, Pay-Pal, direct debit to donor bank account, other Automated Clearing House (ACH) transactions in conjunction with donations and events.

Collection boxes   These are located at racks of small pamphlets, for candles or other memorabilia, around the church for collection of donations, for example in the narthex or parish hall, or even an envelope on the bulletin board.

Mail and walk-in   This is cash or currency received in the parish office through the mail or hand delivered: rental of church property, weddings, funerals, baptisms, pledges or other donations via mail or walk-in.

Financial institution   Interest or earnings on accounts: checking, savings, investment, brokerage, certificates of deposit. Some income may still be held on deposit at the financial institution and shown on the monthly statement, but it needs to be recognized and recorded, too.

Other church entities   This includes bookstore, preschool, school, thrift store, soup kitchen. These will have many processes unique to the nature of the entity.

These sources can be grouped into categories of support based upon their characteristics. The objective in using categories is to create as few processes as possible. For example, all financial institution accounts—checking, savings, investment, endowments—should go through the same process for recording and reconciliation. There is usually no good reason for creating separate processes for each individual account or for each type of account. The more processes you create, the more you compound the inspection, accountability, and oversight needed to administer the process and prevent defalcations. The better-designed processes are simpler and more straightforward. You will need to identify all the sources of income for your church and select the process where each income stream fits in the categories described.

Categories

Collection plate and collection boxes can be combined into a single processing category because they represent previously unseen cash of an initially unknown origin and amount. Fund-raising and events can be combined because there is at least a known price or a starting (cash register or shoe box) till. Mail and walk-in are combined because they represent funds received in the parish office or directly by parish staff, including clergy. Financial institution and

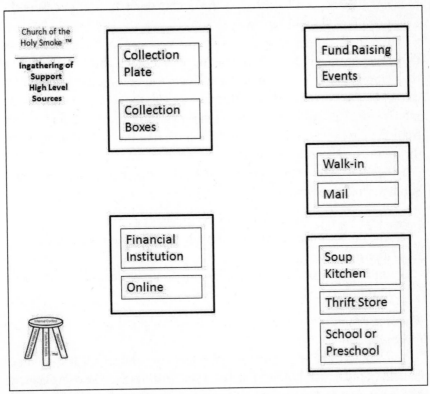

High Level Sources of Support

online can be combined because they represent electronic transactions and not physical currency or checks. Lastly, other church-related entities will have their own set of processes that must be devised, some of which may dovetail with the church's processes and many that will not.

Do not confuse the processes of internal control with the posting of transactions in the accounting system. Processes deal with the flow of money through the church, from income source to the bank, and subsequently out of the bank account for payment for goods, services, or outreach. Posting the general ledger is just one step in the process. Therefore, it is likely that a single event such as a women's retreat will receive designated payments for the event via the collection plate, through the mail, delivered by hand to the church, via PayPal and online credit card, in a collection box, or envelope on the bulletin board.

What we must do is make sure all the money that is received by all the various routes gets properly counted, deposited in the bank, recorded in the accounting records, and that none gets misappropriated along the way. That is what the internal control process is for. In addition, the process will need to identify checks and balances for inspection along the way to ensure the detection of fraud should any occur.

Given these categories of support sources, we can now begin to outline the processes, step by step, to ensure the identification and safeguarding of the support from its source to the bank. There will be some parts that simply cannot be protected. Nothing in the process will stop someone from taking money out of the collection plate as it is passed in church, taking money from the envelope on the bulletin board, making incorrect change in the thrift store or at a fund-raising event.

Collection plate Regardless of when the collection plate is passed— Sunday or other services:

1. There must be two people with the money at all times.
2. The money must be counted immediately after the service or during, if possible.
3. Immediately after counting, the money must be deposited in the bank or dropped in the church safe—every time.

These three principles are not negotiable. Anything less subjects the money to misappropriation.

You would think that the Church of the Holy Smoke, a 3,000-member church, would have this down pat. But one Christmas Eve, the offering made it to the sacristy, but never got counted. The entire offering, tens of thousands of dollars, disappeared—checks and currency. No one knows who was supposed to count the money. The vestry person of the day did not come for the service and a second vestry person was never assigned. After the discovery of the missing offering, the parish was notified of the event and members were asked to cancel their checks with their bank and reissue them. No one knows how much was missing from visitors, non-members or cash donors. Most did cancel and reissue checks, but seven families did not cancel the checks with their bank.

On Easter Sunday, the missing Christmas Eve checks appeared in the collection plate. The counters did not notice the date on the checks and deposited them. Seven families had bounced checks as a result. Seven families left the church. Based on previous years' Easter cash offerings and Christmas Eve cash offerings, it appears that over $10,000 of Christmas Eve cash was not returned to the church.

Collection Plate Counting, Depositing, and Reconciliation

Counting, depositing, and reconciliation process

Presented on the next page is a high-level process that the Church of the Holy Smoke™ uses for counting, depositing, and reconciling. We will carefully examine the rationale for each section and any documentation created as it relates to internal control.

The process is the same regardless of when the collection is made. Some churches will simply put the Saturday night collection, 8:00 a.m. Sunday collection, or other collections throughout the week into a bank bag and drop it in the safe uncounted. There are several problems with this. First, if a locking bank bag is not used, then anyone opening the safe for any other reason would have unfettered access to uncounted funds. Second, if a locking bank bag is used, the keys to the bank bag are in the possession of someone who could help themselves to uncounted funds regardless. Third, how many people have access to the safe? This is one of the areas that some churches are lax in controlling.

Use the three non-negotiable rules of handling cash every time a collection is made. Dropping uncounted money into the safe is acceptable if the safe is never opened prior to the weekly counting, but that is not likely. Follow the counting process each time with independent documents prepared as a result of counting that ensure the money from each collection makes it to the bank.

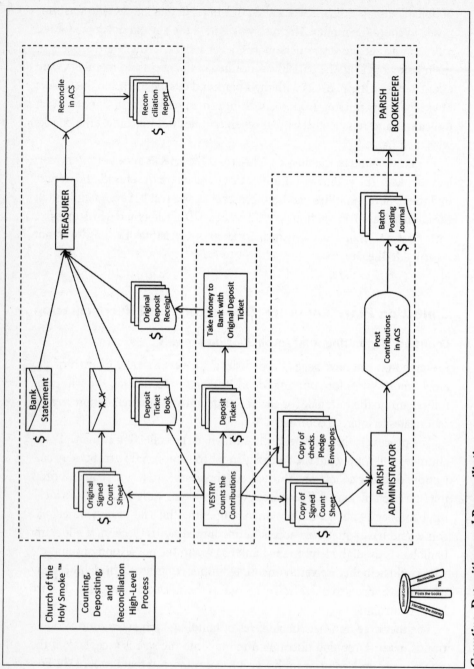

Counting, Depositing, and Reconciliation

An old term, *batch integrity*, still applies today. It is easier to protect against fraud, detect fraud, and manage transactions that are in batches. The reason is simple: the batch total is the amount each step in the process calling for reconciliation or verification uses to determine if the batch is still intact with all its transactions present. Think of a check or an item of currency as an element of this batch. The offering received on Sunday morning is a batch. The total receipts for the book sale for the day is a batch. A batch can be counted again and again, and the total dollars in the batch should be the same.

This is the reason each collection needs to be counted—for batch integrity. What do we do with this total? It should be the same amount that is on the counters' count sheet, deposit ticket, the bank deposit receipt, the bank statement at the end of the month, and the batch posting of contributions and receipts in the contributions or general ledger. Do you see the audit trail created by the batch total? At a minimum, follow the counting process CP1 (shown on the next page) each time there is an offering. The flow on CP1 is represented by a single box following the "Start" indicator in the counting, depositing, and reconciling high-level process.

Follow the counting process CP1 for every collection. Whether the offering is subsequently put in the safe or taken to the bank, each offering becomes a traceable batch. This means there will need to be a locking bank bag for each collection.

Some banks use clear plastic bags with separate compartments for currency and checks, rather than the familiar bank bags. These are acceptable, as long as the money is counted first. The glue used to seal the pockets on those bags must have come from an alien spacecraft. The only way to open them once sealed is to cut them open, destroying the bag. There is a place on the bag for the signatures of those who prepared the deposit ticket and put the money in the bag. The counters should sign that, too.

The vestry counts the money. With the fiduciary liability, why would they let anyone else count it? The vestry can delegate the task, but they cannot relieve themselves of the fiduciary liability. Two people accompany the collection plates to a separate, locked counting room. Do not count the money where people can walk in, interrupt your counting, possibly distract you, and help themselves to a twenty or two. Have a specific place in the church, away from exterior doors, that can be locked to keep people out until the counting process is completed. There should be at least two printing adding machines available for the counters.

The first task is to separate the contents of the collection plates into piles of currency, checks, and envelopes. The envelopes are presumed to be

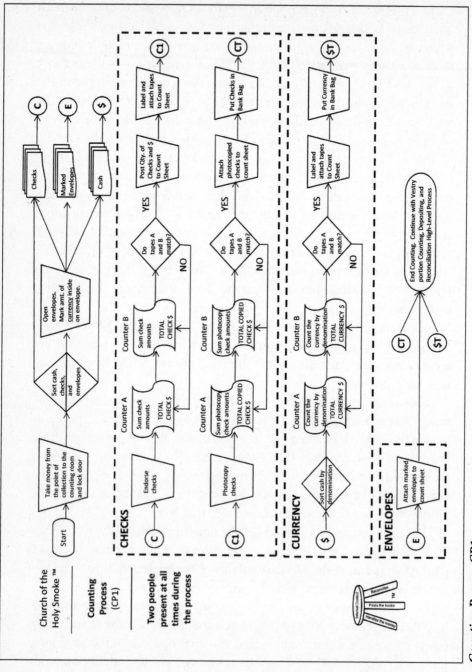

Counting Process CP1

numbered envelopes corresponding to parishioners for the purpose of making pledge donations and other special contributions throughout the year. The presumption is that any contribution inside a numbered envelope is a pledge commitment fulfillment and not considered plate offering. Only loose change and undesignated checks in the plate are considered plate offering. This is important on the day of the bishop's visitation service or if the vestry has designated certain services' plate donations for a specific purpose, for example, the rector's discretionary fund.

A problem arises if there is currency inside the envelope. How would anyone know how much was intended to go toward a pledge if the currency in the envelope was commingled with the loose plate currency? Yet, the count sheet does not make the distinction. The solution is to count the currency in the envelope only (not any checks that may also be in the envelope) and write the dollar amount of currency on the outside of the envelope. Put the currency from the envelopes in the pile with the plate currency. Put any checks in the envelopes in the pile with the loose checks. Set aside the envelopes on which you wrote the amounts for later handling.

Now the counting and cross counting can begin. We will call the two counters Counter A and Counter B. Counter A will separate the coins and bills by denomination. He or she counts the currency by denomination and writes down the results along with the total currency received. Counter A should not tell Counter B the count of the currency.

Meanwhile, Counter B endorses the back of all the checks with the church's stamp that usually reads something like this: "For deposit to the Church of the Holy Smoke™ only." Once all the checks are endorsed, Counter B sums the dollar amount of the checks by creating an adding machine tape of the checks. Counter B also counts the checks to get a quantity of checks received. Counter B does not tell Counter A the totals.

Then the two counters exchange the respective piles of currency and checks. Counter A repeats the summation of the checks by creating an adding machine tape of the checks in the same order in which they are given and counts the number of checks received. Meanwhile, Counter B counts the currency by denomination and writes down the results along with the total currency received.

Once both have completed their counts, they disclose their totals to each other and determine if they match. If they do not, then the items in disagreement must be recounted until both totals agree. Once they agree, the count sheet can be updated.

The faces of the checks are photocopied, preferably in the sequence they appear on the adding machine tape. This is so the person posting the contributions can have a copy of the check from which to post. They can see on the face of the check if the check is designated for some purpose. They can also post in the comments the donor's check number, if desired. Also, any new contributors not previously in the rolls can be added and noted for a pastoral follow-up to welcome them to the church. Once all the photocopies are made, the checks on the photocopied pages are totaled again with an adding machine tape. This is done first by Counter A and then by Counter B, who then compare the totals. Why? Checks left on the copier glass cause a mess when they are not included in the bank bag. Likewise, checks can be dropped and disappear under a piece of furniture on the way to or from the photocopier.

Count Sheet

Once all the information is on the count sheet, it should be signed by Counter A and Counter B and photocopied. The original signed count sheet should be sealed in an envelope addressed to the treasurer. Both counters should also sign across the seal on the back of the envelope before sending to the treasurer. Most likely, that means putting the envelope in the treasurer's mailbox in the church's mailroom. This should be done as the counters are leaving for the bank. Do not leave the counting room with just one person in it while the other goes to put this in the treasurer's mailbox. What is the rule? Two people are with the money at all times.

Once the count sheet is completed, the bank deposit ticket can be prepared. It should list total currency and total dollar amount of the checks. The parish should be using a pre-numbered deposit book that creates a carbonless copy of the deposit ticket. Put the deposit ticket, the currency, and the checks in the bank bag and lock (or seal, if the plastic bags are used).

Now that the bank bag is complete, the next step is to assemble the documentation package to send to the person posting contributions. Attach the envelopes that contained currency to the photocopied count sheet so the person posting contributions can properly allocate the currency between pledge and plate. Also attach the photocopies of the checks. Put this package in an envelope and give to or leave for the person posting contributions for the church. Return the deposit book to the treasurer and take the bank bag to the bank. If for any reason the bank bag is not going to the bank now, put it in the safe. Eventually, one of the count teams will be going to the bank. The objective is to get the deposit to the bank as soon as possible. Money in the bank is safer than money in the safe.

COLLECTION COUNT SHEET   Date: _____

Currency		
Coins	Quantity	Extended Totals
1 ¢ X	_____ =	_____
5 ¢ X	_____ =	_____
10 ¢ X	_____ =	_____
25 ¢ X	_____ =	_____
50 ¢ X	_____ =	_____
$1 coin X	_____ =	_____
Total	$	_____

Paper		
$ 1.00 X	_____ =	_____
$ 5.00 X	_____ =	_____
$ 10.00 X	_____ =	_____
$ 20.00 X	_____ =	_____
$ 50.00 X	_____ =	_____
$ 100.00 X	_____ =	_____
Total	$	_____

Checks		
	Quantity	Total
Total	_____	$ _____

TOTAL COLLECTION $ _____

$ _____

Signature
Name (Print): _____

Signature
Name (Print): _____

☐ Are the envelopes that contained cash
    attached with the $ amount indicated?
☐ Are the photocopies of the checks
    attached?
    Are the adding machine tapes attached
    ☐ Total checks?
    ☐ Total cash and checks?

Collection Count Sheet

We now have a batch that can be traced through the process and reconciled with integrity.

Check readers

Recently, banks have made available the electronic capture of checks via electronic check readers located in their customer's offices. This saves manually summing the checks, endorsing them, and taking them to the bank. What it does not eliminate is counting and depositing currency. The better check readers and banks offer the ability to scan the image of the check and reproduce it via printout in the customer's office along with the dollar amount captured. This must be carefully compared with the dollar amount on the check to verify the check reader interpreted the dollar amount on the check correctly. In the end, there may be some checks that cannot be read, and the CP1 process will need to be followed for those checks.

From the bank's perspective, the process for check readers is this: Once you scan the image of the check, the image is sent to the bank's operations center. Previous federal regulations allowed banks to produce images, called Check21, instead of returning the physical check to the customer. This is the image you see on your own personal bank statement. The scanned check is converted into a Check21 image at the bank's operations center. The Check21 image is sent to the Federal Reserve where the Check21 image is cleared and the funds are sent to your church's bank. The funds are credited to your bank account. Voila, you have a bank deposit.

From your end, the church needs to maintain batch integrity. Scan all the checks at one time, a batch total that the bank acknowledges and one you can reproduce by adding machine tape. This verifies the completeness of the deposit. Attach the adding machine tape and the printout from the scan process to the photocopied count sheet. If your bank's printout includes the check images, include that, too. Otherwise, put the checks that were scanned into an envelope and pass that along with the count sheet package to the person posting contributions. If you are using ACS, posting is the push of a button and the check image appears in the donor's contribution records. Because there are so many different variations of this method, I have not provided a flow chart. Use the general description above to modify your flow to encompass a check scanner for deposits.

Bank Deposit

We can now continue to the next step of preparing the bank deposit. Ensure that all checks are endorsed "for deposit only". The bank deposit book should be one that provides for an original bank deposit (usually white in color) and a carbonless duplicate (usually yellow in color). The deposit slips in the book should be sequentially numbered such that the white and yellow copies have the same number on them and the next pair has a progressively higher number. This may seem innocuous, but suppose there was no till count sheet, sales book, or cash register total (like the Wednesday night supper wicker basket). Anyone with access to the money after counting has occurred could tear out the yellow copy from the book, open the bank bag, remove any or all money, and create a new bank deposit slip. No one would be the wiser. How many people are present when the bank deposit is being prepared? You guessed it, at least two.

Put the original bank deposit slip in the bank bag along with the cash, checks, and—depending on your situation—credit card slips. Take the deposit to the bank—accomplished by two people. If it is after hours, put the deposit (in a locked bag) in the night depository. If given to a teller, get the deposit receipt from the teller, put it in an envelope, seal and sign the back of the envelope (both persons). Either mail it to the church marked for the treasurer, or put the envelope in the treasurer's mailbox in the church mailroom.

Everywhere in the process flow you see the "$", this is exactly the same number. By the time the documents get to the treasurer, there are multiple sources of the correct dollar amount of the deposit that will be used to verify that what was sold was paid for, and that the money was deposited into the bank.

Additional comments regarding counting

You may see a problem arising. What does the person posting contributions do with checks that were loose in the plate without a specific designation, yet the donor is known to have an outstanding pledge and probably forgot their envelope? This is where policy comes in. The vestry will need to both educate members to put "pledge" on the bottom left of their check and create a policy that checks are either applied to the pledge or are applied to plate.

I was observing the counting process one time and noted that the dollar amount in numerals on the check was $80. The written amount on the check was "eight dollars and no/100". You may have even had to read that a couple of times to determine the difference. The counters did not catch it. The bookkeeper loved me for days after. Had the bank noticed, the written amount overrides the numerical amount. The bank would have credited only $8.00 while all the documentation from the counters in their counting and depositing process would have used $80. Can you imagine the bookkeeper's nightmare of looking for $72, $144, $36, any combination that would have identified the discrepancy—none of which even existed, or worse yet, what if one was represented by another check? When you endorse the checks, examine them carefully to see if problems exist: the date is wrong, the check is unsigned, the amount in either place (numerical or written) is blank, the amounts do not match, or any other problems. What do you do if there is a problem with the check? *Do not deposit it.* Return it to the donor and ask him or her to correct the check to match his or her intentions.

Do not leave the collection plates in the narthex between services. People will put their contributions, including cash, in them. And there are usually not two people keeping an eye on the donations. Either put the plates away or have two people standing with the plates—or find other alternatives, such as a locked collection box.

Collection boxes

The problem with collection boxes is that while some points of collection around the church are locked boxes, some are not. The ones that are not locked pose a different problem from those that are. However, having a locked box does not prevent theft if the box is left unattended and available to general traffic at hours when other people are not around. It is common practice for thieves to pilfer an unattended locked box. They may use a pencil, paper clip, or another type of rod with gum or duct tape affixed to one end, insert it through the slot, and retrieve cash from the box. This works best if the slot is on top of the box, the slit is large enough for a paper clip, and the opportunity exists to do this with no one watching. The mouse has defeated the mousetrap. Do you want to build a better mousetrap? Here are some suggestions:

1. Put the slot on the side of the box.
2. Empty the box daily and at different times.
3. Always have two people with the money from the time the box is opened until the money is counted and deposited in the safe or the bank.
4. Even better, find a way to get the money into a more secure process and get rid of the box altogether.

Unlocked collection boxes, envelopes on the bulletin board or outside offices, mailboxes in the mailroom or elsewhere—open collection boxes—present a different problem. People will put checks and cash in them. The problem with unsecured cash is obvious. The problem with checks takes a little criminal thinking to understand. Besides your own parishioners, do other groups use your building? Remember the question asked earlier, Who steals the money? Anyone with access may.

In case you are saying, "But the check is made out to the church," remember the parish administrator who altered the payee on the checks and put it through her ATM? Regretfully, many people do not reconcile their personal checking accounts or even look at the image of the returned check. The perpetrator can get away with theft for a while. Worse, if the perpetrator were part of a more sophisticated ring of thieves, he or she could get the routing and transit numbers, as well as the checking account number, off the bottom of the check. They do not need to steal the check to do that. All they need is access to the check and to write down the numbers. There are many independent check printing companies that will take a check order online, through the mail, or over the phone, thus generating fraudulent checks with a false name and the parishioner's account number on them. It looks like the real thing. With false identification to match the check, it will not take long to go through the parishioner's money in the bank—and maybe not get caught if they are not too greedy. The scheme lasts as long as it takes the bank to notify the parishioner that their account is overdrawn.

Provide members a small, sealable envelope in which to leave their check or cash before putting it in the open container. Together, two people need to check the boxes at least daily, particularly if the open containers are in a part of the church that is accessible at all times, such as the mailroom or the parish hall. A better approach is to use locked boxes instead of unsecured places. The best approach is to find a more certain and secure way to receive the money.

Fund-raising and Events

My comments here address both fund-raising and non-fund-raising events. Fund-raising and other events may have many sources of money coming into the church in advance of the event—mail, walk-in, online. I will address those methods of receiving money, but for now I want to focus on money at the event itself.

Most likely, there will be a till. A till is the cash register drawer that contains the money. Besides a physical cash register, there are many things that can suffice as a till—a shoebox, cigar box, bank bag, paper bag, or wicker basket. Usually, there is a starting amount of money in the till at the beginning of the event, to make change. Lobster Hoopla, raffles, silent auctions, bake sales, book sales, flea markets, Wednesday night supper, Sunday morning breakfast—all sorts of events can create the need for a till.

You may have heard the expression "too many fingers in the till." There is a reason for the saying. If you have an event where something resembling a till is present, then you need to take steps to protect the money. Have as few people in the till as possible. Two is the right number for any time cash is present in the church for any reason. Have these people work as a team. One assists the customer with the sale while the cashier handles the money as the only one in and out of the till. It is a heightened risk of fraud and a total lack of accountability and internal control to have only one person present with the money. Worse still is using an open wicker basket with no one attending it.

First and foremost, do not leave the money unattended. Do not put out a wicker basket and a) hope everyone pays, and b) no one pilfers what money is there. Who will steal the money? Those with access. There should be a table with two people (cashiers) seated at it to greet the event-goers and oversee the money. There should be at least one person in relief available at all times should one of the cashiers need to leave the table. All who might sit at the table should be trained in advance. If credit cards are accepted, everyone should be trained in advance in how to accept and process the cards.

Fund-raising and Event Till Process Flow

Tills originate from all kinds of sources. Regardless of whether it is from the bank, the safe, or someone's pocket, two people need to be with the money at all times. When the money for the till arrives at the table, it should be counted. If the people at the table are different from the people who brought it, the two who brought it do not leave until the two at the table have counted it. An opening till count sheet should be completed and signed by the two counting the till.

Why do I present this level of detail? Because the likely place of theft is from the till. As part of the checks and balances of the process, there is a corresponding balancing amount that can be reconciled with the ending till amount—sales. As part of the event, there should be one, only one, place where all sales are captured.

If you have a cash register, clear your daily totals before you start selling anything. You can find information on how to do that in the manual that came with the cash register. (Most manuals are online these days for most electronic machines.) Once the daily totals are cleared, you can begin selling. At the end of the day, the total daily sales flash (readout) will be the amount used to balance the till and make the daily deposit.

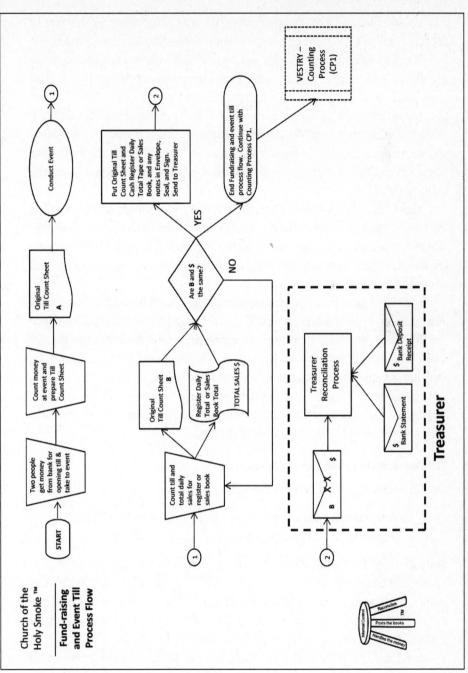

Fundraising and Event Till Process Flow

If you do not have a cash register, there must be some other mechanism to capture each sale. It could be a sign-in sheet indicating the name and number of adults and children meals purchased. The information provided on the sheet could then be totaled to indicate the amount of dollars that should have been collected. It could be more formal with a two-part sales booklet that records the sale, leaving a carbonless copy in the book and providing a receipt for the purchaser. Whatever the method, *this entire process will fail if you do not keep a record of every transaction* and total them at the end of the day, or event, to compare the expected sales support with the totals on the till count sheet.

Checks must be endorsed "for deposit to (your church name) only" at the time they are received. This prevents what is known as two-party checks where further endorsements and cashing/depositing is possible. Endorsing the check "for deposit only" prevents any other endorsements and banks will likely not cash it.

Credit card sales pose an additional problem for till balancing. Total sales accumulated by the cash register will reflect cash and credit sales. To balance the till, there must be a total for cash in the till, a total for checks in the till, and a total for credit card sales slips in the till. The credit card sales slip is the one that is signed by the customer and retained by the cashier.

When sales are finished for the day, total the daily sales.

Prepare the till count sheet at the end of the day *using the one that was used to open the till at the beginning of the day.*

Till Count Sheet and Reconciliation

The till balancing equation is as follows:

Total sales $ + Opening Till $ + Credit card = Ending Till $
(register)   (Till Count Sheet)   Sales $

Shift Change Till Count Process The deposit ticket for the bank can now be made if the above equation balances. If it does not, then stop and determine why. If, after recounting, the equation still does not balance, one of two possibilities exists. If the cash is short from what the total sales amount is, there have been errors made or theft has occurred from the till. If the cash is more than the sales, and you have correctly subtracted the opening till amount, then not all sales have been properly recorded. A note regarding the irreconcilable situation should be attached to the original count sheet and included in the envelope for the treasurer. The process now continues with the counting, depositing, and reconciling high level process on page 182.

TILL COUNT SHEET   Event: Date:

| OPENING TILL | | | | CLOSING TILL | | |

OPENING TILL

Currency

Coins	Quantity	Extended Totals
1 ¢	X _____	= _____
5 ¢	X _____	= _____
10 ¢	X _____	= _____
25 ¢	X _____	= _____
50 ¢	X _____	= _____
$1 coin	X _____	= _____
Total		$ _____

Paper

	Quantity	Extended Totals
$ 1.00	X _____	= _____
$ 5.00	X _____	= _____
$ 10.00	X _____	= _____
$ 20.00	X _____	= _____
$ 50.00	X _____	= _____
$ 100.00	X _____	= _____
Total		$ _____

Checks

	Quantity	Total Dollars
Total	_____	$ _____

TOTAL OPENING TILL $ _____
                                         A

CLOSING TILL

Currency

Coins	Quantity	Extended Totals
1 ¢	X _____	= _____
5 ¢	X _____	= _____
10 ¢	X _____	= _____
25 ¢	X _____	= _____
50 ¢	X _____	= _____
$1 coin	X _____	= _____
Total		$ _____

Paper

	Quantity	Extended Totals
$ 1.00	X _____	= _____
$ 5.00	X _____	= _____
$ 10.00	X _____	= _____
$ 20.00	X _____	= _____
$ 50.00	X _____	= _____
$ 100.00	X _____	= _____
Total		$ _____

Checks

	Quantity	Total Dollars
Total	_____	$ _____

Credit Card Sales, net of returns

	Quantity	Total Dollars
Total	_____	$ _____

TOTAL CLOSING TILL* $ _____
                                         B

Signature _____
Name (Print): _____

Signature _____
Name (Print): _____

Signature _____
Name (Print): _____

Signature _____
Name (Print): _____

*bank deposit   ☐ Check if this is a change of cashiers and attach to opening count sheet for the day.

Till Count Sheet

Church of the
Holy Smoke ™

**Till
Reconciliation**

Register Daily
Total or Sales
Book Total

TOTAL SALES $

+

Till Count Sheet

TILL COUNT SHEET   Event: Date:

OPENING TILL   CLOSING TILL

Currency				Currency		
Coins	Quantity	Extended Totals		Coins	Quantity	Extended Totals
1¢	X	=		1¢	X	=
5¢	X	=		5¢	X	=
10¢	X	=		10¢	X	=
25¢	X	=		25¢	X	=
50¢	X	=		50¢	X	=
$1 coin	X	=		$1 coin	X	=
Total		$		Total		$

Paper				Paper		
$ 1.00	X	=		$ 1.00	X	=
$ 5.00	X	=		$ 5.00	X	=
$ 10.00	X	=		$ 10.00	X	=
$ 20.00	X	=		$ 20.00	X	=
$ 50.00	X	=		$ 50.00	X	=
$100.00	X	=		$100.00	X	=
Total		$		Total		$

Checks			Checks		
Quantity	Total Dollars		Quantity	Total Dollars	
Total			Total		

			Credit Card Sales, net of returns		
			Quantity	Total Dollars	
			Total	$	

TOTAL OPENING TILL $ **A**   TOTAL CLOSING TILL * $ **B**

Signature   Signature
Name (Print)   Name (Print)

Signature   Signature
Name (Print)   Name (Print)

* Bank deposit   ☐ Check if this is a change of cashier and attach to opening count sheet for the day.

= B

Internal Controls
Reconciles
TM
Posts the books
Handles the money

Till Reconciliation

Shift changes You may have had shift changes in the interim. Use a different till count sheet to reconcile the till before letting the next shift take over. Do not use the original till count sheet that opened the till for the day. If you do, you will not know on whose watch anything went missing. Accountability for the till belongs to the two people operating the till, and there should be a clear handoff of the till to another cashier team only after it is balanced. (Do not clear the register daily totals at this point.)

If the shift change is the first one of the day, copy the opening till information from the original till count sheet onto a new one into the opening till information. Use this new sheet to perform the steps to count and balance the till with sales up to the end of the first shift. Use the closing till column once sales and the till are counted to determine if they balance. If they do not, persevere until you understand why not and correct. Once they balance, this till count sheet should be retained until the till balances for the day.

If there is another shift change before the end of the day, repeat the process. There is no need to complete another interim count for shift two. Most likely sales will be more easily determined as a total for the day, and the till should simply be counted. Using a new till count sheet, copy the opening till information from the original till count sheet onto a new one into the opening till information. Use the closing till column once sales and the till are counted to determine if they balance. If they do not, persevere until you understand why not and correct. Once they balance, this till count sheet should be retained until the till balances for the day.

At the end of the day, use the original till count sheet used to open the day. Complete the process and use the closing till column to close out the day. Notice that this does not end the process for the event. Even though the sales are known and reconciled with the till, the money in the till still needs to get into the bank. Use the previously described Counting Process CP1 to complete the event's process.

Walk-in and Mail

The difficulty with money that is delivered to the church is that counting, depositing, and reconciling are impossible without a central point for the collection of the money. ("Walk-in" is any money that is hand-delivered to church staff, for example, the secretary, parish administrator, music or youth minister.) Yet, there still must be two people with the money at all times. At times during the week small churches may have only one person at the church, making the two-person rule impossible. Have the person who hand-delivered the money sign as the second person on the log.

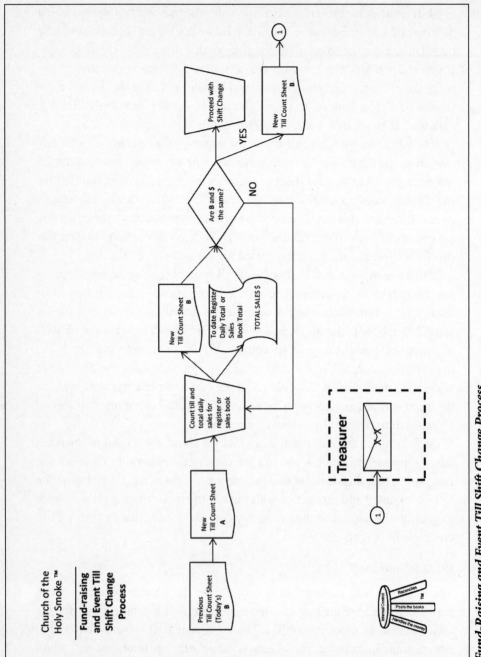

Fund-Raising and Event Till Shift Change Process

WALK-IN OR MAIL DELIVERED MONEY LOG

DATE	DONOR Last Name	First Name	Phone No.	METHOD	AMOUNT	PURPOSE or DESIGNATION	RECEIVED BY 1	RECEIVED BY 2

Walk-In Or Mail Delivered Money Log

Church of the
Holy Smoke ™

**Walk-in and
Mail Process**

Treasurer

At the end of the
month, put log in
envelope, seal,
sign, and give to
treasurer

VESTRY –
Counting
Process
(CP1)

Two People

Walk-in and
Mail Delivered
Money Log

Post Money to
Walk-in and
Mail Delivered
Money Log

Put money in
envelope . Put in
drop box or slot in
the safe. Do not
open safe.

Endorse checks
"for deposit only
. . ."

Walk-in or
mailed
money

Start

Reconciles
Posts the books
Handles the money
™

Walk-In and Mail Process

Many times, the secretary's desk is staffed by volunteers. They could accompany the parish administrator when receiving money or opening the mail. Other times there may be other staff members available. This is a great way to use volunteers who want to be a part of the church, but, like me, are better off not singing in the choir or arranging flowers. Ask them to assist with opening the mail as a second person who can sign the log. It is a good idea to rotate people in this position so there is always the awareness that they will not be the only person performing this task.

You'll notice that clergy have not been mentioned in connection with these processes. It is best if clergy do not accept money for any reason, but rather direct its delivery to the parish administrator or parish secretary. Ultimately, that is where the money would be recorded in the cash receipts log. Clergy are often (and appropriately) focused on pastoral concerns whether greeting parishioners following worship, attending the ECW fundraiser, or participating in a committee meeting. The risk is that sometimes clergy delivered money is not accompanied by the verbal designated purpose for which it is given. Separating that pastoral focus from serving as a money collector is a good and healthy thing both for clergy and for the parish.

The mail should not be opened unless there are two people present and the log is used. The checks should be endorsed "for deposit only" as soon as they are received. Any money should be put in an envelope and marked with the date received. Then the envelope should be sealed and signed by the two people who were present when the money was received and put into the safe. If sufficient quantities of checks arrive, then consider executing the CP1 process followed by the depositing process. Holding a large accumulation of checks and cash should be avoided, even if in the safe.

At month's end, a copy of the log should be made and retained by a person who does not post the contributions or make deposits. The original log should be put in a sealed envelope and given to the treasurer to assist with batch reconciliation. The checks that were put in the safe should be counted the next time the counting process is done (CP1) and included with the deposit. It should be obvious by now that whenever there is counting to be done, the CP1 process is used, regardless from where the money comes.

Financial institution and online

Financial institution and online transactions, while different in the sources that generated them, nonetheless represent transactions even without physical checks or currency to count or deposit.

Financial institution   What I am calling "financial institution transactions" are those that are found only on monthly or other statements coming from financial institutions. Some of them are:

- Interest earned
- Interest charged
- Late fees
- Returned check fees
- Processing fees
- Low balance or over balance fees
- Net proceeds from sales of securities
- Purchases of securities
- Transfers
- ACH transactions
- Wire funds
- Credit card transactions
- Debit card transactions
- Lock box fee
- Safe deposit box fee
- Analysis fee
- Maintenance fee

The only person to see these transactions initially is the treasurer, because the treasurer receives *all* correspondence from the financial institutions. Mostly, these are transactions that require entry into the general ledger, many in order to reconcile the financial institution accounts. Once these transactions are known, the treasurer should compile a list for the bookkeeper, who then makes the entries. This is not automatic. The vestry needs to give explicit blanket approval to the treasurer for such types of transactions, or approval will need to be obtained before each transaction is recorded. Regardless, these are journal entries and should be a part of the monthly treasurer's report and included in the vestry minutes. The treasurer should never post the books, regardless of the reason. That is a violation of the Three-Legged Stool™ of internal control.

Online transactions   Online transactions are totally different in source but are similar to financial institution transactions in that they are both electronic only. Online transactions include PayPal, credit card transactions, and direct debit bank transactions entered on the church's website. These could be recurring transactions or one-time transactions. They can be for most any purpose, including pledge fulfillment, designated giving, purchasing items, registering for an event. The difficulty is that they are going to show up in your bank account perhaps without any indication of their intended purpose. A memo field note or other method of indicating intention included with the electronic transaction is critical.

Some churches' websites will include ways to receive electronic payments and contributions. These will be done through an intermediary requiring a secondary reconciliation. The intermediary should have information that is particular to their way of processing and interfacing with your bank account. They will also have reports that list transactions, fees, and net proceeds. These will also have to be reconciled with the totals deposited by batch into your checking account. Because of the myriad ways these get processed and interfaced with your bank account, you will need to devise a process that uses the principles of internal control. Ultimately, reconciliation falls to the treasurer to perform.

Other Comments

Church safes   First, do not put the safe near the outside wall of the church. The Church of the Holy Smoke™ tried bolting the safe to the floor. Someone broke a hole through thick exterior masonry walls, wrapped chains around the safe, and snatched it, bolts and all, out of the floor. Then the church tried putting in a wall safe that resembled a filing cabinet drawer. The thieves broke through the exterior wall and snatched the drawer, leaving nothing but the front of the safe. Now the safe is well inside the building, bolted to the floor, and behind a locked door. The safe should have an opening in which to drop things. There are some that work like a night depository at the bank. There are others that have a rotating drum. Get either one if you do not have one with the drop opening. It is better to have as few people as possible with access to the contents of the safe. While you are at it, get a safe that has an electronic combination—a keypad. This allows frequent changes to the combination, at least every ninety days. It also allows the combination to be changed immediately should there be need.

Records retention   Particularly as technology changes the way deposits are made and transactions recorded, remember that all donor records are the permanent records of the church (including lists and contributions accounting records). Donor transaction documents, such as count sheets, pledge envelopes (if they contained currency), and scanned checks, should be kept in their batch integrity until an audit is completed on them, plus four years. Some records retention recommendations can be found in Records Manual for Congregations at www.episcopalarchives.org.

Government notices Correspondence from the local, state, or federal government that is from any of those various departments of revenue, labor, or taxation is to be opened *only* by the treasurer. Do not permit anyone else to open mail of that nature.

We have gone through many of the processes that involve the receipt, counting, depositing, and reconciling of money. You should be able to identify your church's receipts with one of the categories and processes described and modify these flows or create other processes for your own church's needs.

CHAPTER

10

Disbursements Internal Control

D isbursements internal control involves more policies than in support internal control. This chapter will discuss many of those policies that must be determined before the process can be designed. Often when designing a process, the need for these policies appears at steps along the way. Below is a high level disbursements process for the Church of the Holy Smoke™.

Disbursements High Level Process

We will use the disbursements high level process multiple times. All disbursements from the church should go through a single process. This allows for oversight and accountability to be simplified, yet implementing the Three-Legged Stool™ of internal control.

The process has at its core the reimbursement package consisting of original invoices and receipts, approved for payment by those accountable for the funds, proper general ledger account codes, a check with stubs, and proper signatures affixed to the checks. How this gets done is where the process comes in.

Just as support has internal control processes, so do disbursements. However, there are policies that need to be in place first before the process can be described.

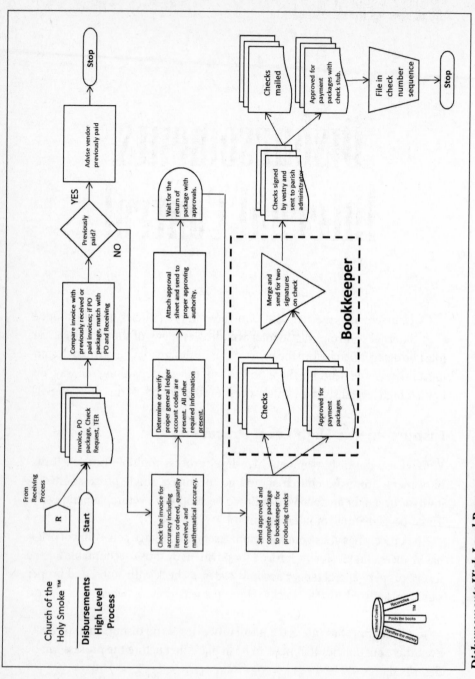

Disbursements High Level Process

Disbursement Policies

One Bank Account

There should be only one checking account. If you are using proper software for your church's accounting, there is no need for more than one checking account. If you are not using software that is designed specifically for church accounting, you are probably using physical checking accounts to try to keep unrestricted and temporarily restricted funds separate. In doing so, you compound the opportunity for error and add additional effort to check procedures.

I have only seen a couple of churches using multiple checking accounts that have the correct amounts corresponding to the general ledger's view of unrestricted and temporarily restricted. Almost always the balances at the bank are incorrect.

Two checking accounts double your effort; four quadruple it. No Sunday school class, ECW, youth group, or even clergy discretionary account needs a separate checking account. What these persons or groups need is a way to access their funds, know their available fund balances, and have ease of use. There are processes that allow for all those goals to be met.

In short, the funds are accessed using the disbursement process and some church operating policies. The balances are known with targeted reports from the accounting system for their fund balances and transactions. The ease of use involves keeping the processes simple and the requestor learning the process and policies, and executing them.

Each of these—Sunday school class, ECW, youth group, clergy discretionary—is a designated account in the chart of accounts in the general ledger. There is no need to have multiple checking accounts for operating or designated funds. The treasurer not only has to reconcile the bank accounts, but also has to reconcile whether the cash in each is the appropriate amount per the general ledger. The treasurer will attempt this once, and then become a believer in the one checking account approach. Easily, up to one-fourth of my audit time has been performing this reconciliation for clients.

There are occasions when the money is separated as required by bequest or other legal agreement where check disbursement capability is necessary. The best example is an endowment fund that is kept at a brokerage house that has check disbursement capability or is required by the legal agreement to be the location from which funds are disbursed.

For example, the Ma Barker Scholarship Fund is held at a brokerage house that has the capability to issue checks to the recipients as requested by the church. Since this activity happens once each year with few checks being issued, there is no need for a checkbook held by someone at the church. With a vestry resolution and proper authorization to the brokerage house, the checks will be issued directly to the scholarship recipients. The reconciliation by the treasurer will provide oversight for the disbursements if the proper documentation is forwarded to the treasurer at the time the check request is made of the broker. If there is a need for checks to be written frequently, then question whether the money is held in the proper type of account.

Checks

All disbursements must be made by a computer-generated check. Whether paying an invoice, reimbursing an individual for purchases made from their personal funds, providing support to individuals or other organizations, all disbursements require a check. Barring catastrophic events that prevent the use of the computer, no checks should ever be written by hand. Writing checks by hand means the church records and financial statements are inaccurate until they are posted later. Many times, this causes reconciliation problems, inaccurate designated fund balances, and increases the likelihood of fraud.

Check Signers

If the vestry is fiduciarily liable for the church's money, then they should be the only ones signing checks. In large churches, the task may be delegated to a few individuals on staff, but remember the Three-Legged Stool™ of internal control. The check signers can have no access to the accounting records and are not involved with reconciliation. Treasurers, clergy, and bookkeepers do not sign checks.

My opinion is that this is not a delegated task. Not all vestry members need to be signing checks. Four authorized signers are plenty to allow for personal schedules to be accommodated and still have checks signed on a timely basis. This will likely necessitate updating the authorized signature card at the bank each year as new members are elected. Best practices suggest rotating this duty annually so there is not a consistent set of signers.

Credit and Debit Cards

Credit and debit cards in the name of the church are an opportunity for fraud. I have heard dozens of excuses for why a church needs a credit or debit card, and none of them are convincing.

Debit cards are like a blank check. How can you manage cash flow with a spigot attached to the checkbook that can be opened at any moment? What about written authorizations prior to purchase? What happens if the card gets lost or stolen? Where do you keep it secured? Deposits are made with a bank teller or the night depository, not through the ATM. Who would be getting cash out of the ATM? There is no good reason for a debit card to be issued. If you have one, shred it.

Credit cards are just as bad. Who is going to pre-authorize the purchase? What about personal purchases? We have heard some say, "I will borrow it just this once and pay it back." If you have a church credit card, shred it. That includes cards for the clergy, too.

What about purchases online? What about the youth minister traveling with the youth? What about . . . ? The answer is simple, requires no new additions to the processes, and is far safer than a credit card in the church's name. Each employee is required to use his or her own personal credit card and go through the reimbursement process. (If the employee cannot obtain a credit card in their name for credit worthiness reasons, why would you ever give them one from the church?) It is that simple. Then there will be no lost or forgotten cash register receipts. For reimbursement, they will need to attach receipts to an invoice approval form and submit the package for approval and payment.

If you establish a policy that all checks will be written on one particular day of the week, then all receipts for reimbursement must be submitted two days prior. If people use personal credit cards and you reimburse them, at most, within eight days, they will have the money in hand to pay the credit card bill.

Whether online or at the gas station with the church bus, the purchase should be made with a personal credit card and reimbursed. Do not have credit or debit cards that are connected to church accounts.

Travel and Entertainment Expense Reimbursement

Notice the operative word—*reimbursement*. This is another area where a personal credit card is used. All travel and entertainment for church business—clergy, employees, or volunteers—is submitted on a travel and entertainment reimbursement form with all original receipts attached. The information on the form is what the IRS requires for any travel and entertainment documentation. The reimbursement for the expense is considered non-wage income to the individual. It is up to the individual to document the expenses to the satisfaction of the IRS. Filling out this form completely and attaching original receipts is the only option. There is no excuse for not having the documentation and receipts to support a claim for travel reimbursement.

CHURCH OF THE HOLY SMOKE™ TRAVEL AND ENTERTAINMENT EXPENSE REIMBURSEMENT

NAME

GL Code

TRAVEL

Purpose

Week beginning

Approval 1

Approval 2

(Required over $200)

(Prepare a separate form for each out-of-town trip)

	Sun.	Mon.	Tues.	Wed.	Thurs.	Fri.	Sat.	TOTAL
Date								
Mileage								$
Parking								$
Air fare								$
Room & tax								$
Auto rental								$
Taxi/Rail/Bus								$
Meals Breakfast								$
Dinner								$
Other:								$
1 -								$
2 -								$
3 -								$
4 -								$
5 -								$
TOTAL	$	$	$	$	$	$	$	$

ENTERTAINMENT

(Attach Separate Sheet If Necessary)

Purpose							
Name							
Title							
Where							
B/L/D/Ent.							
Amount	$	$	$	$	$	$	$

REQUESTOR SIGNATURE

PAGE TOTAL $

Less: Advances $ (   )

NET CHECK $

Travel Expense Reimbursement

"Travel" is local travel by car or longer distance travel by any means—bus, train, air, rental car. "Entertainment" does not mean a gala at the church. Primarily, it means a meal at which the business of the church is discussed. The entry for single business meetings goes in the entertainment section regardless of other travel expenses that might be applicable. The cost of a meal while attending a conference is a travel expense and not entertainment, unless the church representative buys someone else's meal. Examples include:

- Clergy discussing counseling or business matters over a meal
- Search committee member dining with a potential candidate
- Personal gift under $25 given in lieu of lodging

Alcohol for personal consumption should be clearly identified on the receipts. The church should have a written policy regarding expense reimbursement for alcohol and include whether and what type is reimbursable. My opinion is the church's liability is too great to reimburse alcohol purchases. It is a personal preference item, like videos-on-demand in the hotel room, which should not be reimbursed.

The travel and expense form above is intended to show the type of information that is required. Use of a spreadsheet instead of a printed form allows for the inclusion of more complete information than will fit inside a box on a printed page. The documentation should be clear and complete. Regardless, some of these items on the form need further explanation.

Each travel and expense reimbursement form (TER) should be for a calendar week, regardless of the span of time of the event. It is easier to keep records in this manner. If done weekly, there is no question regarding completeness of the expense documentation and reimbursement. It is easier to write a check with the remittance advice stating "for the week of February 1," than that states "for the general convention, clergy conference, and general mileage." I suggest using Sunday as the first day of the week.

Sometimes the travel will be expensed to more than one general ledger account code. There will need to be a clear delineation of how much expense is to be charged to what account code on the form submitted to bookkeeping.

The approver(s) should not affix their signature for payment without all information on the form. The church should establish a dollar amount threshold policy above which there is the requirement of a second approver. These approvals are needed prior to the check being cut. Travel and entertainment expenses are one of the most abused and fraudulent activities in any entity, church or business, and scrupulous oversight is needed.

Each travel activity needs to have a purpose identified. It could be as simple as "local mileage," if it involves traveling around town. If travel is out of the general area of the church, then there must be some other purpose specified. Of course, using a spreadsheet will allow for greater explanation to be included.

The individual needs to keep a mileage log for IRS purposes. The log needs to show origination and destination, and odometer mileage starting and stopping. Some churches will require this to be attached to the TER and the total for the day to be entered as a summary number. The individual is required to have it for his or her personal taxes, so requiring it be attached isn't an added burden.

Parking, airfare, auto rental, taxi, rail, and bus fare are self-explanatory. Attach the receipts to the form.

"Room and tax" means only the hotel room and tax should be entered here. Other incidentals are entered in the appropriate lines. For example, room service meals are entered on the meals line.

There is a reason that lunch is not included on the form for meals. The IRS does not allow a deduction for lunch and the church should not provide reimbursement for lunch. The IRS theory is that most people will eat lunch out anyway. Your church policy may be different, but if reimbursed, the person will need to deal with it on his or her personal tax return. The caveat is that if lunch is for entertainment (business of the church) purposes, then the church may reimburse the person's lunch. It becomes a personal tax return item for the individual reimbursed.

"Other" items that could be listed beg the question what is the church's policy? The church should have a reasonably detailed policy regarding all manner of expense reimbursement. It is good fiscal prudence and good human resources practice to have a written expense reimbursement policy for the church.

Entertainment documentation requires identifying the purpose of the meeting and what was discussed, who attended by name, their titles if representing in some official capacity, the name of the location where the meeting took place, which meal it was or if entertainment only, and the dollar amount. For meetings of a confidential nature, such as counseling, the purpose and what was discussed could be simply "marital counseling" or "pastoral counseling." The details of the discussion should not be listed, but what the IRS in interested in is the nature of the discussion pertaining to business and not a social meeting only.

If there are cash advances outstanding for travel or any other reason, they should be deducted from the travel expense amount and a net check paid.

Receipts for everything must be attached. The church should not reimburse expenses without a receipt—not just travel, but any reimbursement. It is amazing how compliance from all concerned occurs after the first individual without a receipt fails to get reimbursed.

Check Stock

Take every precaution to safeguard blank checks, as if they were cash on hand. Today's copiers and printers reproduce realistic-looking documents, including checks. The check stock should contain anti-fraud features. Some examples:

- Watermarks that are the result of high pressure manufacturing techniques that allow the watermark to be seen from both sides of the paper.
- Parallel lines on the back of the check make it more difficult for fraudsters to cut and paste partial checks, either physically or with imaging systems.
- A pantograph is an image or word, such as void, that appears only when the check is photocopied.
- Small text printed on the check that creates a black line when scanned or copied.
- Color-changing features built into the printing process that cause colors to change when the check is held at different angles, smudge if erased, or even create holograms.
- Signature block with printing that makes it difficult to scan or photocopy signatures.
- All checks must be pre-numbered and customized with the church's name and address. There must be no non-customized blank checks.

Check stock should be in a locked location, with only the bookkeeper having access to the checks. This limits the risk of stolen checks. Periodically, the treasurer should ask the bookkeeper to allow the inspection of the check stock. The treasurer should reconcile the numbered checks in the check stock with those in process, outstanding, voided, and cleared. All checks should be accounted for, and those missing cancelled with the bank. The bank will likely issue a fraud alert in their records and prevent paying any checks that are cancelled. The bookkeeper should keep the following log to assist the treasurer in locating all checks and check stock.

Keep the check inventory with the check stock. Every time the bookkeeper retrieves a check and uses it, the inventory should be updated. When the treasurer inspects the check stock, all checks should be accounted for, including those voided.

CHURCH OF THE HOLY SMOKE™ CHECK INVENTORY

Check Number Used			Voided		Next Starting		
Beginning	Ending	Date Used	Beginning	Ending	Check Number	By	Signature

Check Inventory

Voiding a Check

Checks to be voided are presumed to have been created by the computer accounting system, and should be voided there first before defacing the check stock. Check stock to be voided should have *void* written across the face of the check in large letters. Also, write *void* across the date, amount, and signature blocks. Cut or tear the account number and a portion of or the entire signature block off the check and shred. Put the voided check in a voided check folder and put in the locked location where the check stock is kept. Update the check inventory to reflect the account numbers voided.

Making a Check

There are ways to make checks that assist in preventing fraud. Here are some of them:

- Leading asterisks should fill the numerical dollar amount box, leaving no room for the insertion of a digit.
- Use different fonts when printing the payee's name and written dollars.
- Under no circumstances should blank checks be signed. Ever!
- Two signatures from only vestry members should be affixed to the checks. No one else should be authorized as a signer, especially clergy, the bookkeeper, and the treasurer. Although banks accept only one signature on checks and do not honor a second signature requirement from the organization, two signatures are a point of internal control. The purpose is that two people inspect the invoice, approvals, and check for appropriateness and accuracy.
- Checks should not be signed and left for another signer. Once a check has one signature, it is cashable.
- Never give a signed check back to the bookkeeper who wrote the check or to anyone else with access to the general ledger. Remember the scenario of the perceived needed operation and the scanner-created fraud?
- Use a check that also prints two remittance advices, one to accompany the check to the payee, and one to be attached to the invoice for filing.

The Payment or Reimbursement Approval Package

The bookkeeper should never write a check for which the appropriate documentation, approvals, and general ledger (GL) codes are not affixed. If the payment or reimbursement approval package is not complete, the bookkeeper should reject it and not write the check. The bookkeeper is held accountable for rejecting packages for payment that are not complete. This

Church of the Holy Smoke™
123 Elm Street
Paxtown, Agape 12345

12345

Pay to the
order of:

Dollars

1234567890   123456789012345

Remittance Advice

Vendor:

12345

Invoice: Date: Amount:

Church File Copy

Vendor:

12345

Invoice: Date: Amount: GL Code:

Check

should be periodically inspected. The following documents should be in a payment approval package when sent to the bookkeeper for cutting a check:

- If an invoice or receipt is received (by mail, walk-in, fax):
  - Original invoice stamped with date received and signed by receiving individual
  - If a receipt for reimbursement, the original receipt with items purchased circled, totaled, and initialed by the purchaser requesting reimbursement
  - In either case, invoice approval form with all information correctly attached and approvals
- If a check is needed for which there is no invoice:
  - Check request form with all information correctly attached and approvals
- If goods were received as the result of a purchase order
  - Purchase order with all information correctly attached
  - Receiving report with date received, quantity received, and signed by receiving individual
  - Original invoice stamped with date and receiving individual
  - Invoice approval form with all information correctly attached and approvals
- If a reimbursement is requested for travel and entertainment
  - Travel and entertainment reimbursement form with all information completed in sufficient detail and approvals
  - Original receipts and other documentation attached
  - Verification there are no outstanding advances before writing check

Why do I insist the original receipt be turned in, that the church keep it, and not return it? What if someone bought supplies for Wednesday night supper, did not use all of them, got reimbursed for the full amount of the purchase from the church, and with the original receipt in hand returned them to the store for a refund? Provide a photocopy of the receipt if the person wants one, but do not give him or her the original receipt. This is also a high-risk area for fraud.

Do you see why the ACFE estimates that five percent of any entity's revenue is lost each year to fraud? It does not have to be by overt theft of large amounts, but can be a bleeding of money a little at a time from various sources and means.

Invoice Approval Process

Invoices come into the church a number of ways—mail, included with goods received, walk-in from parishioners wanting reimbursement, fax. All requests for payment are treated the same.

Check Request

A check request is used when there is no accompanying invoice, but only when it involves normal business practices. There are few good reasons to request a check be written without an invoice. Some are:

- A substitute nursery worker (must have Social Security number and address)
- A musician or vocalist for a one-time performance (must have Social Security number and address)

CHURCH OF THE HOLY SMOKE™ INVOICE APPROVAL FORM

If no invoice, use check request form or PO form

Received Date: _____/_____/_____
Received By
Name: _____Signature:_____

Approval
Name: _____Signature:_____

Name: _____Signature:_____

GL Account Code to Charge: _____ $_____.___
_____ $_____.___
_____ $_____.___
_____ $_____.___

TOTAL $_____.___

BOOKKEEPER – DO NOT PAY UNLESS ALL SIGNATURES AND GL CODES ARE PRESENT

Invoice Approval Form

```
┌─────────────────────────────────────────────────────────────────┐
│            CHURCH OF THE HOLY SMOKE™ CHECK REQUEST                │
│                                                                   │
│  DATE                                                             │
│  NEEDED ___/___/___  REQUESTED ___/___/___  REQUESTOR: _____ │
│                                                                   │
│  PAYEE:                                                           │
│  ┌──────────────────────────────────────────┐  CHECK AMOUNT      │
│  │ Name      _____ │                   │
│  │ Address 1 _____ │  $ _____.___   │
│  │ Address 2 _____ │                   │
│  │ Address 3 _____ │  ┌──────────────┐ │
│  │ City      _____ State ___ Zip ___-__ │  │ Tax ID is    │ │
│  │                                            │  │ required     │ │
│  │ Phone  (  )___-_____                      │  │ for checks to│ │
│  │                                            │  │ individuals, │ │
│  │ TAX ID # _____                  │  │ sole         │ │
│  └──────────────────────────────────────────┘  │ proprietors, │ │
│                                                 │ and certain  │ │
│                                                 │ aliens.      │ │
│                                                 └──────────────┘ │
│  GL ACCOUNT   _____   $ _____.___                  │
│  GL ACCOUNT   _____   $ _____.___                  │
│  GL ACCOUNT   _____   $ _____.___                  │
│  GL ACCOUNT   _____   $ _____.___                  │
│                                                                   │
│  1st APPROVER: _____   IN BUDGET:      YES   NO          │
│                                                     (CIRCLE)      │
│  2nd APPROVER: _____                                     │
│               (Required if over $500)                             │
└─────────────────────────────────────────────────────────────────┘
```

Check Request

- Rent paid to an apartment complex for a person in need
- Prepaid gas, grocery, or merchandise cards for pastoral purposes
- Hotel bill due on arrival for youth ski trip

The problem with check requests is that the internal control process is not complete with the production of the check. It is rare that the only documentation is a check request form. If registering for a convention, for example, a printout of the registration fees due should be attached to the check request. Check requests without any attached substantiation should be rejected. In the case of a substitute nursery worker, a sign-in sheet is a method of substantiation.

To complete the documentation package prior to filing in the archives, a receipt will be generated after payment is made in most situations and must be attached. In the case of the nursery worker or musician, there may not be an invoice, but we have name, address, and Social Security number as a part of the check request so a 1099 can be generated at the end of the year, if applicable. For the rest of the situations, a receipt will be generated either at the cash register when the cards are purchased or at the hotel when the final payment is made. That receipt must be turned in to the bookkeeper for attaching to the approval package after the fact and before filing the package. There is no gray area in disbursement processes.

Purchase Order Process

Purchase Orders

Purchase orders are used in larger churches for cost control and staying within budget. For smaller churches, purchase orders are generally not practical. Purchase orders allow pre-approval for expenditures before ordering items or paying invoices. When the general ledger has a large number of accounts—many committees with authorization to make spending decisions, many who do not have the authority, multiple entities within the church, such as a school—then purchase orders may be appropriate. For at least two-thirds of parishes, purchase orders probably are not appropriate. The processes are different depending on whether your church uses purchase orders or not.

The process begins with the need to buy something, place a deposit, or prepare a check for payment to a supplier of services for which an invoice has not been received. The latter might be a check for a supply priest or Christmas cantata vocalist. It is not used for recurring expenses, construction, maintenance, or repair services. Those should have an invoice submitted before payment.

Once a decision is made by a committee or person authorized to make purchases, a purchase order (PO) is completed. (Note that the item has not been purchased at this point. If it has and you need to get the invoice paid or reimbursed, this is not the process to use. Go to the invoice payment process.) The purchase order is sent to a central location, such as the parish administrator, who determines the appropriate approvals needed and sends the PO to the approvers for signature (of approval to pay) and verification of general ledger account codes from which budget the funds will be expended. The process from here is identical to that of the invoice payment process. The check processing, filing, and reconciliation processes are the same. To maintain as few processes as reasonable and to keep the processes as simple as possible, the PO process integrates at this point with the disbursement process.

Church of the
Holy Smoke ™

**Purchase Order
High-Level
Process**

Purchase Order Process

CHURCH OF THE HOLY SMOKE™ PURCHASE ORDER

VENDOR:
Name _____
Address 1 _____
Address 2 _____
Address 3 _____
City _____ State ____ Zip ____-____

SHIP TO: Church of the Holy Smoke™
123 Elm Street
Paxtown, Agape 12345

SOLD TO: Church of the Holy Smoke™
123 Elm Street
Paxtown, Agape 12345

Incomplete shipments accepted: YES   NO
(circle one)

REQUESTOR: _____
1st APPROVER: _____
2nd APPROVER: _____
(Required if over $1,500)

ITEM	QUANTITY ORDERED	QUANTITY RECEIVED	ITEM NUMBER	DESCRIPTION	COST EACH	TOTAL COST	GL ACCOUNT
1							
2							
3							
4							
5							
6							
7							
8							
9							
10							

AUTHORIZED BY: _____   PHONE: (__)__-___   DATE: _____

Purchase Order

Receiving Process

Sometimes the receiving process is a second step in the purchase order process. If a PO was generated, it must be matched with a receiving report of some kind to be attached to the approval package. There must be some proof that the goods ordered were in fact delivered and verified as received before payment can be made. Sometimes the invoice accompanies the goods. No invoice should be paid for goods ordered unless someone has verified they were delivered, as ordered, in the right quantity, and undamaged. *Verified* means someone has deliberately matched the PO with the packing list and contents of the box, put their initials next to each item ordered indicating correctness of that line item, and signed the PO that they were delivered correctly.

The PO and packing list and/or invoice are sent for the appropriate approvals for payment. If the invoice did not accompany the goods, whoever is receiving invoices should hold the receiving package until the invoice arrives and match the invoice with the receiving package before payment. At that point, the invoice must be verified with the PO and receiving package to make sure what was invoiced was what was ordered and invoiced.

Church of the
Holy Smoke ™

**Receiving
High-Level
Process**

Receiving Process

Other Disbursement Policies and Procedures

Filing Check Stubs and Invoices

Some habits die slowly. Others decay at the speed of mountains leveling. Did you ever wonder why six-part forms or forms filled out in triplicate were used back in the days of carbon paper? The reason is that copies were needed so filing could be done of the same invoice in multiple locations. For example, copies were filed in vendor name sequence, check number sequence, budget number sequence, by month, sent to receiving, sent to the originator, etc. That is why there were people who did nothing but file documents.

The question is how do you file checks now? There is one simple answer— by check number sequence. Once filed, the likelihood of having to retrieve a check is remote. Use the computer to run an inquiry of the check register by vendor name sequence, check number sequence, budget number sequence, or by month. Then use the listing to pull the check stubs that have the approval sheet and the invoice attached.

Further, it is an internal control checkpoint to ensure all checks are accounted for by filing the check stubs in check number sequence. Some churches also file the voided checks in check number sequence along with the check stubs to account for all checks.

I once conducted an audit of a medium-sized church that had recently hired a filing clerk. When an audit is conducted, the auditor will randomly select invoices for examination from the check register. They will not be selected in alphabetical sequence, by vendor, or any other logical manner. The church is not given the list in advance; they are asked to pull them while the auditor is there. It took this church six hours to pull the invoices because they filed them by vendor name most of the time. If there was a fund-raiser or project, they were filed by that name. If there was a committee that always wanted to see their invoices, they were filed by that name. After the exasperating fiasco, they asked the filing clerk to pull all the invoices and put them in numerical sequence. The next year, when the invoices were filed by check stub number they were able to pull them in less than an hour.

Employee Advances

Because employee advances are problematic they should not be given readily. If the advance is not handled properly, both the church and the employee can run afoul of the IRS. An advance needs to be cleared by the submission of original receipts, and if necessary, repayment of any outstanding amount.

If not, the IRS will deem the advance to be a non-accountable plan, similar to a housing allowance or a car allowance.

For employees, if the advance is not fully cleared in a reasonable time as mentioned above, withholding, FICA, and FUTA are required, along with other normal payroll taxes. For clergy, it is added to box 7 on the W-2 and SECA is required, or it could be regular W-2 income, depending on the circumstances. Do not be casual about giving advances—give them only in rare and extenuating circumstances. Insist that they need to be cleared within a short time frame.

To avoid problems with the IRS, follow these three rules regarding advances:

1. There must be a business reason for the advance.
2. There must be documentation for the expenditures from the advanced funds.
3. Any unexpended funds must be reimbursed to the church within 120 days.

Employees should sign for an advance on a form that explains the IRS implications for the employee if the rules are not followed. Failure to comply with the rules will result in a reversion to a non-accountable plan and generate tax liability for the church and the individual. To prevent losing sight of advances, use a separate general ledger account number and investigate any balance monthly. A statement requesting the return of the advance and documentation should be sent monthly with prominent indication of the 120-day due date and resulting consequences.

Petty Cash

I generally do not like petty cash accounts, but some churches will have one. Unless there are multiple locations, as in mega-churches, there should be only one petty cash account. Only one person should have access to it, and only one person should be held accountable for it.

Petty cash is usually kept in a box, jar, or large envelope in a desk drawer that is locked unless the accountable person is present. Change should not be made out of the petty cash fund, not even for the soft drink machine in the parish hall.

Establishing a petty cash fund requires documentation. The person responsible for the cash should sign for the initial amount when received, and the treasurer should keep the signed document. The document should also indicate that the owner is personally responsible and liable for any shortage, but that overage belongs to the church. If the responsible person is an employee, the statement should read that any shortage may be deducted from his or her payroll at the church's discretion.

There is a fixed amount (called the imprest amount) of petty cash on hand. It should be no more than is necessary to accomplish its function—such as paying postage due—and never more. The amount in petty cash should always be the sum of receipts in the box and the cash on hand. Monthly, and sometimes mid-month by surprise, the treasurer counts the cash and receipts. They should total the imprest amount. If they do not, an investigation should discover why not.

Each month, the receipts should be gathered, attached to a check request, and a check issued to reimburse the petty cash box for the receipts paid during the month, thereby replenishing the cash to the imprest amount each month. There should also be a low amount threshold that when reached triggers the keeper of the petty cash to go through the process to have the amount replenished mid-month.

Online Bill Payment

Online bill payment is never a good idea because of the difficulty in providing oversight and approvals required. The process to get the proper documentation together is onerous and reconciliation is worse.

Sometimes a mortgage company will require automatic drafts for payment, but that is rare and should be avoided if possible. If not avoidable, there should be a resolution taken by the vestry so the authorization for the draft is documented. Online bill payment might be more convenient, but it is highly susceptible to fraud. The bookkeeper, the treasurer, and anyone with access to the general ledger should not have online bank account access.

Under no circumstances should there be online transacted bank transfers between accounts. Think about the implications and about how you might provide oversight, inspection, accountability, completeness, and proper recording in the general ledger. The process involved is so complex it simply is not worth the effort.

Summary

We began our discussion of internal control in chapter 8 with people, organization, technology, and process, and the Three-Legged Stool™ of internal control. It was not initially obvious that process and policies were intertwined.

There is no substitution for drawing boxes and arrows as a means of designing internal control. There are a number of decisions that must be made regarding what is the church's policy regarding the steps along the way, who will actually perform them, who will inspect them, and what is the demonstrable evidence (traceable checks and balances) that indicates successful implementation and execution of the processes.

What I have presented in chapters 8, 9, and 10 are many of those processes and policies with numerous suggestions, many of which have been learned the hard way in parishes.

Habits take time to change, but they take leadership to initiate the change process. In the absence of documenting and adhering to these policies and processes, people will make their own regardless. The problem is that they will be made from a perspective of convenience and shortcut, and not from the perspective of internal control.

Internal control does not just happen. It is deliberate, documented, and inspected frequently to ensure the safeguarding of assets. It is the vestry who is responsible for the design, but it is the rector who is responsible for its implementation with staff and volunteers. It is the clergy and the vestry who are responsible for the inspection and oversight of the execution of the processes. With good documented design, full implementation, diligent execution, and persistence of inspection, the processes should protect the assets of the church.

11

Taxes

"I thought a church was a not-for-profit, which means it pays no taxes." In my work, I often hear this. The church does pay taxes in a number of ways. However, there may be ways a church should be paying taxes that it is not, and if it is deliberate, that choice is tax evasion. Whether deliberate or not, failing to pay taxes can ultimately be costly.

Who is an employee and who is not is often debated because IRS regulations are not hard and fast. Clergy taxes pose one of the most confusing areas of compensation of any class of employees. This chapter will first discuss what is meant by tax-exempt status, followed by employee taxes, then Unrelated Business Income Tax, and finally other miscellaneous tax matters. Tax laws change frequently and at the will of legislatures. If you have not read the disclaimer on page v, please read it now.

The Parish and Taxes

The use of "not-for-profit" in describing a church or church-related entity conjures thoughts of being tax exempt. While the former is an IRS classification, the latter is vague and needs further explanation.

Tax Exempt

People think of tax exempt in different ways. Some will think of tax exempt as it relates to sales tax. Others think tax exempt means not paying income tax. Neither of these perspectives is precise enough to be accurate.

Sales Tax

Sales tax is levied by state and local governments, not by the federal government. Being exempt from income taxes does not make the church exempt from sales tax laws. Each state will have its own set of laws regarding whether churches pay sales tax on goods and services they purchase. If the state does not require churches to pay sales tax on purchases, most likely the church will need to make application for a sales-tax-exemption license. That number is then provided to vendors at the time of purchase.

Regardless, most states require churches to collect sales tax on goods sold, and in some states, on services provided. For example, if a church provides counseling services for a fee, some states will require the church to collect and remit sales tax. The treasurer of the church should become familiar with the state and local sales tax laws as they relate to the payment of sales tax and the collection of sales tax.

Unrelated Business Income Tax (UBIT)

Unrelated business income [tax] is the income from a trade or business regularly conducted by an exempt organization and not substantially related to the performance by the organization of its exempt purpose or function, except that the organization uses the profits derived from this activity.

The term "trade or business" generally includes any activity conducted for the production of income from selling goods or performing services. An activity does not lose its identity as a trade or business merely because it is conducted within a larger group of similar activities that may or may not be related to the exempt purposes of the organization.

. . .

A business activity is not substantially related to an organization's exempt purpose if it does not contribute importantly to accomplishing that purpose (other than through the production of funds).[38]

The vestry, treasurer, finance committee, or others who are considering a fund-raising activity or other venture should carefully examine *IRS Publication 598, Tax on Unrelated Business Income of Exempt Organizations.*[39] It contains pages of examples of unrelated business incomes and pages of exclusions. Many times *how* an activity is conducted will determine its taxability. With a little flexibility in design and execution, an otherwise taxable activity may be excludable. However, the penalties for not filing a 990-T and paying tax on UBIT are severe. If there is any question or doubt about whether your event is taxable, consult a CPA specializing in NFP before conducting the activity.

---

38. *IRS Publication 598, Tax on Unrelated Business Income of Exempt Organizations* (Washington, D.C.: Internal Revenue Service, 2012), p. 3.

39. *IRS Publication 598, Tax on Unrelated Business Income of Exempt Organizations* (Washington, D.C.: Internal Revenue Service, 2012).

The current threshold amount for reporting and paying taxes on UBIT is only $1,000 gross (not net) income. This is not per fund-raising activity, but the total for the year from all activities. Some of the many activities that could generate potential UBIT liability are:

- Sale of advertising in bulletins, newsletters, magazines, or websites
- Sale of merchandise and publications (including cookbooks), if they do not have a substantial relationship to the exempt purposes of the organization
- Rental income on property, if the property has a mortgage
- Charging for the use of the parking lot

Rental management is not the purpose of a church, so if the church rents property to a local individual or other entity, it falls under UBIT rules. But, there is a loophole if the property is not mortgaged. If the parking lot is not mortgaged and is leased to a third party who charges daily parking to the general public, it is not taxable. If the parking lot is mortgaged, it is taxable, per IRS code.

Incidental fund-raising activities that do not have a material impact on the church monetarily are probably not going to invite inquiry by the IRS. There are criteria for fund-raising events that are not considered to require UBIT, but all of the conditions must be met:

All of the goods sold must be donated.

- All workers at the event must be volunteers (not employees of the church volunteering their time).
- No single item can be sold for more than $9.60 (inflation adjusted annually).
- Gross income for the year must be less than $1,000.
- The activity must not be conducted regularly.

You may have a bake sale, bazaar, raffle, cookbook sale, or other fundraiser and may not have to pay taxes as long as the unrelated activities are not a substantial part of the organization's activities. In addition, they would have to also avoid meeting the next three tests. The income from such activities will be subject to the UBIT if the following three conditions are met:

- The activity constitutes a trade or business.
- The trade or business is regularly carried on.
- The trade or business is not substantially related to the organization's exempt purpose. (The fact that the organization uses the income to

further its charitable or religious purposes does not make the activity substantially related to its exempt purposes.)

The penalty is severe for not paying the UBIT tax. Basically, the IRS goes back and taxes your organization for all years the activity occurred, with no statute of limitations. In addition, in egregious situations NFP status may be revoked.

Stand-alone Organization vs. Church-Affiliated Organization

Generally, if a church-affiliated organization uses the church's Federal Employer Identification Number (FEIN), they follow the tax laws as they apply to the church. (Think of the FEIN as the corporate version of a person's Social Security number.) Church-affiliated organizations can include camps, preschools, schools, hospitals, soup kitchens, thrift stores, and bookstores. Of course, any of those could be stand-alone organizations, too.

If an organization has its own separate FEIN, that organization may or may not be tax exempt and is a stand-alone organization from the church. Indications of income tax exempt status are an IRS form 1023 previously filed, the resulting determination letter from the IRS, and a separate FEIN that establishes the organization as a separate entity from the parish. Further, a separate incorporation of the organization with the Secretary of State should be on file. Consider the following situation of Church of the Holy Smoke™ Preschool:

Scenario: Separate Entity?

Background The Church of the Holy Smoke™ Preschool has been open for twenty-five years. From just a few students in the beginning to more than 125 today, it has grown to meet the needs of the community. It is located on the same property as Church of the Holy Smoke™. It shares the same signage on the road and the same driveway into the property, and connects to the church parish hall by a covered walkway. In the community, the preschool is instantly recognized as connected to the church, because they have the same name and address.

Operational expenses The preschool started as a quasi-mission to the community, but also as a vehicle for identifying new members. The preschool is regarded as a marketing tool by the church, as many new communicants are families who first started taking their children there. The church supports the preschool by paying the electricity, water, Internet, cable, and telephone bills as a part of the church's budget. The bills come directly to the parish administrator. Even the phones at the preschool are extensions of the phone system at the church.

The preschool pays the administrative staff and teachers' salaries by reimbursing the church for them. The church includes the teachers and staff in the church's 941, W2, and 1099 filings by using the church's FEIN for payroll only. The preschool uses most of its funds from tuition for salary reimbursement, cleaning and supplies, books, tables, chairs, and videos for the classroom. The preschool collects its own tuition, makes its own deposits, and has its own checking account in the name of Church of the Holy Smoke™ Preschool. When the preschool is not in session on the weekends, the building doubles as Sunday school space.

Organization and legal   The preschool is a separate corporation registered with the state. It files its own IRS Form 990 with its own FEIN (but uses the church's FEIN for payroll). According to the Corporations Division of the Secretary of State website, the rector at Church of the Holy Smoke™ is the CEO of the not-for-profit Church of the Holy Smoke™ Preschool, Inc. The treasurer at Church of the Holy Smoke™ is the CFO of the corporation, and the preschool director is the corporation's secretary. A board of directors consists of parents and the corporate officers. The board makes decisions on all financial and operational matters for the preschool.

Analysis   This is not a good situation. While there is a legally established separate corporation, it appears to be a thinly veiled attempt by an attorney to limit the liability of the church from the preschool by establishing a separate corporate entity. This is the argument the IRS would likely make:

1. All the employees of the preschool are paid by the church by using the church's FEIN for payroll. The fact that the tuition is used to reimburse the church is not relevant.
2. The church pays the pension of the preschool employees at nine percent to the Church Pension Group with no reimbursement from the preschool.
3. Most of the operating expenses are paid for by the church. The rest of the tuition is used for program and furnishings.
4. Two of the three legal corporate positions are the same as the church— CEO of the preschool corporation is the rector of the church, and the treasurer of the preschool corporation is the treasurer of the church. Only the secretary of the preschool corporation is different—the preschool director.

5. The signage, logos, and lettering are all the same at the street. In fact, the sign says: Church of the Holy Smoke™ and Preschool, giving the appearance as being one single entity.
6. The preschool is on property owned by the church and pays no rent.
7. The building is not a single-use building, but was built as a Sunday school classroom building and is still used for that purpose today.
8. The buildings are of the same architecture and physically adjoined.
9. The phones are answered by the parish secretary, with no direct phone line or number for the preschool.
10. The preschool would not have enough funds to operate a stand-alone company, as its revenue only pays for less than half its expenses. If fair market value rent were paid, the preschool could only pay twenty percent of its expenses from its revenues.

A similar list would probably be included in any legal attempt to pierce the protection of the corporate veil of a separate corporation and include the church in any legal action against the preschool. The separate corporation was created strictly as a limitation of liability on the part of the church for running a preschool. My opinion is that the church is not likely protected for the reasons above. My recommendations are either:

• The corporation is dissolved and the church takes the preschool back into its organization, pays the insurance rates through Church Insurance Companies, and adequately insures against loss. (The Church Insurance Companies have a number of recommendations regarding a preschool and the protection from liability, such as the Safeguarding God's Children program.)
• The church removes the preschool from the property, creating a clearly visible separation so that the casual observer recognizes two different organizations. If left at the property, signage, infrastructure, and all costs—including payroll and rent to the church at fair market value for commercial real estate in the area—shall be paid for by the preschool only. This would mean significantly increasing the tuition, probably six hundred percent. The legal officers of the corporation are all non-church members.

This gets complicated when entities are formed unnaturally to achieve an improper purpose. It is important for tax purposes to understand that the IRS has its own set of rules regarding taxation that override many other legal situations. When talking about taxes, we need to look to the IRS for information.

Scenario: Thrift Store—A Separate Entity?

Background Church of the Holy Smoke™ Thrift Store began as an outreach to the poor in the community. A strip mall of four shops and its parking lot were left to the church in a bequest from a lifelong parishioner. The church leases three of the four shop spaces (now one large contiguous space) to a national NFP organization. The last shop is used by the thrift store.

Operations Unless a holiday intervenes, the thrift store is open weekly. Every Monday, the thrift store is open to accept donations of goods. These goods are sorted and priced, generally by a single individual who does this as a donation of her time. On Tuesdays and Fridays, the thrift store is open for business to sell good, well-maintained items of clothing, books, music, and bric-a-brac. Each item on the shelves has a price tag placed there during the pricing exercise on Monday. Some items that are donated are visibly used or not in a good state of repair. Many of these items are simply given away to people, many homeless, who come to the back door of the store on Monday afternoons. Other items are offered to larger thrift stores, as they have the ability to repair items. Some are simply discarded, if not usable.

The thrift store had trouble finding and keeping enough dedicated volunteers from within Church of the Holy Smoke™ to maintain operations, so they enlisted the aid of several other churches in town. The thrift store now has over sixty volunteers from various denominations who come in pairs to make up a crew of four each day the thrift store is open. Often, the thrift store is staffed by retired couples. A schedule for volunteer rotation is kept by the president of the board of directors who contacts the volunteers to fill the time slots needed.

There is no cash register, and sales tax is not paid to the state. There is a sales receipt book, but since returns are not accepted, the book is only filled out if a customer asks for a receipt. Consequently, there are few records of sales transactions. The till is a cigar box kept under the counter. Anyone volunteering in the store can make a sale, accept money, and make change from the cigar box. Sometimes if a customer has only a limited amount of money but the need is great, discounts are given on a per-case basis. Anyone working in the store can make that decision.

One of the couples or an individual picks up the bank bag from the bank and brings it to the store each Tuesday and Friday. This is the starting amount for the cigar box. Only the bills arrive in the bank bag, as all coinage is kept from one day to the next in a coin tray. At the end of the day, the bills, and any coins overflowing the tray (a rare occurrence), are taken back to the bank for deposit into the thrift store account. All but the fixed till amount is taken from the bag by the bank and deposited. The store key is kept in the bank bag for the next couple when they pick up the bank bag for the next business day, but most volunteers have one anyway.

Operational expenses   The thrift store has its own checking account into which the money is deposited. It pays its own utilities, but has no other expenses, as all the goods are donated and there are no salaries. Only the director of the thrift store has the checkbook and receives all the bank statements. There is no reporting to Church of the Holy Smoke™.

Organization and legal   The thrift store is an outreach of the church. Accordingly, the thrift store used the FEIN of the church to open its bank account. It has a board of directors comprised of interested individuals in the community. They meet twice each year to disburse their profits to needy individuals, local charities, sick and suffering persons, and organizations such as the Red Cross. These funds are disbursed directly to the recipients. Various volunteers nominate recipients of the disbursements.

The thrift store has done well over the years, and has a certificate of deposit in reserve totaling $22,000.

Analysis   The thrift store may be in trouble for not collecting sales tax and remitting it to the state. State laws are beyond the scope of this book, so be sure to inquire of your applicable local and state sales tax requirements from your taxing authorities. The problems posed by the way this operation is conducted are:

1. Separate board of directors is comprised mostly of individuals who are not members of the church.
2. The accumulation of direct earnings from an affiliated organization is likely to require the filing of an IRS 990-T by the church and paying income tax on the earnings (UBIT).
3. Direct payment of funds to individuals rather than other 501(c)3 organizations is not permissible coming from the thrift store bank account as a charitable deduction for the purposes of UBIT.
4. The state may have laws that require a cash register or other record of all sales transactions.
5. The thrift store may need to keep a record of all donations of goods, including a description of each item, its condition, estimated value, and sales price; in other words, keep an inventory of items in accord with state law.

The best thing the church can do, and should do, is to run the thrift store as a part of the outreach commission. There should not be a separate bank account. Any deposits should be made as a deposit designated for the outreach commission. Under the IRS definition of charitable purposes, donations to individuals are possible (although I do not recommend giving money directly to individuals. See chapter 4.). You should have identified a number of holes in the internal control of the scenario as well.

Scenario: Consignment Sales, Unrelated Business Income Tax

Background   Church of the Holy Smoke's™ preschool has a consignment sale every spring and every fall. They have been doing this for the last twenty-five years. Everyone looks forward to the sale, and a big white banner with letters three feet tall is hung from one end of the building to the other so anyone passing by cannot help but see it. There are people who are regular consignors who come year after year to sell clothing, electronics, handmade items, and all sorts of things. The event is held in the parish hall, and some four hundred tables are decked with consigned goods. It is held on a Saturday from 9 a.m. to 4 p.m., but setting up the sale starts the prior Monday.

Operations   The consignors bring their goods to their assigned tables, set their prices, and mark their goods. On Saturday, when a patron selects an item to purchase, the item is taken to the cash register near the exit. The purchase is made at the marked price. The preschool staff runs the cash register and manages the consignment sale. At the end of the day, the sales for each consignor's booth are totaled, and seventy percent of the purchase price is given to the consignor, while the preschool keeps thirty percent.

As this consignment sale has been conducted for years, it has come to be the social event of the weekend and draws a large crowd. The average net income is $40,000 per event, or $80,000 per year. This represents roughly seventy-five percent of the total net income of the preschool and about half of its total income. The other half is from tuition.

Analysis   The following is an excerpt from a letter to the Church of the Holy Smoke™ from their CPA:

> As previously mentioned in the letters to management during our audits of the financial statements of the years ended December 31, 20WX and 20XX, our opinion is that the current and past structure of the Preschool's Consignment Sales are problematic as potentially being interpreted by the Internal Revenue Service (IRS) as unrelated business income. If the gross income is more than $1,000 in a year, then the requirement is to file a 990-T.

> Feeder organizations, such as preschools, thrift houses, and others that provide funds to a parent or other organization are not exempt from taxation.

Two of the exceptions are when the work is performed by volunteers and when the goods are donated. It is our opinion that the Preschool Consignment Sale does not meet these two conditions for exemption under the present structure of the sale.

From the IRS Fact Sheet, Reporting Auction Income and the Tax Gap:

"Many [churches] don't realize the income they earn from auctions and consignment sales may be taxable.

What's Taxable

All income from auctions, traditional or online, and consignment sales is generally taxable unless certain exceptions are met. This income is usually considered either "business" or "ordinary" income. In certain circumstances such income can qualify for capital gain treatment. There are also some exceptions where income can be excluded from taxable income.

Business income resulting from an auction or consignment sale is subject to the same taxes as the income of any other retail or service business. That may include income tax, self-employment tax, employment tax, or excise tax.

Income resulting from auctions akin to an occasional garage or yard sale is generally not required to be reported. However, there may be exceptions. If an online garage sale turns into a business with recurring sales and purchasing of items for resale, it may be considered an online auction business."[40]

Based on our understanding of the Consignment Sale, the following are problematic:

1. The acquisition of goods—The very word consignment means the offering of goods for sale that were purchased. In fact, the goods are purchased from the consignors for 70 percent of the purchase price. The sequence of the transactions does not alter the facts.
2. The use of employees—school and church employees conduct the sale.
3. The sale of goods, such as work clothes—not for use in furthering the business.
4. Sale to customers—the general public is invited to the event as any store.
5. Use of the net proceeds of the sale for operations—greater than 10 percent.

---

40. IRS, Reporting Auction Income and the Tax Gap, FS-2007-23 can be retrieved at http://www.irs.gov/uac/Reporting-Auction-Income-and-the-Tax-Gap

6. The activity conducted on a consistent basis—twice per year, year after year

Not all fund-raising activities are subject to UBIT. If in doubt, it is best to contact a CPA that specializes in UBIT, and IRS tax regulations surrounding not-for-profit organizations.

Scenario: Rental Property

Church of the Holy Smoke is located in downtown Paxtown. It occupies one-half of a city block. Recently, the building housing the Big Bank, which occupies the other half of the block, became available for sale. Big Bank wanted to get out of the real estate business, and was selling the bank building and offering a twenty-year leaseback. How could the vestry lose? Besides, the building was of the same time period, and the architecture matched the church. There were additional offices and conference rooms on the upper floors that were leased to local small business and professional persons (insurance agents, attorneys, accountants, realtors). In the remaining empty space the church could establish additional formation classrooms and conference rooms.

The vestry had received an endowment that provided $800,000 of the $1,000,000 purchase price, and with the rent guarantees from the bank, financing of the remaining $200,000 and making monthly payments was more than workable from a cash flow standpoint.

The deal was done, and everything looked good. However, at the end of the year, Big Bank sent a 1099 for the rent paid to the church of about $100,000. In July, a letter came from the IRS deeming the entire transaction to be the establishment of a 501(c)(4) Private Foundation. (A Private Foundation pays hefty taxes.) At the next vestry meeting, there ensued a discussion about whether this was a Private Foundation or unrelated business income.

Analysis There is a quirk in the tax code. The problem with the above scenario is that there is a mortgage on the building. "Rents from real property, including elevators and escalators, are excluded in computing unrelated business taxable income. Rents from personal property are not excluded. However, special rules apply to 'mixed leases' of both real and personal property. This exclusion does not apply to debt-financed income (producing real property) . . . "[41] The moral of the story is: If you rent a building or parking lot, for example, be sure there is no debt financing on the property.

---

41. *IRS Publication 598: Tax on Unrelated Business Income of Exempt Organizations* (Washington, D.C.: Internal Revenue Service, 2012), p. 9.

Employee Taxes

Determining Who Is an Employee

An area of potential disfavor with the IRS is payroll taxes. One example is paying someone who is in the eyes of the IRS an employee as if they were a 1099 contractor. The IRS determines who is an employee on a case-by-case basis using the common law definition of an employee. There are three major elements that help in determining a common law employee—behavioral control, financial control, and relationship. Each has subsidiary elements that help determine if one of the common law employer-employee conditions exist. Not all conditions need to be present to determine a person is an employee. Even one element being present could cause the IRS to rule in favor of an employer-employee relationship given other circumstances in a particular instance.

Behavioral Control   Behavioral control refers to facts that show whether there is a right to direct or control how the worker does the work. A worker is an employee when the business has the right to direct and control the worker. The business does not have to actually direct or control the way the work is done—as long as the employer has the right to direct and control the work. The behavioral control factors fall into the categories of:

- Type of instructions given
- Degree of instruction
- Evaluation systems
- Training

Types of instructions given   An employee is generally subject to the business's instructions about when, where, and how to work. All of the following are examples of types of instructions about how to do work.

- When and where to do the work
- What tools or equipment to use
- What workers to hire or to assist with the work
- Where to purchase supplies and services
- What work must be performed by a specified individual
- What order or sequence to follow when performing the work

Financial Control   Another test the IRS will use to determine if an individual is an employee is financial control. Does the worker pay his or her own expenses out of pocket (presumably from the pay received from the church), or is the worker reimbursed for expenses? Does the worker bring his or her own tools, computers, or other equipment, or does the church provide them? Does the worker have a webpage or an online ad, or use a contract for time and materials, or is the church the only place this person works? Does the church pay the worker on a percentage of completion basis, or when the job is finished, or do they pay him or her every time he or she works?

Financial control refers to facts that show whether or not the business has the right to control the economic aspects of the worker's job.

Type of Relationship   The IRS examines the relationship between the church and the other party. If the church directs the activities of the individual on a regular basis, then the church exerts a level of influence that is more than a casual contractor relationship. Type of relationship refers to facts that show how the worker and business perceive their relationship to each other. If there is or is not a written contract does not determine the relationship. How the parties actually work together determines whether an employer relationship exists. Does the employer offer benefits that are commonly afforded employees? Is the relationship for an indefinite period of time or for a specific project? Does the worker provide services that are key to the business and does the business have the right to direct and control the worker's activities?

Besides the common law tests for employer-employee relationship, there is one situation that could arise in a church that determines if a person is a statutory employee rather than a contractor regardless of meeting the common law tests for a contractor. That occurs when a person works at home on materials or goods that are supplied by the church and that must be returned to the church, if the church also furnishes specifications for the work to be done.

Scenario: Church Sexton

The Church of the Holy Smoke™ had the same sexton for decades. Eventually, he became frail and could not work every day. Because he lived at or below the poverty level, the church had never given him a W-2; they provided him with a 1099, and sometimes not even that. Many times over the years, the rector took money out of his pocket or the discretionary account and gave it to the sexton. This money never made it onto the 1099. The church had never provided him a pension capability and felt remorse when he could no longer work.

But the vestry thought they had a solution. Remember the thrift store? The sexton also cleaned the thrift store next door. When he retired, the thrift store board, with the church's knowledge, began paying the sexton a pension. It said so in the vestry minutes, and even on the pension check's memo line. The sexton lived another three years, and was at least comfortable with his pension from the church.

Analysis Was the sexton an employee? Yes. The church provided him the tools with which to work, compensated him for his time and efforts, and directed his every action. With the pension, what did the church do? Even though the sexton would have been considered an employee of the church anyway, they reaffirmed it with the pension.

Other employee relationships may exist. Nursery workers, preschool, or school workers may be employees if the conditions are such that they meet some of the tests above. Likewise, summer camp workers probably do, too.

So what is the big deal? The issue is that if a person is an employee and not a contractor, then there are withholding, FICA, State Unemployment Tax (SUTA), Federal Unemployment Tax (FUTA), workman's compensation coverage, and tax filing and payment requirements that have probably been violated if the employee is given a 1099 rather than a W-2 Wage and Tax Statement at year-end. For an Episcopal parish, there are also benefit requirements that may have been missed in the form of pension and healthcare.

The IRS is unrelenting about employee taxes, and the penalties and interest they impose. There is a further implication for the vestry, bookkeeper, or anyone connected with the decision to file a 1099 instead of a W-2. The IRS will hold the vestry liable and, in this one instance, those who were on the vestry at the time the misrepresentation as a 1099, instead of a W-2, employee was made. It gets worse if the IRS decides those involved in the decision to use a 1099 did so deliberately to avoid the church paying its share of the taxes. That is tax evasion, and that is how the feds got Al Capone. There is no amount of grief worth not classifying an employee appropriately and paying the tax.

The employer is considered a trustee of federal trust funds—amounts withheld from employees and amounts due from the employer. The rationale is that those funds are for social security, Medicare, and federal income taxes, and are considered to be held in trust for the U.S. Department of the Treasury until timely and full remittance on a predetermined schedule. Woe to those who deliberately fail to file and pay. They are now potentially personally liable for the amount due plus a one hundred percent penalty. The IRS can choose to assess the individual(s) involved and not the church. Once the IRS shows the court the penalty is due, the burden of proof rests with the defendant, not the prosecution (IRS).

Trust fund recovery penalty. If income, social security, and Medicare taxes that a corporation must withhold from employee wages are not withheld or are not deposited or paid to the United States Treasury, the trust fund recovery penalty may apply. The penalty is the full amount of the Income

Tax, Information and Other Returns, to request an unpaid trust fund tax. This penalty may apply to you if these unpaid taxes cannot be immediately collected from the business.

The trust fund recovery penalty may be imposed on all persons who are determined by the IRS to be responsible for paying the tax for collecting, accounting for, and paying these taxes, and who acted willfully in not doing so.

A responsible person can be an officer or employee of a corporation, an accountant, or a volunteer director/trustee. A responsible person also may include one who signs checks for the corporation or otherwise has authority to cause the spending of business funds.[42] (emphasis added)

Based on the above, I hope you see that simply giving someone a 1099 instead of a W-2, failing to file and pay withholding taxes on time, or failing to report wages to an employee is a serious offense. Notice that any member of the vestry, staff, or volunteer is liable. When it comes to payroll taxes, the IRS will go back as many years as they can determine the tax due and come after anyone who can pay.

Other Taxes

Here are some of the IRS publications that a church may need during the year. There may be others. These publications change constantly, are superseded, deleted, or new ones added. Be sure to get tax assistance from a CPA who specializes in the area of taxation in question. Initial investigation into the tax topic of interest begins with a visit to www.irs.gov and the search engine there.

In addition, the Church Pension Group issues several publications that are updated at least annually, and are also good resources for the summarization of many of the publications above. As the Web pages change frequently, it is best to go to the homepage of Church Pension Group (www.cpg.org) and use the search engine there to locate the most recent publication. Some applicable publications are:

- Clergy Tax Guide
- Federal Reporting Requirements for Episcopal Churches
- Small Employer Tax Credit Memo

42. *IRS Publication 542: Corporations* (Washington, D.C.: Internal Revenue Service, 2012), p. 6.

SOME COMMON IRS PUBLICATIONS APPLICABLE TO A CHURCH

Publications

15	Employer's Tax Guide
15A	Employer's Supplemental Tax Guide
15B	Employer's Guide to Fringe Benefits
505	Tax Withholding and Estimated Tax
509	Tax Calendars
515	Withholding Tax on Nonresident Aliens and Foreign Entities
517	Social Security and Other Information for Members of the Clergy & Religious Workers
525	Taxable and Nontaxable Income
526	Charitable Contributions
538	Accounting Periods and Methods
551	Basis of Assets
557	Tax Exempt Status for Your Organization
561	Determining the Value of Donated Property
571	Tax-Sheltered Annuity Plans (403(b) Plans) For Employees of ... Certain Tax-Exempt Organizations
575	Pension and Annuity Income
598	Unrelated Business Income Tax
946	How to Depreciate Property
966	Electronic Choices to Pay All your Federal Taxes
969	Health Savings Accounts and Other Tax-Favored Health Plans
1518	IRS Tax Calendar for Small Businesses and Self-Employed
1542	Per Diem Rates (For Travel Within the Continental United States)
1771	Charitable Contributions - Substantiation and Disclosure Requirements
1779	Independent Contractor or Employee Brochure
1828	Tax Guide for Churches and Religious Organizations
1932	How to Make Correct Federal Tax Deposits (FTD)
3079	Gaming Publication for Tax-Exempt Organizations
3637	Exempt Organization's Introductory Brochure
4220	Applying for 501(c)3 Status
4221-NC	Compliance Guide for Tax Exempt Organizations
4302	A Charity's Guide to Vehicle Donations
4303	A Donor's Guide to Vehicle Donations
4341	Information Guide for Employers Filing Form 941 or Form 944 - Frequently Asked Questions About the Reclassification of Workers as Employees
4573	Group Exemptions
4862	Small Business Health Care Tax Credit Flyer

Notices

844	Federal Tax Obligations of Non-Profit Corporations
931	Deposit Requirements for Employments Taxes
989	Commonly Asked Questions When IRS Determines Your Work Status as "Employee"
1360	New Donor Record Keeping Rule
1422	Extension of the 4.2% Employee Social Security Tax for Employee Wages

Forms

1099-MISC	Statement for Recipients of Miscellaneous Income
940	Employer's Annual Federal Unemployment (FUTA) Tax Return
941	Employer's Quarterly Federal Tax Return
944	Employer's Annual Federal Tax Return
W-2	Wage and Tax Statement
W-3	Transmittal of Wage and Tax Statements
W-4	Employee's Withholding Allowance Certificate
W-9	Request for Taxpayer Identification Number and Certification
990	Return of Organization Exempt From Income Tax
990-T	Exempt Organization Business Income Tax Return
1023	Application for Recognition of Exemption Under Section 501(c)(3) of the Internal Revenue Code

Some Common IRS Publications Applicable to a Church

Clergy Compensation

Tax laws, particularly as they relate to personal income tax, change constantly. The information in this book should be regarded as general in nature and not be used to prepare tax returns. Always consult a CPA for professional assistance each year, as clergy personal income taxes are unlike any others. Always go to www.cpg.org for the latest version of *20XX Tax Guide for Episcopal Ministers for 20XW Returns*. You can call the authors of the Guide for consultation for:

- Tax return preparation questions
- Compensation packages for new positions
- Housing allowance explanations
- Advantages of reimbursable expense allowances
- Saving through the RSVP program
- Taxes after retirement

Clergy are a hybrid type of employee. While the church issues them a W-2, the church is not required to withhold FICA, unless requested by the clergy on the W-4, Withholding and Exemptions form. If the clergy does have FICA withheld, it is credited to the SECA that clergy are required to pay as self-employed. If that sounds confusing, it is.

Clergy Wages

Clergy salaries paid by churches are presumed by the IRS to be for the purpose of conducting religious services and other pastoral duties. If an ordained individual gets a job at a local business besides the one at the church, the local job is considered outside the boundaries of pastoral duties. The distinction is important because clergy, when being paid for performing pastoral duties, are exempt from FICA (Federal Insurance Contributions Act). When they are performing a secular job, they pay FICA and are subject to withholding of taxes. However, clergy do pay self-employment tax, SECA (Self Employment Contributions Act), on their earnings in their religious vocation.

Clergy are considered self-employed for the purposes of withholding. That means that the church is not obligated to withhold federal, state, or SECA taxes from their paycheck. The unusual part is that their salary still gets reported on a W-2 rather than a 1099. However, the clergy can file a W-4 with the church or church organization and elect to have federal, state, or SECA taxes withheld. Then the church is obligated to withhold, report, and pay them along with the non-clergy employees. SECA is calculated at the time the clergy files their tax return. Any withholding is applied to any taxes due at that time or refunded.

Purse or Love Gift

The assistant rector of Church of the Holy Smoke™ was leaving to become rector at another church. She had been at Church of the Holy Smoke™ for several years, was well liked, but deserving of the new role. The senior warden thought it fitting to send her off with a gift of money from a special collection designated for that purpose. The response was overwhelming and $20,000 was collected for the "purse." Parishioners used every method of payment, including collection plate, walk-in, online credit card, PayPal, and mail.

Since that was a special collection and a gift to the assistant, is the money taxable? Yes, as wages, and appears in box 1 of the W-2 along with the rest of the salary paid that year. In addition, the assistant rector will pay SECA, federal, and state tax on the additional $20,000 as if it had been a part of her salary, because in the view of the IRS, it is part of her salary. Being a special collection has nothing to do with any tax determination. What if the church calculates the additional tax and adds that to the purse to ease the burden? That additional amount is also taxable to the assistant rector. That means that some part of the donations went to pay taxes, not to benevolence for the clergy.

There are several problems with the above scenario that makes the income taxable to the assistant rector:

1. The assistant rector is still in the employ of the church or recently left, and the IRS views the purse as compensation for prior services performed by the assistant rector.
2. The church collected the money and paid it to the assistant, thereby passing the money through the church's books. Is that not what happens every day and twice on Sunday in the normal course of business of the church? Yes. The IRS does not view the purpose for which the money was collected as having any bearing on the determination that it was anything other than business as usual.
3. The collection gave the appearance that it was sanctioned and operated by the church (in this case it was). The bulletin, the bi-weekly newsletter, a letter from the rector and senior warden, e-mails, announcements from the ambo, and the bulletin board in the parish hall were all used to advertise the special collection.

There is a way around this, but it is precarious at best. If a parishioner not in any official capacity—that is, only a pew dweller and nothing else—advertised and collected the money on his or her own without the use of church assets, the gift would be private individual gifts outside the realm of wages. The donors could also give the money directly to the assistant rector. The assistant rector would have to be careful to deposit the money into a personal checking account and not one belonging to the church.

Allowances and Expenses

Critical vestry requirement   Some members of the clergy receive a housing allowance, car allowance, or other stipends intended to cover expenses. If not properly declared and paid, the church can cause a potentially devastating tax problem for the clergy. The problem is avoidable, but totally in the hands of the vestry. *Prior to* the first paycheck of a newly-arriving clergy at the parish, and *prior to* the start of every subsequent year thereafter, the vestry must make the determination regarding how much of the compensation package is salary and how much is allowance.

The December vestry meeting is probably the last chance to do this. Otherwise, the IRS will deem all of the allowance to be ordinary income (Box 1 of the W-2). The worst part is that no deductions would be allowed for housing, car, etc. for the entire taxable year. There is no opportunity to correct a mistake. If the vestry does not make this designation, documenting it in the minutes dated before the issuance of the first paycheck or first paycheck of subsequent years (even if nothing has changed), and providing a copy of the minutes to the cleric, the entire amount will be taxable. If the cleric were audited by the IRS, and had a housing, car, meal, or other allowance, the IRS would ask to see the minutes in which those were approved prior to the commencement of employment and prior to the commencement of the first payroll in January each year thereafter. My recommendation is that the vestry use a resolution process that highlights the documentation of their decision. For example:

Be it resolved that the vestry of the Church of the Holy Smoke™, desirous in providing for the welfare of its rector, do hereby resolve this 23rd day of November, 20XX, that the compensation of the rector for the year beginning January 1, 20XY consists of the following:

Salary	$50,000
Housing Allowance	30,000
Car Allowance	3,600
Total Annual Compensation	$86,600

Signed: Senior Warden   Signed: Treasurer
Date: November 23, 20XX   Date: November 23, 20XX

Housing allowance   Even if everything is handled correctly, the allowances are taxable under certain conditions. All of the housing allowance is taxed for the purposes of SECA. The housing allowance is taxable, but there are expenses that are uniquely deductible to the extent of the housing allowance. This is another uniqueness of taxes related to clergy. If the deductible expenses do not exceed the amount of the housing allowance, that remaining portion is taxable as ordinary income. It is the responsibility of the clergy to take those deductions on their tax return. There is a place on the W-2 that is provided for including the amount of the housing allowance separately from the wages.

Church-owned housing   The fair rental value, including furnishings, plus utilities must be included in the calculation for SECA by clerics at the time they file their taxes.

Car expenses   The IRS uses the terms *accountable* and *non-accountable* to determine whether the clergy is being reimbursed for expenses or given a car allowance. *Accountable* basically means that the clergyperson must account for expenses according to IRS guidelines for business expenses in the commercial environment (e.g., submission of receipts). *Non-accountable* means that there is no accounting for the purpose of reimbursement, but rather the clergy is given a fixed amount each month and not required to submit an expense report or receipts.

1. Accountable. The church can help the cleric by requiring complete documentation before paying the reimbursement. This is a policy decision by the vestry that should be made for everyone seeking reimbursement for expenses from the church, including clergy.

Accountable expense reimbursement must follow IRS business expense guidelines for documentation

- Receipts
- Purpose
- Participants
- Location
- Date
- Nature of the discussion

In the accountable plan, there are specific requirements for receipts. Failure to keep the detailed information and receipts required will cause the IRS to disallow the expenses deducted. However, the reimbursement will still count as income. A receipt and the items above are required.

Some may wonder about the term *nature of the discussion*. This does not mean a full disclosure of the content of the conversation. However, an appropriate nature of discussion is marital counseling or personal counseling. There is no reason to reveal confidential information.

2. Non-accountable. The non-accountable plan means that the cleric does not have to keep receipts to be reimbursed by the church. The church will automatically pay the allowance amount, usually each month. However, the cleric will need to keep the receipts in the manner described above to be able to deduct the expenses from the income.

An allowance of most any kind is income. It is just that as clergy the IRS is clear about what is tax deductible and how that must be documented.

Donor records   Donors are ultimately responsible for keeping accurate records of donations in proper form and substance for the IRS to allow the deductions.

A donor cannot claim a tax deduction for any single contribution of $250 or more unless the donor obtains a contemporaneous, written acknowledgment of the contribution from the recipient church or religious organization. A church or religious organization that does not acknowledge a contribution incurs no penalty; but without a written acknowledgment, the donor cannot claim a tax deduction. Although it is a donor's responsibility to obtain a written acknowledgment, a church or religious organization can assist the donor by providing a timely, written statement containing the following information:
  • Name of the church or religious organization
  • Date of the contribution
  • Amount of any cash contribution
  • Description (but not the value) of non-cash contributions

In addition, the timely, written statement must contain one of the following:
  • Statement that no goods or services were provided by the church or religious organization in return for the contribution,
  • Statement that goods or services that a church or religious organization provided in return for the contribution consisted entirely of intangible religious benefits, or
  • Description and good faith estimate of the value of goods or services other than intangible religious benefits that the church or religious organization provided in return for the contribution.[43]

43. *IRS Publication 1828: Tax Guide for Churches and Religious Organizations* (Washington, D.C.: Internal Revenue Service, 2011), p. 24.

This means that every time someone makes a cash or cash equivalent donation, the church has to acknowledge it in writing. When this ruling first came out, common wisdom was that it meant making out receipts every week for every donor making a donation of over $250. The IRS quickly issued a (non-binding) opinion that listing each separate donation over $250 on the quarterly and/or annual contribution letter given to all donors would suffice. When the church does provide the documentation of a donation (of any type, cash or property), the church must supply the information shown above, including name of the church and date of contribution.

Quid pro quo   When there is a donation that exceeds $75 (not $250) in the context of a fund-raising event, the church must make a statement about how much is a donation, and how much covered the cost of the meal, for example, or other benefit. My church has a Valentine's Day dinner-dance costing $100 per couple. Since filet and lobster tails are the fare, a sizable amount of the donation is actually a quid pro quo for the meal, DJ, and other expenses. The church, in that case, must list on a ticket, or better, on the charitable contribution statement, that the $100 consisted of $55 for the meal and $45 in donation. The $45 is the only amount I can deduct. Now we see an IRS requirement that is placed on the church. Of course, if I wrote a $150 check on Sunday as an offering, there is no need to list the check separately on my contribution statement, but there is a need to state that all $150 was a donation. This could be done anywhere on the face of the statement for all contributions, except for those specifically identified.

Losing Not-For-Profit Status

It is possible to lose NFP status with the IRS, even if the organization is a church. The criteria to establish and maintain a NFP are:

- the organization must be organized and operated exclusively for religious, educational, scientific, or other charitable purposes
- net earnings may not inure to the benefit of any private individual or shareholder
- no substantial part of its activity may be attempting to influence legislation
- the organization may not intervene in political campaigns
- the organization's purposes and activities may not be illegal or violate fundamental public policy

Inure

The term *inure* comes from Middle English. In this sense, it means "to get benefit from." In other words, we could not start a NFP for hungry children, collect $1 million, pay ourselves $950,000, give the remaining $50,000 to Feed the Children and call the group a NFP simply because we have no money left. The IRS is attuned to this type of scheme.

Inurement is likely to occur in the context of "insiders." This means employees, owners, stockholders, and their family members cannot receive undue benefit. In church-related settings, insiders could include the priest, vestry, wardens, and in some cases, employees. Technically, a church could pay so much of its income out in a rector's salary that inurement could be construed, although it is unlikely to happen. Examples of prohibited inurement are:

- payment of dividends
- payment of unreasonable compensation to insiders
- transferring property to insiders for less than fair market value

The prohibition against inurement to insiders is absolute. Therefore, any amount of inurement is, potentially, grounds for loss of tax-exempt status. In addition, inurement could invoke excise taxes on each transaction.

Insiders are different from those who receive private benefit. Notice that it is best to give to other charitable organizations. Remember the thrift store? They gave thousands of dollars away every six months as the board was convinced of need. Some of those benefactors were "for private benefit." Hence, the better practice is to bring all the revenue to the outreach committee for disbursement according to church policy.

The issue of inurement should not be dismissed out of hand. Once inurement is deemed to have occurred, there is no gray area. Gifts of less than fair market value could be inurement. If the church owns a rectory that they gave to the rector, inurement has clearly occurred, and the consequences are ugly for all. In fact, the value of the inurement is not the deciding factor. What is implied is intent and outcome, too. If the gift, transfer, or payment were made with the intent, or eventual outcome without intent, that taxes were avoided by either the church or the individual, and if the inurement falls outside the realm of the pastoral purposes of a church, NFP status may be jeopardized.

Private interests

Churches must not provide substantial benefit to private interests. This may sound innocuous. However, consider this: A church called to ask if they should accept a $50,000 donation. The donation was being given to the church with the intention that the church would then pay an elderly relative's excess medical expenses—which amounted to $50,000. This not only sounds like money laundering on the part of the individual and the church, but tax evasion on the part of the donor. It is a substantial amount for the benefit of a private interest, and would cause the church to be in jeopardy of losing its NFP status.

Political campaigns and public policy

Corporations that are 501(c)3s cannot be involved in affecting public opinion, endorsing, providing a venue for, or by any means exercising political influence or influencing legislation. That being said, buried in the IRS publications are strict regulations for ways these corporations can participate in the political process. It is just not advisable to go in this direction. This prohibits advocating a stance that attempts to influence public opinion on any legislation, popular, controversial, ethical, or otherwise.

Remember the comments about the group determination, and that the diocese really holds the 501(c)(3)? If a church causes a loss of NFP status, since it does not have its own 501(c)(3), does it mean the diocese and every church and organization under it loses their NFP status? Theoretically, they could; the status is the result of an overt action in forming the groups and not the use of the statutory status in the IRS code. It has never come to that, but I would not want to be the one to cause it to be tested.

Tax audits of churches

Contrary to popular belief, the IRS does audit churches when there is sufficient reason. The IRS cannot choose to audit a church unless there is credible information leading it to believe there is reason to do so. Often, a credible informant provides the documentation to authorize an audit. The religious for-profit bookstore down the street may have complained to the IRS that the church had a large area for book sales open two days per week. Credible evidence may also be gained through auditing a parishioner and discovering the church is complicit in some way that raises reasonable suspicion, for example, a 1099 when a W-2 should have been issued.

In 2006, the IRS announced it was hiring an extra 7,000 agents and training them for a year. Their target was the NFP industry. Beginning with 2008, for the first time every NFP, except churches, had to file a Form 990 of one kind or another. At the end of 2010, those NFP 501(c)(3)s that had not filed for three years lost their NFP status. Every state had thousands of NFP organizations lose their status. The IRS has cleared the books of marginal NFPs. Now they can focus on what is left, and all the churches are left. I am waiting for the next shoe to drop.

CHAPTER
12
Budgets

Budgets and the budgeting process are a mystery to some vestries. To others it is rote execution for the finance committee. The remainder vacillates somewhere in between. Why do some vestries have an easy time of budgeting while others have difficulty?

Budgeting is not difficult if:

1. there is a realistic estimate of revenue
2. a budget of expenses is based on realistic expectations of revenue
3. planned expenses do not exceed the expected revenue
4. progress is clearly and honestly monitored throughout the year
5. the budgeting process requires committees and commissions to justify their needs for funds annually

The budget must reflect the financial implementation of the long-term mission of the church. If the stated objective is to involve young people from an early age through young adulthood in the life of the church, then why does the budget not reflect that? Why does it include more money for Wednesday night suppers than for EYC and youth formation materials? I am not advocating one over the other, but pointing out that the budget is an opportunity to be more about mission than money. Another way of looking at it is that money is put where the mission is. The budgeting process can be used as a catalyst to involve the church in the discussion about priorities. It can also be used as a way to meet the changing needs of the organization as new people come in, others leave, and existing members move from one stage of life to another.

The budget process can be a time for reflection on how to keep the church vibrant and conscious of its mission. Does the budget reflect the goals of the parish? With an influx of young new parents, then why is the nursery still hit-or-miss with sign-up sheets and volunteers? Why not allocate part of the budget for paid, professional nursery workers so even the most nervous parent can enjoy worship knowing his or her child is under trained supervision?

Keep in mind the budgeting process is about more than money. This is the opportunity to assess, reconsider, plan, reset, and change direction in small steps, when needed, to keep the church meeting the needs of its parishioners and the world. Budget setting should be a thoughtful, careful, and thorough process that gathers information from all relevant sources. The emphasis should be on the process. Following a process that helps the church walk through the development of a budget in a meaningful way generates a budget that is seldom altered to any great degree unless unforeseen situations arise. Constantly altering budgets in mid-stream is usually an indication of an inadequate planning process.

The same concept that applies to internal control also applies to the budget—trust the process, not the person(s). Without a process to follow in developing the budget, disagreements occur. This sets up taking sides on a range of similar interests. The next thing you know, the cleric is left wondering what happened. Why is there division in the congregation when there should be peace and harmony? For those readers who are clergy, here is some simple advice: If you stand on the sidelines and hope by some miracle that the finance committee or vestry is going to craft a budget somehow, then it is anyone's guess how useful or accurate it is going to be. Make sure there is a process in place, that it is followed, and that you stay connected to it throughout.

Vision, Mission, and Goals

If the church does not have a set of vision, mission, and goals statements, create them—before you start the budgeting process. This is not an easy process, but one that has to be done before budgeting can begin. The reason is that the vision, mission, and goals will become the arbitration anchor to which to turn when factions are competing for the same limited resources and there is not enough to go around.

The question to ask is, "which of these funding requests more closely matches our vision, mission, and goals for the church?" Do not underfund multiple projects or commissions for the sake of appeasement by spreading the limited amount of money among them. Likely, they will all fail. Fund the one that most closely matches the vision, mission, and goals that were determined before the budgeting process began. There are many books written on the subject, and I will not go into the development of vision, mission, and goals in this one.

Budgeting Processes

While there are many approaches to the budgeting process, let's examine the two most common. In the end, most churches use a combination of the two. However, in too many churches, the new budget seems to "happen" rather than be the result of a process intended to achieve certain results.

There are several characteristics of a successful budget. It must:

- be realistic and based on the best estimates of those in the best position to make the prognostication
- be consistent and represent in financial terms the mission, goals, and objectives of the church for the long-term and for the budgeted period
- be a line-item budget: every revenue and expense account in the general ledger must have a value associated with it, even if the estimated amount is zero. This zero amount represents a conscious decision by the vestry not to engage in expenditure, activity, or fund-raising in this area in the coming year for that item.
- have some amount of flexibility should conditions arise necessitating a change in the budget
- be monitored closely by the vestry, not only as a fiduciary responsibility, but also to allow adjustment based on actual revenue

There are also characteristics of budgeting that make for difficult management:

- not creating the budget using the general ledger accounts
- mathematical errors when estimating
- not being thorough in estimating all anticipated expenses
- not being realistic about expected revenues and over-projecting income
- estimating revenue based on the amount of expenditures desired rather than matching expenditures to realistic expectations of revenue
- budgeting all the revenue for expenditures, allowing no room for error or adjustment throughout the year
- assuming that the total expended for the current year is the correct amount to budget for the next year

- dividing the annual expenditure amount by twelve, not recognizing that some expenditures are annual or semi-annual and cash reserves need to be built up to pay for them
- not saving the detailed calculations for each line item for reference later in the year

General Budgeting Process

Although there are two fundamentally different approaches to budgeting, there is still basically one process. The baseline budget approach is more straightforward and does not involve as many steps as the expanded zero-budgeting approach. However, do not presume that because one approach may appear to be easier, it is the correct one for your situation. Below is the full process, after which are the two approaches.

Step 1: Evaluation   Whether it is done by the full vestry, a subset thereof, a finance committee, an interested group of people, or the bookkeeper, there needs to be some reflection regarding the prior year's results. Evaluation of the prior year involves comparing the actual revenues and expenditures to the budgeted revenues and expenditures to determine where the variances (differences) are. That is not reflection, though most will stop there. The next step is more important—to determine *why* there are variances. What caused there to be a variance in each category—plate, pledge, designated, fund-raising, or expenses. If the answer is not obvious, delve into each category, into each general ledger account code—transaction by transaction if necessary—to determine why the variances occurred.

Scenario: Impact of significant donors   Church of the Holy Smoke™ called a new rector. Within six months, the rector wanted to call an assistant rector. Since this was March and the budget did not include an assistant rector, the church made an appeal for additional financial support. Donations and pledges of $50,000 were received for the purpose of calling the assistant (designated funds, by the way, since they were pledged for a specific purpose). At the end of the year, a new budget was adopted that included the new assistant rector. However, by July of the next year, it became apparent that there was not enough support to sustain the additional position. The parish struggled the rest of the year. The only place to take the money from the budget was the diocesan commitment for the year—and that did not make the bishop happy. The assistant was let go in December.

Analysis   The vestry set up the March appeal toward the funding of the new assistant rector position as a means to determine the general support for this new post. Donations or pledges of no more than $1,000 per household were allowed, requiring fifty households to pledge before an assistant rector would be called. The assumption on the vestry's part was that the additional increased pledging would continue the next year. It did not. While there appeared to be general support for calling an assistant initially, the vestry's campaign never acknowledged the ongoing increased pledges required.

To make matters worse, three families left the church at different times throughout the next year, and each had pledged $25,000 to the general budget, creating a $75,000 shortfall. The two situations combined left the Church of the Holy Smoke™ with less overall pledged revenue than before the assistant's position was considered. Now the church is behind an entire year's annual commitment, and a new year with a new commitment is looming.

The same is true for expenditures. Any variance, positive or negative, must be understood. Sometimes it is simply caused by inflation. Sometimes it is the result of changing vendors. For example, the cleaning service may have become ineffective and a change needed. The next vendor may charge more, but do a better job. The monthly expense for that line item has now increased mid-year. If the new budget had been prepared by using the year's total expenditures for cleaning as the amount needed for the next year, the budget would be wrong. For example:

> Old Cleaning Service—6 months at $500 per month = $3,000
> New Cleaning Service—6 months at $700 per month = $4,200
> Total annual cleaning expense $7,200

The correct budgeted amount for the next year is $8,400 (12 months at $700 per month), not the experienced amount of $7,200. Only an analysis of the transactions would have revealed that fact. This is a common error made when budgeting. However, had the details of the transactions not been examined, then the error would have made sense to those who did not know or understand the underlying events. Remember—the budget process is often conducted by a subset of people who have no knowledge of the events that cause variances in the actual vs. budget expenditures. Third, if there are variances in the revenue, then it may be necessary to go into actual individual person or family pledge and giving accounts to determine shortfall or opportunities. There are no secrets in the church, and the idea that no one knows what you give is wrong. It may not be broadcast, but several have to know. Those preparing the budget must have access to all the transactions in the general ledger for the year—and prior years, and access to all the pledge and giving records, too.

Step Two: Determine next year's expenditure requirements This is probably the most critical part of the process, yet is the most underperformed. It asks the question "what will be different about next year?", but most often, the answer is not well understood.

The difficulty is that the broader congregation is not involved in the development of the budget. Vestries have commissions or some designation that indicates a division of responsibilities among vestry members—for example, outreach, worship, formation, building and grounds. Each vestry member should meet with their committee chairs and request a plan for the coming year's activities and any necessary budget allotments for them. For example: the worship commission vestry member would meet with the choirmaster, the healing service team leader, the person who prepares the bulletins and newsletters, the Lay Eucharistic Minister (LEM) team leader, the altar guild committee chair, the flower guild committee chair, and so forth.

Each individual (working in concert with their committee) would need to provide the worship commission vestry member a detailed, preferably by month, list of activities and expected expenditures, if any, for the coming year. This sounds like overkill and a lot of work. Not if you want an accurate budget—and a church where programs work in concert with each other and other parts of the church. Besides, it is the vestry member's personal fiduciary responsibility, liability, and obligation of oversight in holding the committee chairs and team leaders accountable for their actions, including plans and expenditures.

Sounds like a great retreat opportunity for team building and brainstorming. Multiply this by each vestry member, and you have a congregation deeply engaged in the plans for the coming year. Under those circumstances there are dozens and dozens of parishioners who are involved and taking personal ownership of and pride in their piece of the puzzle. When it comes time for stewardship, those who have been involved in the process of planning for next year will view the church as being significant to them in their daily lives. They have a say in how things get done, and a view of how their activities (and they) fit into the life of the parish as a whole. The budgeting process can be used as a way to connect people to the church to make it more relevant and meaningful to them. Budgeting is more about the process than about the money.

The expenditure requirements are gathered first to allow for creative thought and planning that may lead to new ideas and programs. The challenge is that often there will be more good ideas than funds. That is not a bad thing, and if carefully managed all the way through the process, may yield an expansion or replacement of existing programs.

This step needs to be performed not only for operating expenses, but also for non-operating expenses. Examples include:

- Fund-raising activities—expenses that are uniquely attributable to the activity. Who does this? The fund-raising chair.
- Building campaigns—hopefully, this is under competent project management. Who does this? The building campaign chair with the help of the contractor.
- Youth ski trip—understand the full expenses required, including any reimbursements anticipated for adult volunteers as well as all directly-related costs per youth and number expected in attendance. Who does this? The youth minister.
- Easter sunrise service and a new brunch—how many people are estimated to attend and what is the cost per person for the brunch? Who does this? The worship commission chair with whoever is in charge of the brunch for the coming year.

Do you get the sense of broad parish involvement in this process? These events must have had some planning and forethought put into them before beginning the budget process. This can be drudgery or fun. Largely, it depends on the approach taken by vestry and the leadership skills they employ.

So how to make it happen? There are many ways:

- The divide-and-conquer method: Send out the marching orders via e-mail to each person from whom you expect input, along with a deadline when the task is due. This may get it done, but is probably the least effective in generating the desired results unless all of the people are Type A overachievers.
- The Kumbaya method: Everyone within a work area gathers in the parish hall after church or one evening and tries to develop the year's plan with the commission chair. This works if there are good group dynamics that allow for open and honest conversation, brainstorming, and prioritization. However, the method requires excellent facilitation skills on the part of the discussion leader. Facilitation skills are learned and do not come as standard equipment at birth. Few have actually been trained in facilitation.
- The vestry-knows-best or budget-committee-knows-best method: Vestry members or the budget committee hold a retreat or a series of meetings and put together the budget without input from anyone who will be performing the functions.

- The workshop/pizza party method: A planned agenda that includes the elements for success. I think this works best because it provides:
  - adequate time for an explanation of the objectives of this part of the budget process
  - materials for each participant to use in assessing and preparing their plans and expenditure needs for next year
  - an opportunity for those who have similar interests to get together for brainstorming
  - a forum for those who may have never been involved to step forward and join a process
  - other resources to be available as needed
  - camaraderie and consensus-building
  - food, an Episcopal tradition for everything successful. This approach still requires facilitation skills, but because of the pre-planning and preparation, has a higher likelihood of success.

Example: Youth Ski Trip The church expects the youth to cover their ski rental and lift costs, which is the first cost identified. It is anticipated that the church may need to provide the funding for a couple of youth to attend and is the second cost identified. (Scholarships do *not* come from the rector's discretionary account, but are a budgeted expense from the operating budget.) Costs for the adults are listed next, which include ski rentals and lifts, mileage, and meals and lodging.

To determine the amount that is an expense to the church, a column is created that lists from where the money will come to pay for all the expenses. Some will be paid by the youth, some by the adults, and some by the church. It is assumed that the youth have been contributing toward the ski trip for the last several months and that some of the money will come from the designated account in the general ledger established for the purpose of the ski trip. The rest will come from the operating budget.

Notice that the revenue sources are listed ("paid by" columns). Notice also that the general ledger account name is listed so there is no guesswork involved in where to accumulate the funds designated for the ski trip and from where the payment will be made. In addition, the amount requested to be funded by the church is clearly identified, with detailed documentation, and the operating general ledger account is listed. If this plan ultimately is approved by the vestry, then this documentation, or any alteration thereof, should be kept available in the church office for the bookkeeper to know

Youth Ski Trip		Paid by		
		Youth	Adults	Church Youth Budget
Ski rentals and lifts, $200 each person:				
Number of youths participating	18	$ 3,600	$ -	$ -
Number of youth scholarships	2			400
Number of adults participating	4		800	
Travel expenses:				
Mileage or gasoline				250
Food for adults				
4 adults, 3 meals each				540
Lodging @ $50 each				
Adults				200
Youth		900		100
Total from youth:		$ 4,500		
GL DESIGNATED SKI TRIP ACCOUNT:		881100		
Total from adults:			$ 800	
GL DESIGNATED SKI TRIP ACCOUNT:			881100	
Total from youth budget:				$ 1,490
GL OPERATING YOUTH ACCOUNT:				481100
TOTAL REQUESTED FOR THE SKI TRIP TO BE INCLUDED IN THE 2013 BUDGET:				$ 1,490

Youth Ski Trip

where to properly post items and the parish administrator or others to be able to answer questions should they arise as the ski trip approaches.

This is an example of the kind of detail I would expect from the committees and commissions to be brought to the budget committee or whatever body is preparing the budget. This is a budget request, not a foregone conclusion that the money will be provided, and the proper expectation needs to be set with the person preparing the budget for the ski trip so there is no surprise if all of the funding is not provided.

Step 3: Estimate the revenue requirements and allocate revenue to expenditures There are reasons I start with expenditures before revenue. First, starting with expenditure requirements allows for all the various committees to conduct the planning process to determine their budgetary needs for the new year. Second, there is never enough money to go around, so ultimately determining the priorities for the allocation of money will have to occur. Third, if the requirements step was properly developed and there are more requests for money than there is money to go around, that is a good thing. That means that the congregation is engaged in visioning for the church at a level that is personal to them. It is also an opportunity to justifiably ask that people consider raising their pledge and other giving so that there is enough money to fund the proposed activities. The process provides for much more visibility and interaction than if development of the budget is done in a back room.

There are core operating expenditures that must have revenue provided for them or the church will not operate—salaries, electricity, mortgage, and the like. The first allocations of revenue must be assigned here. There is a tendency to gloss over these core items and not understand their funding requirements in detail. For example, the cost of carrying a member of the clergy on the payroll is often assumed to be only the salary and housing allowance, a view that overlooks the cost of all benefits associated with that employment. This fails to acknowledge that non-clergy members of the staff have other expenses that must be considered, such as the church's portion of payroll taxes. The example on the next page illustrates the level of detail to which the budgeting process should go. Every general ledger account code should be considered. If there is not one to address new events or activities, make one.

This will often mean having the discussion about any changes in personnel, salaries, or benefits before the budget can be completed. That is a good thing because it gets the topics on the table and gets them discussed, preferably completed in advance of budget conclusion time.

It is important to note that only pledged and anticipated plate revenue can be allocated to operating expenses. Designated revenue is allocated to designated expenses. For example, one pledge made annually and only for the flower guild is not an operating expense pledge. It is designated only for the flower guild, and in allocating revenue, all of that pledge must be allocated to the flower guild. However, undesignated pledge revenues are allocated to operating expenses first, and only if any remains after all operating expenses are covered and the revenues allocated to programs, activities, or reserves.

Once the necessary core expenditures are allocated adequate revenue, allocate the remaining revenue to non-core expenditures. If there is not enough to go around, that will mean prioritizing the remaining events, programs, and other expenditures. Now would be a good time to pull out the church's vision, mission, and goal statements to use as an arbiter in determining what gets funded and what does not. If the church's mission is to spread the gospel through outreach, then the youth ski trip might stand a better chance of getting funded if it were the youth mission trip to assist Hurricane Katrina

General Ledger Account Code	Core Operating Expenses:
	Salaries
	Wages
	Clergy
400100	Rector's Salary
400110	Rector's Housing Allowance
400200	Rector's Pension
400300	Rector's Medical Insurance
401100	Assistant Rector's Salary
401200	Assistant Rector's Pension
401300	Assistant Rector's Medical Insurance
401400	Assistant Rector's Car Allowance
	Non-Clergy
405100	Parish Administrator's Salary
405120	Church portion of PA's FICA and FUTA, SUTA
405200	Parish Administrator's Pension
406100	Music Minister's Salary
406120	Church portion of MM's FICA and FUTA, SUTA
406200	Music Minister's Pension
407100	Youth Minister's Salary
407120	Church portion of YM's FICA and FUTA, SUTA
407200	Youth Minister's Pension
	Utilities
420100	Water and Sewer
420200	Gas
420300	Electricity
	Telephone
420410	Church phones
420420	Rector's cell phone
420430	Assistant Rector's cell phone
420400	Youth Minister's cell phone
	Internet
420510	Internet Service
420520	Web page hosting
XXXXXX	Etc.

Budget Account Codes

victims or Haitian earthquake victims. Using the vision, mission, and goals of the church as an arbiter, some projects will quickly fall into alignment and others will quickly be identified as outliers.

Now comes the hard part. You must decide which projects, events, fundraisers, and outreach are funded with the remaining projected revenue. Some sacred cows and a few new-idea calves will be sacrificed along the way. Some really good ideas may fail for the lack of funding. One pitfall to avoid is failing to adequately fund an item in an attempt to spread the wealth around. Avoid the temptation to fund everything. Using funding as a means of placating parishioners is wrong and not defendable fiduciarily. This is the honesty part of the process. Be honest with yourself and honest with the congregation. Giving a little money to each program so that success is marginalized or programs are set up for failure is no way to budget—ever. Provide for contingencies by not allocating all anticipated revenue to budget line items.

One way to provide for contingencies is to identify those programs and activities that will not occur without adequate revenue. A second way is to have a designated account code in the general ledger used as a reserve fund and allocate income to it. A third way is to make an appeal for increased pledges if the budgetary shortfall will eliminate critical elements of the next year's mission and ministry. How much revenue to hold back is a judgment call. It depends on many different factors. I like to think that ten percent is a good contingency number, but this is where you need some really good prognosticators in the room.

Step 4: Develop a draft budget   In developing a draft of the budget, use the general ledger chart of accounts as the basis for the report. Prepare columns that show last year's budget, last year's actual, this year's budget, this year's year-to-date (YTD) actuals, and the next year's proposed budget. It may be necessary to print this on legal size paper in landscape mode. Make a final column for adjustments resulting from discussions or votes taken with the vestry.

While this report should include all general ledger accounts, they should be arranged in a logical format that groups similar items together. One of the best I have seen groups the general ledger accounts by commissions. This gives each chair a view of his or her oversight and accountability responsibilities. Core operating expenses are shown separately, as they are the responsibility of the vestry as a whole. It is also useful to prepare supplementary schedules that show the direct revenue and expenses for projects and fundraising, as in the youth ski trip example earlier in this chapter. This allows for transparency and clearer understanding of income and expenses that may not be budgeted.

The draft budget should be developed for the full fiscal year initially, then spread throughout the year by month, allowing a view of expenses against the peaks and valleys of giving (revenues are higher at the end of the year than they are in the middle of the year). While some expenditures (such as mortgage) approximate level spending amounts month-to-month, other expenditures occur annually or semi-annually, such as insurance or pension payments. Depending on the timing of income and the timing of the expenditures, a potential cash flow shortfall can be avoided by holding income from earlier in the year or from the prior year.

Step 5: Finalize the budget   The vestry will ultimately decide which activities are provided for in the budget and which are not. Once the budget is finalized, it is a good idea to publish the budget for all to see. There are no secrets in the church, and my experience has shown that the more transparency there is with money, the more freely donations are made.

Once the budget is finalized, the bookkeeper loads it into the software, one general ledger account at a time. This should be a rote exercise since the vestry took into consideration every account in the general ledger and assigned a budget value to it, even if zero. If the budget was not prepared account by account, how is a bookkeeper expected to load the budget into the computer system? A copy of the approved budget should be included with the vestry minutes archived with church records. Because there are so many versions of the budget floating around at this point, it is critical that the clerk of the vestry make sure the correct version is included as an attachment to the minutes.

Timing   Some vestries will develop a budget in time for the annual meeting. Others will develop the budget as their last official act before the end of the year when one-third of the members will be replaced. Still others will wait until the new vestry is installed and have a joint meeting with the outgoing members present to assist with the decision making. There are a number of approaches to determining when the budget should be finalized, not the least of which is precedence or preference. Regardless of when the budget is finalized, the budgeting process for the next year should start as much as six months out. In addition, the budget needs to be prepared in advance of the stewardship campaign.

While this book does not address stewardship, timing of a stewardship emphasis does affect the process. There are two basic approaches to stewardship and its relationship to the budgeting process. Either the budget is prepared prior to the stewardship campaign, and the amount of money needed is set as a goal and communicated to the congregation, or the budget is prepared after the stewardship campaign so there is a known amount of pledge revenue from which to allocate to expenditures.

If the budget was developed in advance of the stewardship campaign, there would be an opportunity to put forth new ideas and changes to existing programs, and the costs associated with them—an opportunity to sell the budget in support of the new programs to the congregation. It is a positive message, particularly if Step 2: "Determine next year's expenditure requirements" was followed, allowing a number of people to be involved in the development of the new budget.

Now that we have seen the full budget development process, let's turn our attention to the two approaches. Again, most churches will use a combination of the two but lean primarily on one or the other.

Baseline Budgeting Approach

The first budgeting approach is probably the most commonly used and most familiar. Formally, it is known as the baseline process. In the vernacular, it is known as the "what did we do last year?" approach to budgeting. Baseline budgeting uses either this year's actual or budgeted income and expenses to prepare next year's budgeted income and expense.

This is an acceptable approach when there is little change in the size or demographics of the congregation, and there are to be no new programs initiated. If your church organization is located in a small town where everyone grew up together in the church and there is little transiency, then this is most likely an acceptable method. However, in churches where those variables are more active, this method can become the black hole approach to budgeting, allowing churches slowly to stagnate and die because the church becomes rote and unresponsive to new needs and opportunities.

There are several positive characteristics of the baseline budgeting approach. The baseline approach is useful when costs are relatively fixed and predictable—salaries, utilities, mortgage payment, telephone, and the like. It allows for trend analysis from prior years to compare revenues by source and expenditures by program, event, and line item in the budget. It saves time and allows the vestry to focus only on the things that are changing significantly.

The disadvantages to the baseline budget are these: While it works in many cases, the method should not be used exclusively more than four or five years in a row because the church has probably had a shift in demographics. On average, seventeen percent of the population in the United States moves every year. That includes across town, off to college, intrastate and interstate moves. Within three years, it is statistically possible that half the population of a parish will be different.

One solution to the demographics issue is The Episcopal Church website (http://www.episcopalchurch.org). It links to a research department that will assist a church in understanding the demographics of the surrounding area. Since the actual Web page URL changes frequently, my recommendation is to search the TEC website using the search term *studying your congregation and community.* Select your diocese, church, and the button "View Community Profile."

Format	Black and White ▼
Diocese	(SELECT) ▼
Church	(SELECT A DIOCESE FIRST) ▼

View Diocese Chart   View Church Chart   View Community Profile

Community Demographic Profile

You will receive a report that includes information from many different sources. For a one-mile radius of the church, the report usually contains the following:

- population, household trends
- racial/ethnic trends
- age trends
- school-aged children trends
- household income trends
- households and children trends
- marital status trends
- adult educational attainment
- employment and occupations
- mosaic household types
- charitable giving practices
- religious practices

Pre-generated as of a certain date and projecting the next five years, the report is useful as a backdrop for your own research. Over time, as the reports are generated, it is useful to compare them for trends and accuracy. A church that habitually uses the baseline approach should include much more zero-based budgeting within its budget process, or switch to zero-based at least once every five years as the new report is issued.

Another problem I have observed with baseline budgeting is a complacency that undermines the attention to detail required for close examination of variances and trends. This possibility is particularly likely if the same budget or finance committee members prepare the budget year after year or if the budget is prepared without the input of the rest of the congregation. If the vestry prepares the baseline budget, then every three years there is likely no one who remembers when the last zero-based budget was created or how long the baseline approach has been used. Baseline budgeting can carry forward errors from prior years, ignore new programs that need funding, and fail to acknowledge changes in the economy or demographics that lead to alterations in donations.

The divide-and-conquer method and the vestry (or budget committee)-knows-best methods are the two methods of constructing a baseline budget that are usually employed. The Kumbaya and the workshop/pizza party methods slow down and befuddle the baseline approach because those methods attempt to get at the details and provide for a planning process based on the details of activities and transactions of the various commissions. Fundamentally, if a budget is crafted after money is pledged, the baseline approach is probably the budgetary method employed. The question then becomes is the parish habituated to cutting items from the budget rather than crafting a budget for a changing demographic, recognizing current economic climes, and allowing for introspection and assessment?

From the general budget process discussed earlier, the baseline budget will alter the steps as follows:

Step 1: Evaluation Usually, the extent of evaluation is the printing of last year's budget vs. actual revenues and expenses, this year's year-to-date budget vs. actual, and performing a "what is different next year" assessment. I am not a fan of limiting this step for all the negative reasons above. An inflation factor may be applied. Rather than pulling that number from the air, look at data from the U.S. Department of Commerce to determine inflation rates, disposable income rates, and direction and rate of change of household income to determine the inflation factor to be used.

Step 2: Determine next year's expenditure requirements As previously described, the baseline approach performs this step cursorily, if at all. The baseline approach assumes a church that is stable in its membership, demographics, and programs. It also assumes that the status quo is the desired status of the church. If that is the case with your church, you are using the right approach. If it is not, then the zero-based budgeting approach should be implemented, preferably starting at Step 1.

Step 3: Estimate revenue requirements and allocate revenue to expenditures This step should be relatively straightforward in the baseline approach. Since a status quo, stable church is assumed, the revenue should be reasonably predictable.

If there is more than a ten percent positive change in expected revenue, then there is reason for pause before continuing. A greater than ten percent positive change in revenue expected may indicate additional families and individuals joining the church or returning to the church. That has implications for such things as staff, programming, and utilities.

If there is more than a ten percent negative change in expected revenue, then there is also a reason for pause before continuing. A greater than ten percent negative change in revenue expected may indicate a loss of pledging families, an economy in peril causing families to struggle with daily bills, or other problems in the church. If a problem or reason for decline has not been identified before, then it must be identified now. Problems ignored are problems allowed to grow. In this situation, baseline is no longer an option, and I recommend starting over using the zero-based budgeting approach. It is back-to-basics time and that is accomplished best with the zero-based budgeting approach.

Step 4: Develop a draft budget Assuming that the baseline budget approach is still the proper approach, then a draft of the budget should be prepared for examination and discussion. Most likely the entire vestry has not been involved with the budgeting process, and it is now time for their inspection and approval or adjustment. One of the dangers inherent in this step is the attempt to summarize the budget in large categories, such as worship, outreach, and youth. Now is not the time for the big picture.

The budget is a document that is derived from the details, general ledger account by general ledger account. It should be examined that way during approval by the full vestry. Once approved, the line item budget becomes the stick against which the actual revenues and expenditures are measured as they occur over time.

This step is not to be undertaken lightly. This is also not a fifteen-minute agenda item at a vestry meeting. This is going to take time. Send out the detailed draft, detailed account by account, at least two weeks in advance of the meeting. Vestry members should raise questions or identify areas for discussion and let the senior warden know in advance so adequate time can be allotted for discussion. If necessary, schedule a special meeting to address the budget, but do not underestimate the time required to perform this step properly. When approved, every vestry member is fiduciarily responsible for everything in the budget.

Step 5: Finalize the budget   The actual budget is loaded into the computer system and a true and correct copy is attached to the minutes of the meeting. Vestry minutes and their attachments are archived forever. They form a legal record and a historical record of the proceedings of the church.

Zero-based Budgeting Approach

If your church organization is in a metropolitan area, including its suburbs, then the baseline approach is likely not the best approach for you. The 2010 Census Bureau data shows that approximately seventeen percent of the population of the United States moves every year. That indicates that in three years fifty-one percent of the population living near the church will be potential new members. While the data is lagging the downturn in housing, historically this has been the case.

Since a large part of the U.S. population lives within what the federal government calls a Metropolitan Statistical Area, more than half the movement occurs in one of those. Rural areas tend to be more stable in their populations. This data also says that the programs required to address the needs of the congregation and community are likely to need reexamination for relevance and applicability more often. Statistically, it would indicate a need for that introspection and examination at least every three years.

The zero-based budgeting approach is best suited for this environment since it recognizes the changing circumstances. Because the transitions are at the individual or family level, the shift in demographics over time, it is easy to miss unless proactively followed. The process to address the needs of a congregation that is in constant transition is the zero-based budgeting approach. Implementing this approach resembles more of the general budgeting process:

Step 1: Evaluation   This step begins with some reflection—who are the members of the church, what community does the church serve, and what are the vision, mission, and goals of the church? It does not assume status quo, but rather assumes that change is occurring at a discernible rate and with discernible outcomes. This step will involve many more than just the budget committee. Consider the workshop/pizza party method of gathering requirements and assessing what works or not, what is still relevant or not, and what is still desirable or not. The end result of this step is the conscious choice that some activities or programs will be updated, replaced, or scrapped altogether, but that each will be examined and a conscious decision made.

Step 2: Determine next year's expenditure requirements Once decisions are made regarding the needs of the church for next year, the zero-based budgeting approach starts with the assumption that funding for the next year is based solely on the year's plans and activities. It does not ever begin with a look back at how much was budgeted last year. The assumption should be that an item or program is not funded until proven viable and selected to be included. As in the youth ski trip example, all requests for funding need to have backup documentation prepared and presented to the budget committee, and to the vestry if necessary. There is no foregone conclusion that any activity or program will be funded from the revenue allocation in Step 3, but rather that it must be weighed against all other requests and matched with the vision, mission, and goals of the church. It is presumed that the dollar amount of budget requests will exceed the amount of available revenue anticipated, making Step 3 more critical in the zero-based budgeting approach.

As in the baseline budgeting approach, some parts are going to be easy. The mortgage, diocesan commitment, electricity, and phone are going to be more readily estimable. As before, all assumptions must be documented and included with the budget request.

Step 3: Estimate revenue requirements and allocate revenue to expenditures This step is more involved here than in the baseline budgeting approach. If there is more anticipated revenue than budget requests, then the step is easier. More likely, the opposite is the case. As in the general budget process, this will require making a choice among many good budget requests.

The approach is to identify any requests that are not in concert with the vision, mission, and goals of the church and set them aside. They will be revisited once all the others are considered. Returning to the remaining requests, determine the total amount to be considered and compare it to the available revenue. Begin by allocating revenue to the necessary operating expenses, such as salary, payroll taxes, mortgage payments, diocesan commitment, telephone, and electricity. There may be a discussion about what is considered "necessary operating expenses." *Necessary* is the operative word; *operating* is merely a descriptor. As an arbiter, ask, is the expense necessary to keep the doors open? If yes, then it is operating. If no, then it is a discretionary spending (not in any way related to the rector's discretionary account). Discretionary spending simply means we could spend it for that if we want, but the roof is not going to fall in if we do not.

Back to allocation of revenue. Allocate the undesignated pledge and plate revenue to the necessary operating expenses. Allocate all designated revenue to designated expenses. What is left? If all the operating expenses are covered by the undesignated revenue, then I suggest the establishment of a temporarily restricted fund to save for a rainy day. Otherwise, the remaining undesignated revenues may be allocated to designated expenditures, or they may be allocated to the budget requests that were set aside initially.

Step 4: Develop a draft budget   This step is the same as the baseline approach. A draft of the budget should be prepared for examination and discussion by the vestry. It is now time for the entire vestry to inspect and approve or adjust the budget. Try to avoid summarizing the budget in large categories, such as worship, outreach, and youth. Now is not the time for the big picture.

The budget is a document that is derived from the details, general ledger account by general ledger account. Once approved, the line item budget becomes the basis against which the actual revenues and expenditures are measured as they occur.

As noted earlier, this step is going to take time. Send out the detailed draft detailing each general ledger account number two weeks in advance of the meeting. Vestry members should raise questions or identify areas for discussion and let the senior warden know in advance so adequate time can be allotted for discussion. If necessary, schedule a meeting to address the budget, but be sure to allot enough time to perform this step properly. When approved, every vestry member is fiduciarily responsible for everything in the budget.

Step 5: Finalize the budget   This step is also the same as the baseline approach. The actual budget is loaded into the computer system and a true and correct copy is attached to the minutes of the meeting. Vestry minutes and their attachments are archived forever. They form a legal record and a historical record of the proceedings of the church.

Economics and the Impact on a Budget

Both the baseline and the zero-based budgeting approaches assume a stable buying power of the dollar and stable costs of services and goods procured—neither of which are reality. When the federal government reports the rate of inflation to the public, it uses what is known as the "core" rate of inflation. What is diabolical about this is that it removes from its calculation the cost of food and gasoline, both of which have skyrocketed since 2008, with gasoline more than doubling. When food and gasoline are inserted into the calculation as they were before 1980, the *real* rate of inflation is over ten percent.

Do churches buy food and gasoline? More than you think. First, as reimbursement for food and gasoline costs turned in by its members; more than that, everything from candles and albs to Wednesday night suppers are affected by the rising cost of fuel. If a budget committee does not take into account the components of the budget that are affected by the *real* inflationary rate, then the use of the federal government reported rate of inflation will lead to a budget shortfall. Hence, trend analysis of actual expenses by budget line item from year to year is important when budgeting. This is not contradictory to either approach. Inflation gets factored into the baseline approach estimates as a multiplier by some percentage increase. In the zero-based approach, each budget request should use some rate of inflation factored into the estimated costs.

Look at a ten-year trend analysis and pay particular attention to the change in the slope of the cost curve beginning in 2008. Apply the Consumer Price Index increase as a compounding multiplier to each year, and the real rate of inflation will become shockingly apparent. This is where the real rate of inflation is being masked by the federal government. Failure to understand this and the resulting trends will leave a vestry wondering why they are faced with actual costs exceeding revenue. Remember, vestry members are at risk of being potentially fiduciarily liable for the shortfall in the budget if failure to properly restrict spending is the cause, and its reasonable predictability was possible.

In order to keep up with the real inflation rate, the church will need donations to increase by a similar amount. When the rate of increase of income at the donor's household is less than three percent, as it is in 2012, and the real rate of inflation is ten percent, as it is in 2012, there is a rapidly widening gap between income and what it will buy. In fact, real disposable income of the U.S. household in 2012 is down ten percent since 2008. If that trend continues, by 2016, the expected level of giving will be up ten percent while the costs could be up thirty-three percent.[44] In inflationary times, the purchasing power of the donations received will be exceeded by the amount of dollars it takes to purchase the same goods in the upcoming year. But with quantitative easing (simply printing more money to pay the nation's bills) by the Federal Reserve, the real purchasing power of the dollar goes down.

---

44. This is calculated by taking the rate of increase in household income (1.03 or 3%) and multiplying that times itself for three years—1.03^3, and the real rate of inflation (1.10 or 10%) and multiplying that times itself for three years—1.10^3.

When Ben Bernanke, chairman of the Federal Reserve, announced in September, 2012, the continual quantitative easing monthly indefinitely for years, it built in permanent inflation in the economy and the permanent decline of the purchasing value of the dollar for years to come. This permanent decline is compounded upon itself every month. This is the worst possible situation the government could have created—a systemic compounded inflation that undermines those who are living on pensions or annuities because they are not indexed to inflation.

When the decline in the value of the dollar for purchasing goods is combined with the decline in household disposable income, it becomes doubly important that the church not take the budgeting process lightly. The vestry must pay very close attention to its demographics by age. Those on fixed income will have less to donate to the church. If the demographics of the church are such that a significant percentage are on fixed income, the decline in donations year-on-year could be dramatic over just three years' time.

It is important that vestries understand the impact of inflation on their budgets, not only in preparing the budget, but also when explaining the situation to donors. The chart below illustrates this point.

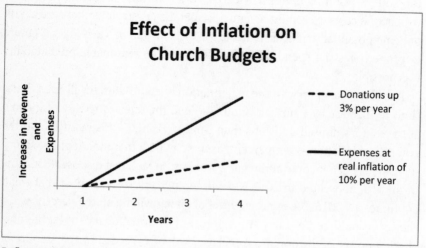

Inflation Effect

The chart above is not a prognostication on my part, but merely to make a point.

While all budgeted expenses will not increase at this rate, it does point to the potential for expenses increasing in cost combined with the purchasing power of the dollar declining much faster than the increase in revenue.

In short, when the most basic of economic principles is ignored, everyone wonders why there is not enough money to spend.

As a final thought, to make the budgeting process easier each year, do not wait until budgeting time to evaluate the impact of events in the life of the church or the economy, and any underlying transactions. Evaluate the budget monthly and document any reasons for variances. The treasurer should make sure the minutes include an analysis of the trends, either directly in the minutes or in the treasurer's report that is attached to the minutes for archiving. *Analyzing* actual vs. budget variances monthly will make the budgeting process easier when the time comes; merely perusing them will not. In the end, it is the responsibility of the vestry to provide this level of oversight and accountability.

CHAPTER
13
Other Items

Miscellaneous

This chapter addresses a number of other financial management issues that are related to previous topics, but need to be specifically addressed or are stand-alone topics. They are presented in no particular order.

One of the areas of financial management of the church that receives minimal attention is insurance. My experience is that most churches, if not obtaining their insurance from Church Insurance, are not adequately insured—particularly for fraud and personal property. Other areas that are often underinsured are sexual harassment, child protection, and vehicle liability.

Insurance

The Church Pension Group (CPG) publishes a number of useful and well-written documents on a variety of financial subjects, including:

- disability insurance
- financial planning
- health plans
- life insurance
- long-term care insurance
- pensions
- preventing sexual abuse
- property and casualty insurance
- publicaciónes en Español
- publications en Français
- retirement savings
- tax publications

Become familiar with the resources applicable to your parish or church organization by visiting their website (www.cpg.org) and downloading the material. One particularly outstanding publication is "Risk Management & Insurance Basics for Episcopal Organizations." Every treasurer, senior warden, and rector should read it. There are many other excellent resources as well.

In light of the prevalence of fraud in churches, I recommend that each parish obtain fidelity liability insurance.

Fidelity Liability Insurance protects your church against dishonesty, fraud and forgery both from those within your church community and people outside your parish. Canon law requires fidelity coverage.

Fidelity Insurance specifically protects:
- Checking and other financial accounts
- Donation, plate collections and other contributions
- Income from daycare, tuition and other revenue-generating sources

Coverage Types
Employee Dishonesty
- Protects against dishonesty by:
  - Employees
  - Directors
  - Trustees
  - Volunteers
- Coverage is per occurrence
- Deductible applies

Forgery & Alteration
- Protects against loss from fraudulent checks, account withdrawals and promissory notes
- Covers actions by those who are not employees, directors or trustees
- No deductible applies

Risk Minimization
The following steps will help reduce the risk of financial loss and must be followed to qualify for immediate coverage:
- Hire an outside CPA to conduct an annual audit
- Have accounts reconciled by someone who does not have check-signing authority
- Countersign every check
- Have at least two people count every collection

How Much Fidelity Insurance Do You Need?
- At least 25% of your total annual revenue or five percent of your total assets

- Do not purchase more than your total annual revenue

Policy Application
- Coverage is immediate—effective the date you are approved
- You must explain your auditing process if:
  - The person in charge of your audits is not a CPA
  - An annual independent audit is required for coverage of the rector's discretionary fund

This is a summary of the coverage provided by the Church Insurance Companies. The actual insurance policy or certificate should be consulted for complete details of coverage. In the event that the information in this book conflicts with the actual insurance policy, the actual insurance policy shall govern.[45]

Please notice that as part of the application process CPG requires an independent audit by a CPA, including clergy discretionary funds, for immediate coverage or an explanation of its absence, for coverage to be considered.

Naming Financial Accounts

The financial accounts—bank, brokerage, savings, and foundation—should all be in the name of the church with all communications, including statements, coming to the church. If subtitled, they should be addressed to the treasurer. For example: Church of the Holy Smoke™ Scholarship Fund, ATTN: Treasurer.

Scenario: Securities Fraud   In chapter 7, I mentioned a particularly onerous audit situation that involved a family and its matriarch who thought they owned the church. She was the treasurer who thought no one but her should know the contributions to the church. In sequestering the church records, I found one financial statement she had misfiled, a pair of stock brokerage statements dated November and December of the prior year. They were titled in the name of the church and addressed to the treasurer, but the financial statement address was her home address.

In November, she had transferred from her personal brokerage account (at the same broker) approximately $20,000 of stock shares to the church's account. In December, she sold the stock in the church's account and transferred the money back to her personal account. She used the church's not-

45. https://www.cpg.org/administrators/insurance/property-and-casualty/policies/fidelity-liability-insurance/

for-profit (income tax exempt) account to sell stock for a capital gain, but pay no income tax on it because it was sold in the church's account. In January, she paid her pledge from her personal account so she could get the tax deduction. However, she only paid in pledge half the amount of what was sold. The rest she pocketed tax free.

Analysis   First, this is securities fraud for which the local broker was an accomplice. Second, the vestry knew about the brokerage account, but did not demand the address be changed to the church's address. Third, the treasurer was corrupt, and everyone knew it, but no one would address the issue with the help of the diocese. When I posed my fraud questions to each member of the church's leadership independently, every one of them said, "Nobody else knows this, but . . ."

Financial account statements should be titled in the name of the church and addressed to the church. If there is suspicion of wrongdoing, get the diocese involved. It sometimes requires personal courage to protect the assets of the church.

Single Checking Account

Using appropriate accounting software (such as ACS), all the church's money should be in one bank account. This greatly reduces the opportunity for fraud. Using designated general ledger accounts to separate those funds from operating funds is more easily maintained using software and a single checking account. With only one bank account, there is only one process to design and maintain, making internal control easier to oversee.

FDIC Limit

If the cash in the bank account exceeds the amount insured by the FDIC, then it will need to be separated. But what church needs more than $250,000 on hand and available? If that much cash is available, then I would suggest finding a good corporate banker at a large institution, not a small hometown bank, and discussing cash management opportunities.

Endowment Account

Endowments that contain a permanently restricted corpus may require a separate account. A copy of the document establishing the corpus and noting the endowment purpose should be given to the financial institution. At that point, they have a fiduciary responsibility to see that the account opened is not at cross purposes with the document. It is still the responsibility of the vestry to provide oversight.

Authorized Signatures

Authorized signatures, and keeping them up-to-date, are often overlooked. There should be a policy, approved and documented by the vestry, that establishes who (what role or position) is authorized by the vestry to sign with what financial institution, and when the signature cards are to be updated. Remember, the requirement of two signatures is only for the benefit of the church, as an important part of internal control by indicating that two people with proper authority have reviewed the documentation of any check request. The policy manual should also indicate who is authorized to sign contracts or authorize stocks to be sold.

Reconciliation

Being current with reconciliation is important. It keeps the vestry knowledgeable about the current assets, but most financial institutions assume that, after sixty days, all accounts are accurate and may not make any corrections after that time.

Fixed Assets

Church of the Holy Smoke's™ parish was growing and a new sanctuary was under construction. On the local news one morning, I saw the rector standing in front of the new sanctuary, which was on fire. The church was two weeks from receiving a certificate of occupancy. The fire burned the new sanctuary to the ground. Because it also burned the education building and parts of the parish hall and old sanctuary, the church had no place to meet. A nearby congregation loaned their building for months while the reconstruction was done. Thankfully, the parish had insurance.

Traditional insurance policies generally cover the replacement of the building and the contents at some percentage of the insured amount of the building, usually twenty-five or thirty percent. However, if the church has a fixed asset schedule, particularly one that has been audited, then the reimbursement can be for actual replacement. Not many rectors or vestries have ever read the insurance policy.

Here is the lesson to be learned. Church of the Holy Smoke's™ insurance policy called for the insurance company to replace the buildings. The check was $1.2 million. The policy also called for the contents to be replaced at thirty percent of the value of the buildings. That would have been $360,000. However, a clause in the policy allowed the church to show proof of contents for actual replacement.

The church had been audited for the last seven years, and there was a fixed asset schedule in the CPA's possession and (properly updated) in the ACS system online. The vestry had an established written fixed asset policy and the bookkeeper had followed it diligently. The check for actual contents replacement was $939,000. By having the audited fixed assets schedule, the church recovered $579,000 more than they would have otherwise. Here are two key points: One, they had the asset and depreciation schedule. Two, they had it audited by a CPA.

There are multiple reasons for establishing a fixed assets policy, diligently overseeing its proper implementation, and causing it to be audited. First, it is required by GAAP. Remember the unqualified or "clean" audit opinion discussed in chapter 6? Second, Canon 7 requires:

(e) Books of account shall be so kept as to provide the basis for satisfactory accounting.
. . .
(h) All buildings and their contents shall be kept adequately insured.[46]

Which of the above insurance reimbursement checks for contents reflects adequate insurance?

Capturing the information for the asset and depreciation schedule at the time of purchase or donation is not burdensome and is good practice. Should you ever question the treatment of an item in fixed assets, the auditing CPA will be glad to offer advice. Of course, if the church has a clearly written fixed asset policy, most questions are easily answered from the guidance found there.

Depreciation

Below is a depreciation schedule example. All assets of the church should be included in this schedule.

Many times I hear that depreciation is not useful in a church because it is a not-for-profit entity that (usually) does not pay taxes. However, you should view depreciation as a management tool. When setting the budget for next year in preparation for the stewardship campaign, it is useful to have a list of the equipment that is reaching the end of its useful life. If the useful life and proper depreciation methods are selected, the depreciation schedule will indicate that.

---

46. *Constitution and Canons for the Government of the Episcopal Church* (New York: Church Publishing Inc., 2009), p. 40.

Item Number	Description	Date Acquired	New or Used	Useful Life (Years)	Depreciation Method	Cost or Donated Value	Prior Depreciation	20XX Depreciation	Accumulated Depreciation	12/31/20XX Book Value	Remaining Life (Years)
1	Leather Chair	1/1/19XA	New	20	SL	1,600	1,360	80	1,440	160	2.00
2	HVAC	4/1/20XP	New	10	SL	10,000	6,750	1,000	7,750	2,250	2.25
	TOTAL					11,600	8,110	1,080	9,190	2,410	

Depreciation Schedule

286 • Financial Management for Episcopal Parishes

If the useful life and proper depreciation methods are selected, the depreciation schedule will indicate just that. No one on the vestry remembers that the HVAC was installed eight years ago. When does an HVAC (heating, venting, and air condition system) die? Good Friday afternoon. (I have known three churches where that was the case.) If the vestry had been given the advanced warning that the HVAC was expected to be fully depreciated in the next three years, a reserve could have been created, budgeted, and included in the last three years' stewardship campaigns so the money would be there to replace it. Otherwise, it is a surprise, and to many churches, a financial hardship. The church is nearing summer when donations decline. Suddenly, there is an immediate need to spend $8,000–$10,000 for a new HVAC.

What to do if the church's fixed assets have not been recorded? From the Church Pension Group's website (www.cpg.org), download the *Parish Inventory* document. If you have fine art, stained glass, or other valuables, download the *Fine Art Appraisals* document from the website as well.

Discovering the documents and transactions from prior years necessary to build a fixed assets schedule is not a single weekend event. It is helpful to have in charge of the project a long-time member of the parish whose memory can provide some history on the donation of the altar or font, for example. Of course, if the font is seventy-five years old, its replacement cost is much greater than the purchase price. It may fall into the area of art instead of simply an asset. The important thing for the appraiser to know is the age and the person or company who may have made it.

One church, built in 1845, had a basement door with no key to its lock. Everyone thought it was a closet, so no one bothered to have it opened. The asset search committee got a locksmith to open the door and found it was a records room with a large old safe situated among filing cabinets. The latest document in the room was dated 1973.

More important, there were documents that detailed the addition of the stained glass windows 125 years earlier. The replacement cost today would be $200,000. The value of the windows as works of art is $400,000. Opening the safe, which contained documents signed by members of many previous generations, was like opening a time capsule.

There is a small pre-Revolutionary War church in Florida with a simple but magnificently beautiful silver chalice. The chalice was so beautiful it was displayed on the altar with a light over it for all to see. The small town had the old church with its beautiful chalice on their local historical tour.

When the parish finally had the chalice appraised, they discovered it was made by a famous silversmith in New York in 1776 from Spanish pieces of eight that were smelted to be used in his creations. Its estimated value was $125,000. Soon after, the chalice was featured at the Metropolitan Museum of Art and traveled to New York from Florida by armored car. It is still on display in the parish for anyone to see, but it is now under protective Plexiglas with alarms—and insured.

Discovering the information necessary for the asset and depreciation schedule is a journey into the history of the parish and can serve to revitalize pride and reinvigorate interest in the life of the local church. The journey may take a year or two, but what you discover is of as much value as the end product asset list.

Records Retention

Proper retention of records is not only a good idea, but is often also the law. There are two sources for a list of documents and their retention period in the church. The first is a chapter dedicated to this purpose in the *Manual of Business Methods in Church Affairs* available online.[47] The second is *Records Management for Congregations: A Manual for Episcopal Parishes and Missions* available online from The Archives of the Episcopal Church.[48] Each church organization of every size should have and use copies of these two documents.

Planned Giving

Planned giving is different from the capital campaign, annual giving, or other areas of stewardship. The opportunities for planned giving are many, though often individuals (and parishes) are not aware of them. This is where the Episcopal Church Foundation (ECF) should enter the conversation with your stewardship committee. If *charitable remainder trust* or *pooled investment income* are unfamiliar terms, visit the ECF's Capital Campaign Resources website and download their brochures and booklets.[49] Then, call them to discuss the opportunities for planned giving and how to conduct parishioner awareness campaigns.

---

47. *Manual of Business Methods in Church Affairs,* available online at http://www.episcopal church.org/page/manual-business-methods.

48. *Records Management for Congregations: A Manual for Episcopal Parishes and Missions,* available online at http://www.episcopal archives.org/Records_Manual_for_Congregations .pdf

49. The Episcopal Church Foundation (ECF) website is found at http://www.episcopal foundation.org/tools-and-programs/fundraising-tools/capital-campaigns/capital-campaign-resources

In addition, ECF has developed an excellent book titled *Funding Future Ministry, a Guide to Planned Giving*[50], which is also available for purchase. The price of the book is well worth the expenditure.

Each state will have differing laws regarding the establishment of certain types of planned giving vehicles, so there is no substitute for a local estate planning attorney. Most are willing to come to the church pro bono to hold an open discussion regarding planned giving. Do not use a local stock broker or investment advisor. Use a local estate planning attorney as there will be different legal documents required by each state and the estate planning attorney can offer a set of options not always found at even the largest of brokerage firms.

Vestry Minutes

The primary purpose for presenting and approving the financial statements in a vestry meeting is the vestry exercising its obligation of fiduciary responsibility in providing oversight of the finances of the church that are summarized in the financial statements.

In churches where the finance committee does not meet regularly, the treasurer's report should include the financial statements we have been discussing: the Statement of Financial Position, the Statement of Activities (with budget vs. actual amounts comparatively), and the Statement of Cash Flows. These statements should be comparative to last month, last year, and to the budget. In churches with an active finance committee, the financial statements and the finance committee minutes should be presented to the vestry.

I recommend that a Statement of Net Assets be prepared. This statement details by account the amounts for each unrestricted, temporarily restricted, and permanently restricted account and provides a detailed look at the designated funds in particular.

The vestry should determine what the key numerical measurements are and track them. These are the non-financial indicators of performance of the parish, such as attendance. Some examples are:

- additions and deletions from the church roll and the financial impact thereof
- pledge performance data
- projected cash flows by month
- other trend data, such as preschool enrollments and church attendance

---

50. *Funding Future Ministry, a Guide to Planned Giving* at http://www.episcopalfoundation .org/tools-and-programs/leadership-tools/funding-future-ministry

Each commission chair (vestry member) should receive the detailed transactions for each account over which they have oversight in advance of the vestry meeting. They then can vet the transactions and have their approval recorded in the minutes. Oversight is thus documented, and the vestry can focus on the financial statements and key performance indicators during the vestry meeting.

The discussion should be centered on matters that require the entire vestry's oversight or decisions, such as changes to the budget or contract approvals. What is not useful is for each committee chair to review his or her budget with the full vestry, unless there is a problem. General matters regarding cash and debt management might be better discussed in detail in the finance committee meeting and a summary brought to the vestry meeting with proposed solutions. The early stages of capital campaigns require full vestry input and vote. Later stages during building may require a separate committee with a summary discussed with the vestry.

Here is a sticking point with auditors. The vestry minutes should contain a copy of the entire treasurer's report, including the finance committee minutes and a copy of any contracts approved. Many times vestry minutes say only, ". . . gave the financial report, which was approved by the vestry . . . ," with no documents attached. If not attached to the minutes, monthly financial statements have a way of disappearing shortly after the meeting is over and are difficult to reconstruct months later. Church records retention documents indicate vestry minutes be kept permanently.

Contracts

A parish decided to add an extension to the sprinkler system for the new memorial garden. The junior warden (building and grounds) suggested the vestry allow him to use the same sprinkler company for this extension installation as had done the entire church grounds a couple of years ago. A motion was made, seconded, and approved. There was no estimate, no contract, no drawings—nothing presented to the vestry and nothing attached to the minutes. The day came, and the sprinkler system extension was installed. The junior warden invited the parish administrator to come see the new addition. Of course, she had been in the vestry meeting when it was approved and was delighted to see the new grass.

A couple of weeks later, an invoice for $1,800 for the installation arrived. The parish administrator approved it and sent it to bookkeeping, a check was cut, two signatures obtained, and the bill was paid. Nothing more was thought about it until the next vestry meeting when the junior warden asked why the building and grounds budget balance was so low. When the parish administrator explained the invoice for $1,800 had been paid, the junior warden emphatically remarked, "$1,800? I had an agreement for $1,080." The overpayment was never returned. The lesson learned is to get a contract or written estimate approved at the vestry meeting and attach it to the minutes.

The minutes become the legal record of the proceedings of the vestry. With that amount of fiduciary liability, get as much documentation as necessary to leave nothing financial to the imagination or misinterpretation.

Summary

This book began with the words of Jesus. In short, it is okay to bring the issue of money to the conversation in the church. We saw that Jesus paid his taxes, had an accountant, Judas, who is the one with access to the money, and Judas stole it. The sin is the *love* of money, and Judas went down that path to his destruction, but money itself is not sinful.

We examined the canons involving money and the treatment of financial matters in the church. We learned that audits are the only method of examination of the financial records that is prescribed by the canons and that CPAs are the only ones who can sign audit opinions.

There are specific roles to be performed by clergy, vestry, staff, and volunteers that are core to the design and implementation of internal control. We also learned of the vestry's fiduciary liability for the finances of the church, which should be a motivation for the vestry members to take their role seriously and not casually.

In speaking about money, we have to use financial terminology correctly. That way, our fellow parishioners, the diocese, and external financial institutions can understand our needs, and we can understand their response. Usage of vernacular terminology is not helpful and confusing. We examined what comprises the church's money and assigned key NFP industry standard terms to those—unrestricted, temporarily restricted, permanently restricted, designated, corpus, and others.

Using that terminology, we were able to read and interpret the financial statements of a church. You were able to follow along with either your GAAP or OCBOA basis financial statements from your church or organization.

Building on the financial statements, we completed the description of an audit with the various opinions and letters to and from management and other entities such as banks and attorneys. You should have a better understanding of the level of examination and work involved in an audit and the deliverables. You should also understand why compilations or reviews are not substitutes for an audit.

In preparation for the chapters on internal control, we took time to understand the prevalence of fraud in the church and some of the characteristics and motivators of the perpetrators. We learned that anyone with access can potentially commit fraud and gained an understanding for the need for internal control.

We spent several chapters on internal control, starting with the introduction to the Three-Legged Stool™ of internal control. We went into detail regarding how to build internal control for both the revenues and the expenses of the church. Extensive examples were offered for your consideration, and you should have a better understanding of the processes.

The church is not immune from taxation and does pay tax under certain circumstances besides payroll and sales tax. We learned of the pitfalls of UBIT and the peril of not properly treating a worker as an employee.

You were given different approaches to budgeting with steps to follow in preparing and producing a budget. What followed were some additional comments and miscellaneous items such as fixed assets and depreciation, the single most prevalent issue for the issuance of a qualified audit opinion.

Throughout the book, there were references to other publications and websites from the church and external sources, such as the IRS, to give you the opportunity to research items further. Also throughout was the theme of examination, accountability, and oversight of the people, organization, process, and technology.

The financial statements are the result of the financial transactions of the church. The financial transactions of the church are influenced by the policies, procedures, and internal control established by the church. A good understanding of financial management of the church is necessary for proper oversight of the financial transactions, policies, procedures, and internal control.

Oversight is the inspection of the accounting records, and individuals' performance of the processes and procedures of internal control. Oversight leads to personal accountability of clergy, vestry, employees, and volunteers. Personal accountability leads to a financially better-run church. A financially better-run church leads to more time and focus on the pastoral purposes of the church. In the end, the results are all in the numbers.

This book should leave the reader with the sense that the church—clergy, vestry, staff, and volunteers—all play an integral role in the safeguarding of the donations and assets of the church. Active leadership from the clergy and vestry are key to the successful implementation of policies, processes and procedures, oversight, and accountability. Well designed and run operations allow for more pastoral time and greater transparency, both of which lead to increased confidence in the church that leads to increased giving and participation by a growing congregation of parishioners.

Workbooks, process flow charts, a blog, direct contact with the author, and other resources are available to assist you online[51] It is my sincere hope that your awareness of the issues of financial management for parishes has been raised. Further it is my hope that you will take action on these issues starting with the tone of the leaders and followed by the implementation of your own version of the recommendations herein presented.

---

51. To schedule a consulting engagement, vestry retreat, education event, or to buy workbooks with templates to implement many of the suggestions, go to www.financialmanagement 4churches.com